Using English

GRAMMAR AND WRITING SKILLS

Using English

GRAMMAR AND WRITING SKILLS

Adrian B. Sanford

Harcourt Brace Jovanovich, Inc.

New York   San Diego   Chicago   San Francisco   Atlanta

ISBN: 0-15-594481-9

Library of Congress Catalog Card Number: 79-83624

Printed in the United States of America

ACKNOWLEDGMENTS

The publisher gratefully acknowledges the contributions of Jo Ann Stewart and Charlotte Herbert to the preparation of the Review Exercises for the series.

For permission to reprint copyrighted material, grateful acknowledgment is made to the following sources:

Harcourt Brace Jovanovich, Inc.: Excerpts from *The HBJ School Dictionary.* Copyright © 1977 by Harcourt Brace Jovanovich, Inc.

Oxford University Press: From a reprinting of *Mulcaster's Elementarie,* edited by E. T. Campagnac.

The H. W. Wilson Company: Excerpt from *Readers' Guide to Periodical Literature.* Copyright © 1977 by The H. W. Wilson Company.

PREFACE

Using English is a brief but complete treatment of English grammar, usage, and mechanics, with a separate section devoted to the process of composing sentences and paragraphs. The book can serve both as a textbook—to be read and studied from front to back—and, for the writer whose skills are already developed, as a compact reference guide to the more subtle or unfamiliar niceties of English prose.

Learning to write well—with clarity and precision—is not an easy task, but neither is it an impossible one. Language, and its manner of expression, carries certain conventions. These conventions, once mastered, make communication easier and more gratifying to both the sender of a message and its recipient. The intent behind my writing *Using English* is to show what these conventions are and how to employ them.

A. B. S.

CONTENTS

UNIT THREE: USAGE

UNIT FOUR: MECHANICS

UNIT ONE

GRAMMAR AND STRUCTURE

Parts of Speech
Phrases
Clauses
Sentences
Sentence Problems

1

PARTS OF SPEECH

Nouns, Pronouns, Adjectives

The building blocks of the English language are the eight *parts of speech*. This chapter shows you how three important parts of speech work. *Nouns* name things. The things can be living or not living, real or imaginary. *Pronouns* take the place of nouns. So pronouns also name things. *Adjectives* help to describe the things that are named by nouns or pronouns.

These parts of speech have different forms to show how they are used in sentences. Using the parts of speech correctly means that you must first choose the right words and then the right forms.

NOUNS

1a A noun is a word or a group of words used to name someone or something.

Nouns are the words you use to name the things you can see or hear or think about. The word *flower* is a noun. So is *guitar. Note* is a noun when it names a sound or something in writing. *Idea* is a noun. *Chicago* is also a noun.

A word used to name a person or thing is a noun.

EXERCISE 1 Number a sheet of paper 1–8. After each number write the nouns from each of the following sentences.

EXAMPLE There are no rules for the new game called "Smash-Up."

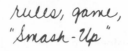

rules, game, "Smash-Up"

1. When you put your little car on the road, you are the boss.
2. You just flick the spinner and move along the boxes on the board.
3. Pretend that you are behind the wheel of a roaring racer.
4. Drive your car in ways that you never would in real life.
5. Smash into your opponents and leave them in a pile of junk.
6. Spend time in the hospital and then roar back out onto the highway.
7. See if you can still move when the other cars and drivers have run out of gas.
8. "Smash-Up" is the exciting game where every player loses!

Common Nouns and Proper Nouns

(1) **A common noun names any person, place, or thing. A proper noun names a particular person, place, or thing.**

Here are some examples:

COMMON NOUNS	PROPER NOUNS
athlete	Chris Evert
state	Iowa
woman	Pearl Bailey
agency	Society for the Prevention of Cruelty to Animals (SPCA)
religion	Buddhism
street	State Street

Hint: A proper noun always begins with a capital letter. If a proper noun has more than one word, each important word begins with a capital letter.

EXAMPLES   **B**ank of **C**hicago, **U**nited **S**tates of **A**merica

---

EXERCISE 2 The following list of words contains proper nouns (without capital letters) and common nouns. On a sheet of paper, write the common nouns in one column, headed *Common Nouns.* Write the proper nouns in another column, headed *Proper Nouns.* Capitalize the proper nouns.

octopus, rocket, new york yankees, bandages,
italy, nickel, atlantic ocean, cement, united
states of america, storm, lucille ball, soccer,
india, detroit, congress, bank, envelope,
tarzan, stevie wonder, peace

Singular Nouns and Plural Nouns

1b A noun may be singular or plural.

If a noun names only one person or thing, the
noun is *singular.* If a noun names more than one
person or thing, the noun is *plural.*

EXAMPLES

SINGULAR NOUNS	PLURAL NOUNS
person	persons
lamp	lamps
hedge	hedges
state	states
table	tables

See Spelling,
pp. 332–334

Most singular nouns form the plural by adding
s. Other singular nouns ending in **s, x, ch, sh,** or **z**
usually form the plural by adding **es.**

EXAMPLES boss, boss**es**
fox, fox**es**
switch, switch**es**
match, match**es**

If a singular noun ends in a consonant followed
by **y,** the noun forms its plural this way: the **y**
changes to **i** and **es** is added.

EXAMPLES fly, **flies**
          berry, ber**ries**

Irregular Nouns

A few nouns are irregular in the way they form the plural. They form the plural in special ways or do not change at all. Nouns made up of more than one word, called *compound nouns,* also form the plural in special ways.

EXAMPLES

SINGULAR	PLURAL
deer	deer
woman	women
goose	geese
mother-in-law	mothers-in-law
attorney general	attorneys general

EXERCISE 3   Some of the following nouns are singular. Some are plural. Number a sheet of paper 1–10. Next to each number, write the missing singular or plural form. You may need to use a dictionary.

EXAMPLE   *box* boxes

1. ridge _____
2. _____ buses
3. stretch _____
4. fuzz _____
5. brother-in-law _____
6. ox _____

7. worry _____
8. _____ monkeys
9. catch _____
10. _____ men

Possessive Nouns

1c   A noun can show possession or ownership.

A noun that shows possession or ownership is in the *possessive case*. Most singular nouns form their possessive case by adding an apostrophe (') and **s**.

EXAMPLES   the mouse**'s** tail, Bebe**'s** shoes, May**'s** flowers, Lois**'s** smile

Plural nouns that end in **s** add only an apostrophe (') to form the possessive case.

EXAMPLES   butterflies' wings, welders' torches

Irregular plural nouns, such as *women,* do not end in **s**. These nouns form the plural possessive by adding the apostrophe (') and **s**.

EXAMPLES   men**'s** umbrellas, children**'s** playthings

If two or more people own something, the possessive ending is added only to the last person's name.

EXAMPLE   Dave and Joanie**'s** house

EXERCISE 4   Number a sheet of paper 1–10. Next to each number, write the correct form of the word or words in parentheses that belongs in the blank.

EXAMPLE   The owners tried to sell as many
_____ tickets as
possible. (children)

Children's

1. _____ circus was considered the best. (Barnum and Bailey)
2. In 1885 the highlight of that circus was _____ cannon act. (Emanuel Zacchini)
3. Before the _____ frightened eyes, Zacchini would crawl into a cannon. (people)
4. Then everyone waited for the _____ signal. (ringmaster)
5. When the signal was given, the _____ fuse was lit. (cannon)
6. As the cannon exploded in a cloud of smoke, _____ body went flying toward the top of the tent. (Zacchini)
7. The _____ act was interrupted by this flying Italian. (lions and the tigers)
8. Zacchini flew the _____ whole length and landed in a safety net. (tent)
9. The excited crowd never knew that the _____ thrust actually came from a powerful spring inside the cannon. (daredevil)
10. The big _____ noise and smoke were added just for the show. (gun)

A few forms of the possessive case sound awkward in speech. Change the wording to avoid the awkwardness.

EXAMPLE

AWKWARD   The Public Broadcasting System's
          best shows
SMOOTHER   The best shows of the Public
          Broadcasting System

EXERCISE 5 Number a sheet of paper 1–5. Rewrite each of the following awkward wordings.

EXAMPLE   Richard Rodgers and Moss Hart's
          songs

*The songs of Richard
Rodgers and Moss Hart*

1. The Westbury Baking Company's new products
2. The Middle East's strife
3. The United States of America's citizens
4. The Chief of Staff's assistants
5. The pen and pencil's holder

PRONOUNS

**1d A pronoun is a word used to take the
place of a noun, a noun word group, or
other pronouns.**

You use pronouns all the time. They help you keep from repeating unnecessary words.

EXAMPLES   I think movies are better than ever.
           They are better than TV shows.
           [The word *they* is a pronoun. It
           takes the place of the noun *movies*.]

The thick yogurt drink gushed out. *It* foamed over the top of the large cup.
[The word *it* is a pronoun. It takes the place of the noun word group *the thick yogurt drink*.]

You and I look alike. *We* could be taken for twins.
[*We* is a pronoun. It takes the place of the pronouns *you* and *I*.]

Sometimes you may use pronouns incorrectly. When you do, your speech and writing become unclear.

Example of unclear use of a pronoun:

Conchita and Mae planned to walk to Anita's house after school. *They* hoped it would be sunny and warm.

It is unclear to whom *they* refers. Does it refer only to Conchita and Mae? Or is it also to Anita?

Example of clear use of pronoun:

Conchita and Mae hoped it would be sunny and warm after school. *They* planned to walk to Anita's house.

EXERCISE 6 Number a sheet of paper 1–6. Rewrite each sentence, substituting a pronoun for each group of underlined words.

EXAMPLE The shirt with the faded numerals is dirty.

It is dirty.

1. The fire burned so fiercely we were not sure we could stop the fire.
2. The chief shouted at us to follow the chief and move toward the fire.
3. We picked up the hoses and carried the hoses with us.
4. Inside, the heat was so bad we could hardly stand the heat.
5. "Hit those flames with water first and put those flames out," the chief said.
6. After fighting the fire for hours, all of us finally put the fire out.

Personal Pronouns

1e A personal pronoun stands for a noun or a noun word group that names a particular person, place, or thing.

People often use personal pronouns when they write or speak. Here are some examples:

PERSONAL PRONOUNS	NOUNS
I	the person speaking or writing
you	the person(s) spoken or written to
he	a man or boy
she	a woman or girl
it	a thing (such as a pencil), an idea, the wind, an unknown animal
we	a group including yourself
they	a group of people or things you speak or write about

1f Some personal pronouns change form depending upon their use in a sentence.

The form a pronoun takes is called its *case*. If a pronoun is the actor in a sentence, it is in the *subjective case*.

EXAMPLE *She* started the engine.
[*She* is the actor.]

If a pronoun receives the action in a sentence, it is in the *objective case*.

EXAMPLE Juanita drove *her* to school.
[The pronoun *her* receives the action.]

If a pronoun shows possession or ownership, it is in the *possessive case*.

EXAMPLE Juanita went in *her* car.
[The pronoun *her* shows that Juanita owns the car.]

Here are the subjective, objective, and possessive case forms of personal pronouns.

SUBJECTIVE CASE	OBJECTIVE CASE	POSSESSIVE CASE
SINGULAR		
I	me	my, mine
you	you	your, yours
he	him	his
she	her	her, hers
it	it	its
PLURAL		
we	us	our, ours
you	you	your, yours
they	them	their, theirs

EXERCISE 7   The following sentences have different cases of personal pronouns in parentheses. Number a sheet of paper 1–8. After each number write the correct case of the personal pronoun.

> EXAMPLE   Many trees shed (them/their) leaves in the fall.
>
> *their*

1. (We/Us) can see the different colors in some parts of the country.
2. In the North and the East, trees show (them/their) colors best.
3. Every tree with color loses leaves from (it/its) branches.
4. (We/Us) people have to clean up leaves in town.
5. Because (I/me) clean our yard, the trees make more work for (I/me).
6. My young sister runs and kicks her feet in the leaves piled up by (I/me) and messes (they/them) up.
7. I told my parents and (she/her) that (we/us) might have a sorry child if (she/her) messes up any more of my leaves.
8. I told (she/her) and (they/them) that she would then look good in a pile of leaves.

The English language that you speak and write uses several other kinds of pronouns as well as personal pronouns. The most common kinds are *relative pronouns, demonstrative pronouns, interrogative pronouns, indefinite pronouns,* and *reflexive pronouns.*

Relative Pronouns

Relative pronouns are used to begin groups of words that tell about someone or something mentioned earlier. A relative pronoun *relates* the word group to what it tells about. Some common relative pronouns are *that, which, who, whom,* and *whose.*

EXAMPLES Toby, *who* paints well, had three entries in the show *that* opened yesterday.

Demonstrative Pronouns

Demonstrative pronouns are used to point out particular persons or things. Some common demonstrative pronouns are *that, these, this,* and *those.*

EXAMPLES *That* belongs with *these.*

EXERCISE 8 Each of the following sentences contains one or more relative pronouns and demonstrative pronouns. Number a sheet of paper 1–5. Next to each number, write the relative pronouns and demonstrative pronouns you find in the sentence.

EXAMPLE Marlene, who collects seashells, gave us those.

who, those

1. This is a shell that she found last week.
2. The grey shell, which echoes in your ear, is bigger than those.

3. These that she has in the case need to be cleaned.
4. The echo, which is hard to hear anyway, sounds loudest in this.
5. Those still dirty might sound louder if cleaned of the sand that clogs them.

Interrogative Pronouns

Interrogative pronouns are used to ask questions. Some common interrogative pronouns are *what, which, who, whom,* and *whose.*

EXAMPLES   *Whose* towel belongs here?
Which do you want?

Indefinite Pronouns

Indefinite pronouns are used to refer to persons or things not definitely known. Some common indefinite pronouns are listed here.

all	each	more	one
another	either	most	others
any	everybody	much	several
anybody	everyone	neither	some
anyone	everything	nobody	somebody
anything	few	none	someone
both	many	no one	

EXAMPLES   *One* of the bees flew off.
Others seemed to follow.

Reflexive Pronouns

Reflexive pronouns are used to refer back to nouns or other pronouns. Some common reflexive pronouns are *myself, ourselves, yourself,* and *yourselves* (and the other forms of personal pronouns with -*self* or -*selves* added).

EXAMPLES   Warren will do the job *himself.*
Zenia gave *herself* a gift.

EXERCISE 9   Each of the following sentences contains one or more interrogative pronouns, indefinite pronouns, or reflexive pronouns. Number a sheet of paper 1–5. Next to each number, write the pronouns you find in the sentence.

EXAMPLE   What will the others do for themselves?

what, others, themselves

1. Who can speak for everyone?
2. No one can speak for all.
3. However, several seem to know everything about the trip.
4. What is the plan for yourself?
5. We will have to discover everything for ourselves.

ADJECTIVES

1g   An adjective is used to modify or describe a noun or pronoun.

An adjective tells *what kind, which one, how much,* or *how many.*

EXAMPLES

what kind	a *tame* bird	a *bent* rod
which one	the *third* row	the *old* one
how much or how many	a *full* bucket	*six* meters

A single adjective may modify more than one noun or pronoun in a sentence.

EXAMPLE   The sea and the sky appeared *blue.*

Also, a noun or pronoun may have more than one adjective modifying it.

EXAMPLE   However, *dark* and *heavy* clouds soon changed color.

The words *a, an,* and *the* are special adjectives. They are called *articles.*

EXERCISE 10   The following sentences contain adjectives. Number a sheet of paper 1–10. After each number write every adjective in the sentence and the noun it modifies or describes. Draw an arrow from the adjective to the noun it modifies. Do not write the articles.

EXAMPLE   Being a space detective in the twenty-first century is not easy work.

space detective

easy work

twenty-first century

1. That is why I charge ninety moondollars an hour.
2. I have decided to be the best detective in the whole galaxy.
3. I was on a dangerous case for a strange person named Q.
4. I had never seen this mysterious boss of mine.
5. But I had heard a rough voice giving crisp orders on the electronic spacephone.
6. I had been given a tough job to find a large gem called the Jupiter Stone.
7. But when I found the precious Jupiter Stone, it was guarded by a powerful robot.
8. After a long battle, I stopped the metal monster and escaped with the priceless gem.
9. Then I heard a familiar rough voice in the moon shadows behind me.
10. "You passed my little test," the low voice said, "and now are you ready for a real assignment, Ms. Hassenfelter?"

The Position of Adjectives

Adjectives usually come before the nouns they modify. Sometimes, however, adjectives come right after the noun.

EXAMPLE The horse, *weak* and *sweaty,* stood
motionless in the dusty road.
[The adjectives *weak* and *sweaty* are
placed directly after the noun *horse,*
which they describe. Note that they
are set off by commas from the rest
of the sentence.]

Hint: When placing an adjective directly
after the noun it modifies, use commas to
set off the adjective.

EXAMPLES

ADJECTIVES BEFORE THE NOUN

The faded old curtain hung
in tatters.
A startled deer bounded
across the clearing.

ADJECTIVES AFTER THE NOUN

The curtain, old and
faded, hung in tatters.
A deer, startled,
bounded across the
clearing.

Sometimes adjectives come later in the sentence and complete the description of a noun or
pronoun. These are called *adjective completers.*

EXAMPLES The napkin is *red* and *white.* It
looks *new.*
[The adjectives *red* and *white*

describe the noun *napkin*. The adjective *new* modifies the pronoun *it*.]

Comparison of Adjectives

1h An adjective may change form to show how one thing compares with another.

Most adjectives add **er** and **est** to show comparisons. These endings are added to the *positive form* of the adjective. If two things are compared, **er** is added to make the *comparative form*.

EXAMPLE

POSITIVE FORM   Her right hand is *strong*.
COMPARATIVE FORM   Her left hand is
                   stronger.

Most short adjectives add **er** to form the comparative.

EXAMPLES   POSITIVE   COMPARATIVE
           old   older
           round   rounder
           tame   tamer

[Note that when the positive form ends in **e,** only **r** is added.]

POSITIVE   COMPARATIVE
fat   fatter

[Note that when the positive form ends in a consonant with a single vowel before it, the consonant is doubled before **er** is added.]

See Spelling,
pp. 338–339

POSITIVE	COMPARATIVE
happy	happier

[Note that when the positive form ends in **y** with a consonant before it, the **y** changes to **i**.]

Most short adjectives add **est** to the positive form to show comparison of more than two things. This form is called the *superlative form.*

EXAMPLES

POSITIVE   North of the equator, the *short* days are in the fall and winter.

COMPARATIVE   The days become *shorter* in the summer and fall.

SUPERLATIVE   The *shortest* day is in December.

Here are the different forms of adjectives.

POSITIVE	COMPARATIVE	SUPERLATIVE
long	longer	longest
square	squarer	squarest
wet	wetter	wettest
funny	funnier	funniest

Long adjectives do not usually add **er** and **est** to form the comparative and superlative forms. Instead, they add the words *more* and *most* in front of the positive form.

EXAMPLES

POSITIVE	COMPARATIVE	SUPERLATIVE
frightful	more frightful	most frightful
vicious	more vicious	most vicious
graceful	more graceful	most graceful

Hint: If you are not sure how to form the comparative or superlative form of an adjective, say the word to yourself in a sentence. A long adjective will sound too long and awkward. Do not use a word like *beautifulest,* for example, because it sounds too awkward. Use *most beautiful.*

EXERCISE 11 Each of the following sentences needs a form of the adjective in parentheses. Number a sheet of paper 1–7. Next to each number, write the correct form of the adjective.

EXAMPLE Two engines are _____ than one. (strong)

stronger

1. That is the _____ freight train ever to climb these mountains. (long)
2. These are the _____ mountains along the entire railroad. (steep)
3. It will be a _____ climb than anyone believes. (hard)
4. I am the _____ engineer on the railroad. (trustworthy)
5. I have never known a _____ job than this one. (dangerous)
6. It would be a lot _____ if we just hauled a load of feathers. (easy)
7. If we have a wreck, think how much _____ those would be to land on! (comfortable)

Irregular Adjectives

Some adjectives form their comparative and superlative forms in special ways. These are called *irregular adjectives*. Here is a list of the forms of the most common irregular adjectives.

POSITIVE	COMPARATIVE	SUPERLATIVE
bad	worse	worst
good well }	better	best
many much }	more	most

EXERCISE 12 Number a sheet of paper 1–15. Write the comparative and superlative forms of the following adjectives.

EXAMPLE   wise

wiser

1. sloppy	6. gracious	11. much
2. strong	7. foolish	12. bare
3. well	8. high	13. hot
4. happy	9. few	14. tired
5. dry	10. practical	15. wide

Adjectival Pronouns

1i   Some pronouns may be used as adjectives.

Certain pronouns may be used with nouns to tell which person, place, or thing is meant.

EXAMPLES *This* hammer is better than *my* hammer.
Which hammer should we use?

These pronouns are called *adjectival pronouns.* They are used as adjectives to help describe nouns.

EXERCISE 13 Each of the following sentences has one or more adjectival pronouns. Number a sheet of paper 1–6. Next to each number write the adjectival pronouns in the sentence.

EXAMPLE Your cap looks warmer than her cap.

your, her

1. These clothes are not my clothes.
2. Whose clothes are they?
3. This coat is too short to be my coat.
4. What child could wear these shoes?
5. Those pants would hardly cover my knees.
6. Which thrift shop could use these garments?

REVIEW EXERCISE A   Nouns

Each of the following sentences contains one or more nouns. Number a sheet of paper 1–10. Next to each number, write all the nouns from the sentence.

EXAMPLE The American alligator can be found in the southeastern United States.

alligator, United States

1. Its dark green and grey skin is tough.
2. The alligator has eyes at the top of its skull so it can see while swimming.
3. It swims by moving its tail.
4. It lives for fifty or sixty years.
5. Females use grass and other plants to make a nest.
6. They lay their eggs in the center of it.
7. In winter, these animals rest under water, in the mud, or in deep holes.
8. They eat turtles, fish, snakes, frogs, and other animals.
9. Alligators used to be seen in North Carolina and in the Mississippi River.
10. The Fish and Wildlife Service does its best to protect them.

REVIEW EXERCISE B   Personal Pronouns

Following is a matching exercise. Number a sheet of paper 1–10. Choose the personal pronoun that fits in each blank and write it next to each number.

PERSONAL PRONOUNS

their	they
she	her
our	you
it	us
we	them
I	his
he	me

EXAMPLE   The queen of the planet Alpha
Magna adjusted _____ tunic.

her

1. "My people," she said, "_____ planet has been invaded."
2. "Strange creatures have brought _____ space ships to this world."
3. _____ fell silent for a moment.
4. "_____ myself have spoken to these alien beings."
5. "As a people, _____ must decide what should be done."
6. "_____ say they want our yellow metal."
7. "I hear how _____ laugh."
8. "Strange as _____ may seem, they feel that this most common of our metals is extremely valuable."
9. "I believe we should give _____ all they want."
10. "Perhaps then they will leave _____ in peace."

REVIEW EXERCISE C   Other Kinds of Pronouns

The following sentences contain one or more of these types of pronouns: relative pronouns, demonstrative pronouns, interrogative pronouns, indefinite pronouns, or reflexive pronouns. Number a sheet of paper 1–10. Next to each number, write the pronoun or pronouns that are found in each of the sentences.

EXAMPLE Hunza is a small country whose
people live to great ages.

whose

1. In this high, mountainous land, everyone must work.
2. Meat, which is very scarce, is rarely eaten.
3. Several of the crops grown are potatoes, carrots, cauliflower, and turnips.
4. In the high country, nobody eats sugar or smokes tobacco.
5. That may be one reason the people live so long.
6. Many of Hunza's people live to be more than a hundred.
7. Yet the land itself is steep, rocky, and harsh.
8. What makes this such a happy place?
9. The people, who are poor, are easygoing.
10. Their lives, which are simple, are rich in peace and health.

REVIEW EXERCISE D Adjectives

Several of the following sentences contain adjectives, but some do not. Number a sheet of paper 1–10. Next to each number, write all the adjectives in the sentence. Do not write the articles *a, an,* or *the.* If there are no adjectives in the sentence, write *0.*

EXAMPLES The cold winter had gone, replaced
by a warm spring.

cold, warm.

"I'm leaving," Joanie said.

O

1. "Do you have dark glasses?" asked the kind woman.
2. "I've got them, an orange towel, and the suntan lotion."
3. "Do you have a good book?"
4. "Yes, and I have the transistor radio and three magazines."
5. "Are you taking along something to eat?"
6. "I've got a bag of fresh grapes and cheese and bread."
7. "The cheese might melt."
8. "I've got a big roll of paper towels."
9. "I guess you have remembered to bring everything."
10. "Well, getting some sun is serious business," said Joanie, as she went out the door into the bright sun.

REVIEW EXERCISE E   Comparison of Adjectives

Following is a list of adjectives. Some are in the positive form. Others are in the comparative or superlative form. Number a sheet of paper 1–10. Next to each number, write all three forms of each adjective, beginning with the positive form.

EXAMPLE   least

less, lesser, least

1. more helpful
2. more
3. greatest
4. colder
5. dangerous
6. latest
7. lower
8. sillier
9. charming
10. beautiful

REVIEW EXERCISE F   Adjectival Pronouns

Below is a list of adjectival pronouns. On a sheet of paper, write five sentences of your own. Use a different adjectival pronoun in each sentence. Underline the pronoun.

this	my	these
which	your	

2

PARTS OF SPEECH

Verbs, Adverbs, Prepositions, Conjunctions, Interjections

This chapter presents the five parts of speech not discussed in Chapter 1. *Verbs* tell of action or existence. *Adverbs* can describe action. They also can modify adjectives or adverbs. *Prepositions* and *conjunctions* show relationships among ideas in a sentence. *Interjections* only express strong feelings.

Remember that each part of speech does special work in a sentence. The kind of work done by a word tells you what part of speech it is.

VERBS

2a A verb is a word used to help tell what happens or what exists.

EXAMPLES   Ed *starts* the bus.   It *appears* full.
The bus *moves.*   *Are* you ready?

There are two kinds of verbs: *action verbs* and *linking verbs*.

Action Verbs

(1) An action verb tells what someone or something does.

Action verbs, as their name shows, tell of action. In a sentence, the action verb helps tell what happens.

EXAMPLES   Charlene *threw* the ball against the wall.
[*Threw* tells what Charlene did.]

The rubber ball *bounced* to the ground.
[*Bounced* tells what the ball did.]

Marilyn *caught* the ball in the air.
[*Caught* tells what Marilyn did.]

EXERCISE 1   Number a sheet of paper 1–10. Next to each number, write the action verb in each sentence.

EXAMPLE   At his home in San Francisco, Charles E. Bolton dressed in fine suits and hats.

dressed

1. On the job Bolton wore a long white coat and a flour sack over his head.
2. People called the man in the white coat Black Bart.

3. In the late 1870's and early 1880's, Black Bart successfully robbed twenty-seven stagecoaches.
4. However, Black Bart never shot anyone.
5. After each holdup, he left a poem about the robbery.
6. Black Bart's last robbery happened November 3, 1883.
7. At that robbery, Bart accidentally dropped his handkerchief.
8. A detective found a laundry mark on the clean, white handkerchief.
9. This mark led the detective to a laundry in San Francisco.
10. At that laundry he arrested one of the cleanest bandits in the West.

Transitive and Intransitive Verbs

(2) An action verb is transitive if its action is received by someone or something.

The word *transitive* means a "crossing over" of action to a receiver. The receiver of the action is called the *object*.

See Sentences, p. 117

Examples of transitive verbs:

Nitosha *bent* the nail.
[*Bent* is a transitive verb. *Nail* receives the action. It is the object.]

Perry *crumpled* the paper into a ball.
[*Crumpled* is a transitive verb. Its action is received by the paper. *Paper* is the object.]

(3) An action verb is intransitive if there is no receiver of the action.

The word *intransitive* means "not crossing over." No person or thing receives the action of an intransitive verb. There is no object of the verb.

Examples of intransitive verbs:

Carmen *laughed.*
[*Laughed* is an intransitive verb. The action it expresses leads nowhere.]

In the morning Carmen *yawns* after waking up.
[*Yawns* is an intransitive verb. No person or thing receives the action it expresses.]

EXERCISE 2   Six of the following sentences have transitive verbs. The others have intransitive verbs. Number a sheet of paper 1–12. Next to each number, write the verb in the sentence. Next to the verb, write *T* if it is transitive. Write *I* if it is intransitive.

EXAMPLE   Thai slithered up the tree.

1. She rested on a wide, low branch.
2. She waited there for a long while.
3. She heard many sounds in the jungle.
4. Far away a lion roared a challenge into the air.
5. The monkeys chattered in the nearby trees.
6. They shook the top branches.
7. But Thai saw nothing.

8. At last something made a crackling noise in the brush.
9. Below her a small wild pig came by.
10. Quickly the old snake dropped from her branch.
11. Thai caught her dinner.
12. The jungle quieted.

Linking Verbs

(4) **A linking verb joins words that name someone or something with words that describe or rename that person or thing.**

There are only a few linking verbs in English. The most common linking verbs are the forms of the verb *to be.* Some of these verbs are *am, are, is, was,* and *were.* Other linking verbs are forms of *appear, become, look, seem,* and *sound.*

Usually a linking verb cannot complete the See Sentences, pp. 118–119 thought of a sentence all by itself. It needs to be followed by another word or words called a *subject completer.* Completers may be nouns, pronouns, adjectives, or adverbs.

EXAMPLES The ants *are* alive.
[*Are* is the linking verb. *Alive* is an adjective that describes the ants.]

Their nest *is* full of eggs.
[*Is* is the linking verb. *Full* is an adjective that tells something about the condition of the nest.]

EXERCISE 3 Number a sheet of paper 1–8. Next to each number, write the linking verb.

EXAMPLE What is wrong with me, Carla?

is

1. My throat feels sore and dry.
2. Carla seemed aware of my feelings.
3. Those two teeth looked so frightening.
4. But Carla's voice sounded soft and friendly.
5. "You are fine now, Gus, exactly like me."
6. In the mirror there was a brand of two red spots on my neck.
7. Suddenly the mirror looked empty, with no reflection.
8. In my nightmare I became a vampire, too.

Hint: Remember that a linking verb joins with another word or words to describe a person, place, or thing. An action verb helps tell of something that happens or has happened.

Auxiliary Verbs

(5) An auxiliary verb helps the main verb tell what happens or what exists.

EXAMPLES The bread *will* fall out of the oven.
[The auxiliary verb *will* helps the main verb *fall*.]

We *can* eat it anyway.
[The auxiliary verb *can* helps the main verb *eat*.]

The most common helping verbs are listed here:

am	have	can	might
are	has	may	must
is	had	should	do
was	shall	would	does
were	will	could	did

The main verb and its auxiliary verb or verbs make up the *complete verb,* also called the *verb phrase.*

See Phrase, p. 405

EXAMPLES Paula *should know* the answers.
She *has been studying* them all night.

In some sentences words come between the auxiliary verb and the main verb. The auxiliary verb and the main verb are still the words that make up the complete verb.

EXAMPLES Kenji *will* most likely *get* a high grade on the test.
Studying *can* often *make* the difference.

EXERCISE 4 Number a sheet of paper 1–10. Next to each number, write the complete verb. Underline the auxiliary verb.

EXAMPLE People had sighted a UFO.

had sighted

1. Some of them had rushed inside for safety.
2. Others were hurrying away from town.
3. Still others were walking carefully toward the object.

4. It had soared in on a beam of light.
5. Its flight was watched by dozens of people.
6. It had made a landing in a field.
7. Some brave people were approaching its side.
8. Strange musical messages were coming from it.
9. Many people had feared disaster.
10. However, a relationship was established between the invaders and the humans.

Tense

2b Most verbs change form to show a change in tense.

The word *tense* means time. Verbs show tense to make it clear in a sentence when the action happened or when someone or something existed.

EXAMPLES
PRESENT She *walks* to work each morning.
SIMPLE PAST She *walked* to work yesterday.
FUTURE She *will walk* to work tomorrow.

See Infinitive, p. 400 The *present tense* of a verb uses the *infinitive* form to show present action. The verb adds **s** or **es** if its subject is *he, she,* or *it,* or any noun these words can stand for.

EXAMPLE

INFINITIVE	PRESENT	
	Singular	Plural
sleep	I sleep	we sleep
	you sleep	you sleep
	he ⎤ she ⎬ sleeps it ⎦	they sleep

Another form of the present tense is made by adding **ing** to the infinitive form of the main verb. This other form is called the *present participle*. The present participle form of the main verb is combined with the present tense of the auxiliary verb *be* to show continuing action in the present.

EXAMPLES

INFINITIVE	PRESENT PARTICIPLE
carry	carrying
slip	slipping
hope	hoping
lose	losing

Estelle *is carrying* bundles.
The bundles *are slipping* from her hands.
Estelle *is hoping* she *is* not *losing* her grip.

Future tense is shown in several ways. Ordinarily the main verb is helped by either *shall* or *will*.

EXAMPLES She *will walk* to work tomorrow.
I *shall finish* the book soon.

Future tense can also be shown in other ways.

EXAMPLES She *might walk* to work next week.
He *is going to hunt* for his wallet.

Regular verbs show *simple past tense* by adding **d** or **ed** to the infinitive. Irregular verbs do not show simple past tense by adding **ed**. Instead, irregular verbs have special forms for the past tense.

Another form of the past tense is called the *present perfect*. This form uses the *past participle* form of the main verb and the present tense of the auxiliary verb *have* to show that an action has been completed in the past.

EXAMPLES

INFINITIVE	PAST PARTICIPLE
speak	spoken
walk	walked
do	done

Elisa *has spoken* to Luis.
Yoko and Tae *have walked* home.
Randy *has* already *done* his homework.

Regular Verbs

2c **Regular verbs add *ed* or *d* to the infinitive form to show the past tense.**

EXAMPLES

INFINITIVE	SIMPLE PAST
climb	climb**ed**
live	liv**ed**
close	clos**ed**

Irregular Verbs

2d **Irregular verbs may change form to show past tense, but they do not add *ed* or *d* to the infinitive form.**

The past tense of irregular verbs is shown in special ways. For example, *break* is the infinitive

form of an irregular verb. Its simple past tense is
broke. Its present perfect tense is *have broken*.

EXAMPLES

INFINITIVE	SIMPLE PAST	PRESENT PERFECT
break	broke	have broken
ride	rode	have ridden
run	ran	have run
stand	stood	have stood
take	took	have taken
throw	threw	have thrown

EXERCISE 5 The simple past tense or the present
perfect tense of each of the following verbs is missing. Number a sheet of paper 1–15. Next to each
number, write the missing tense of the verb. After
each word you write put *R* if it is a regular verb.
Put *I* if it is an irregular verb.

EXAMPLE

INFINITIVE	SIMPLE PAST	PRESENT PERFECT
go	went	_____

have gone, ↙

INFINITIVE	SIMPLE PAST	PRESENT PERFECT
1. run	_____	have run
2. live	_____	have lived
3. blow	blew	_____
4. play	_____	have played
5. hunt	_____	have hunted

ʃ

6. swim	swam	_____
7. look	looked	_____
8. work	_____	have worked
9. catch	_____	have caught
10. tap	tapped	_____
11. fly	flew	_____
12. begin	_____	have begun
13. hold	_____	have held
14. open	opened	_____
15. sit	_____	have sat

ADVERBS

2e An adverb is a word used to modify an action verb, an adjective, another adverb, or a complete statement.

An adverb that modifies an action verb tells *when, where, how, how much,* or *how often* the action occurs.

Examples of adverbs that tell *when* action happens:

Sylvia arrived *late.*
[When did Sylvia arrive? Answer: *late. Late* is the adverb.]

Doc swam across the lake *yesterday.*
[When did Doc swim across the lake? Answer: *yesterday. Yesterday* is the adverb.]

Example of an adverb that tells *where* the action happens:

We put the cat *inside*.
[Where did we put the cat? Answer: *inside*.
Inside is the adverb.]

Examples of adverbs that tell *how* or *how often*
something happens:

Jay picked up the glass *carefully*.
[How did Jay pick up the glass? Answer:
carefully. *Carefully* is the adverb.]

Isabel Grenville practiced *daily*.
[How often did she practice? Answer: *daily*.
Daily is the adverb.]

Certain adverbs can be placed in different positions within a sentence. Unlike adjectives, which
usually must be next to the nouns they modify,
these adverbs are movable.

EXAMPLES   Jay *carefully* picked up the glass.
            Carefully Jay picked up the glass.
            Jay picked up the glass *carefully*.

The words *not* and *never* are special adverbs.
They change the meaning of a verb from positive to
negative.

EXAMPLES   Roberta is here.
            Roberta is *not* here.
            Roberta is *never* here.

EXERCISE 6   Write the following sentences on a
sheet of paper. Skip a line between each sentence.
Underline each adverb. Draw an arrow from the
adverb to the verb it modifies.

EXAMPLE   Alexander the Great fought valiantly in many battles in the fourth century B.C.

Alexander the Great fought <u>valiantly</u> in many battles in the fourth century B.C.

1. At the age of sixteen, Alexander bravely led his troops.
2. By the age of eighteen, he quickly conquered many Greek cities.
3. At twenty he easily won election as king of Macedon.
4. All of Greece soon came under his rule.
5. He moved then to conquer Persia.
6. He later overran Egypt.
7. He drove his troops impatiently.
8. They marched constantly in search of new land.
9. Alexander treated most of the conquered people well.
10. At age thirty-two, he suddenly died of a fever.

EXERCISE 7   Write the following sentences on a sheet of paper. Skip a line between each sentence. Underline the adverb in each of the sentences. Draw an arrow from the adverb to the verb the adverb modifies.

EXAMPLE Two pigeons perched quietly on a high ledge.

Two pigeons perched quietly on a high ledge.

1. "Move forward," the mother pigeon said to her youngster.
2. "Stand here at the edge," she said.
3. "You can soar gracefully on your wings."
4. The youngster stepped fearfully to the edge of the ledge.
5. He looked timidly at the street.
6. "Must I fly down?" he gurgled.
7. "Open your wings now," said his mother.
8. She spread her wings fully.
9. He feebly flopped his little wings.
10. "I think I'll fly tomorrow," he said as he retreated.

EXERCISE 8 Number a sheet of paper 1–6. Next to each number, write the verb and an adverb that tells *where, when,* or *how.*

EXAMPLE play _____ (how)

hard

1. ride _____ (when)
2. eat _____ (how)
3. drive _____ (how)
4. run _____ (where)
5. sleep _____ (when)
6. camp _____ (where)

Adverbs are sometimes used to modify adjectives.

EXAMPLE   Wilma has extremely long
           fingernails.
           [The adverb *extremely* modifies the
           adjective *long*.]

The adverbs *too* and *very* modify adjectives. Other adverbs that modify adjectives include the following:

amazingly	entirely	rather
completely	especially	surprisingly
continually	extremely	terribly
definitely	quite	unusually

Adverbs can also modify other adverbs.

EXAMPLE   The summer rains arrived rather
           late.
           [The adverb *rather* modifies the
           adverb *late*.]

EXERCISE 9 The following sentences contain adverbs that modify adjectives or other adverbs. Number a sheet of paper 1–12. Skip a line between numbers. Next to each number, write the sentence. Underline the adverb. Draw an arrow from the adverb to the adjective or the other adverb it modifies.

EXAMPLE   Weapons have a dreadfully long
           history.

Weapons have a
dreadfully long history.

1. Darts and spears appeared very early.
2. Slings and stones made amazingly powerful weapons.
3. David killed the giant Goliath with a surprisingly accurate shot.
4. Bows and arrows have been used quite widely.
5. The longbow has an unusually interesting background.
6. Its very earliest beginnings are not known.
7. It seems to have been used more widely than any other weapon.
8. The crossbow became an especially powerful weapon.
9. Its arrow could pierce a soldier's armor rather easily.
10. Gunpowder hurls a missile more powerfully than a bowstring.
11. The gun quite soon replaced the bow.
12. Extremely forceful guns and rockets are the rule today.

Adverbs may modify an entire statement.

EXAMPLE *Then* I was too young to understand. [The adverb *then* modifies the statement *I was too young to understand.*]

EXERCISE 10 Each of the following sentences contains an adverb. Number a sheet of paper 1–18. Next to each number, write the adverb from the sentence. Next to the adverb, write the word or group of words the adverb modifies.

EXAMPLE Michiko Endo finally finished the blanket.

finally, finished

1. Jorge Estrada expertly closed the box.
2. In it was an exceedingly noisy animal.
3. The animal definitely wanted to escape.
4. Jorge asked Angela Dye to hold the box carefully.
5. She took it clumsily.
6. The box shook fiercely in Angela's hands.
7. Angela's extremely shaky grip loosened.
8. The box fell noisily to the floor.
9. Jorge and Angela were momentarily stunned.
10. "Grab the beast quickly," yelled Jorge.
11. Angela bent hurriedly toward the box.
12. At that moment a quite speedy animal slipped from the box.
13. It escaped as Angela fruitlessly reached for it.
14. Jorge seemed upset then.
15. "Why did you do that?" shouted Jorge angrily.
16. "That's a surprisingly fast animal you have," said Angela.
17. "How can you say that?" moaned Jorge sadly.
18. "It's amazingly fast, but 'you have' are the wrong words," continued Jorge. "The words should be 'you had'."

EXERCISE 11 Use the following adverbs in sentences of your own. Make up ten sentences to include adverbs that modify verbs, adjectives, and other adverbs. Underline the adverbs you use.

1. extremely
2. truly
3. unusually
4. quite
5. perfectly
6. completely
7. most
8. easily
9. sharply
10. horribly

2f Adverbs help compare the action of verbs.

Most adverbs can show comparison by adding **er** and **est.**

EXAMPLES
POSITIVE Gary Budmind sleeps *late* on Saturdays.
COMPARATIVE He wishes he could sleep *later.*
POSITIVE The parents of Jody Buck let her sleep *late.*
SUPERLATIVE Jody Buck sleeps the *latest* of all our class.

Adverbs that are long words or that end in **ly** do not add **er** or **est** to show comparison. Instead, they add the words *more* and *most* in front.

EXAMPLES
POSITIVE crudely
COMPARATIVE more crudely
SUPERLATIVE most crudely

Irregular Adverbs

A few adverbs show their comparative and superlative forms in irregular ways.

EXAMPLES
POSITIVE   well, badly
COMPARATIVE   better, worse
SUPERLATIVE   best, worst

EXERCISE 12   Number a sheet of paper 1–5. Next to each number, write the correct form of the adverb that belongs in the blank in each sentence.

EXAMPLE   Bunny Clooney brushes her teeth _____ than anyone in her family.   (hard)

harder

1. She also chews carrots _____ than anyone. (loud)
2. She says they make her teeth shine _____ than they used to. (brightly)
3. Her older sister, Honey, chews _____ than Bunny. (fast)
4. Their younger brother, Sonny, chews carrots the _____ of all. (fast)
5. He also chews carrots _____ than his sisters. (often)

PREPOSITIONS

2g   **A preposition connects the noun or the pronoun that usually follows it to other words in a sentence.**

EXAMPLES   The paychecks came *before* the mail.

[The preposition *before* relates the noun *mail* to the verb *came*.]

I put mine *in* the bank.
[The preposition *in* relates its object *bank* to the verb *put*.]

Other members *of* the team cashed their checks.
[The preposition *of* relates its object *team* to the noun *members*.]

Prepositions most often help show relations of time, place, manner, or kind. A list of common prepositions follows:

TIME	PLACE			MANNER OR KIND
after	about	below	near	by
before	above	beside	on	except
during	across	between	over	for
since	against	beyond	through	like
until	around	down	toward	of
	at	into	under	with
	behind	inside	up	

Some prepositions are made up of more than one word.

EXAMPLES
| because of | in addition to | instead of |
| by means of | in back of | on account of |

EXERCISE 13 The following sentences contain seventeen prepositions. Number a sheet of paper 1–12. Next to each number, write the preposition or prepositions that appear in that sentence.

EXAMPLE A picture of you is worth a thousand
words in a description.

of, in

1. Most people like seeing themselves in photographs.
2. The camera is an invention of the nineteenth
century.
3. Cameras of today owe their development to
many people.
4. Before photography, people only drew pictures
or wrote descriptions.
5. Cameras bring people pictures of places beyond
their reach.
6. They have seen astronauts on the moon.
7. The surface of Mars is captured in photographs.
8. One astronaut dropped a camera during a
spacewalk.
9. Probably it is still whirling through space.
10. The manufacturer of that camera offered a reward of a million dollars to anyone who could
find it.
11. Maybe a stranger from outer space will find it.
12. Would the stranger keep the camera or return
it for the reward?

Object of the Preposition

A preposition usually takes an *object*. The object is usually a following noun or pronoun. The
preposition relates its object to some other word in
the sentence.

EXAMPLES   Rachel left *after* the party.
[*Party* is the object of the
preposition *after.*]

She left *with a* friend.
[*Friend* is the object of the
preposition *with.*]

They stopped *at* Maxie's diner.
[*Diner* is the object of the
preposition *at.*]

EXERCISE 14   The following sentences contain
twenty prepositions with their objects. Write each
sentence on a sheet of paper. Skip a line between
every sentence. Underline each preposition and
draw an arrow from it to its object.

EXAMPLE   Many kinds of animals have an
amazing sense of direction.

Many kinds of animals
have an amazing
sense of direction.

1. One example is the sea turtle that swims 1,400
   miles each year from Brazil to a small Atlantic
   island.
2. The female sea turtle lays her eggs on the island in the sand.
3. She leaves the eggs, returns to the ocean, and
   swims toward Brazil.
4. Later the baby turtles hatch and crawl from
   the nest to the sea.

5. They swim toward Brazil and arrive without help.
6. How the turtles know the route is a mystery to scientists.
7. Another example is shown in the migration of birds.
8. Many birds of the northern hemisphere travel south in the winter.
9. They return to the north in the spring.
10. Many of them nest in the same place each year during the summer.

2h   A preposition may have more than one object.

EXAMPLES   Salvatore Dominic lives

in the city and the country.

He works at an office and his home.

EXERCISE 15   Write each of the following ten sentences on a sheet of paper. Underline the preposition. Draw arrows from each preposition to both objects of the preposition.

EXAMPLE   The Saint Bernard is a dog of large size and intelligence.

The Saint Bernard is a dog

of large size and intelligence

1. This dog is recognized by its great size and sad face.

2. Its fur is a mixture of brown and white.
3. Its front and back are marked by floppy ears and a bushy tail.
4. It walks with a lumbering step and rolling motion.
5. The breed was trained to rescue travelers trapped in dangerous snowdrifts or sudden snowstorms.
6. It also could lead hikers over mountains and high trails.
7. It brought them safely to food and shelter.
8. It has done its work in the high Alps and other mountainous regions.
9. It is blessed with excellent ears and nose.
10. Many victims owe their lives to this dog's keen sense and courage.

CONJUNCTIONS

2i A conjunction is a word used to join other words or groups of words.

Conjunctions are of two types: *coordinating* and *subordinating*.

Coordinating Conjunctions

Coordinating conjunctions connect words or word groups that are equally important. The most common coordinating conjunctions are *and, but, for, nor,* and *or.*

A coordinating conjunction may join words.

EXAMPLE   Rhythm *and* blues have been mixed by Stuckey *and* Grange.

A coordinating conjunction may join short word groups.

EXAMPLE   They make records *and* give concerts.

A coordinating conjunction may join longer word groups.

EXAMPLE   They had hoped to break up their group, *but* their fans forced them to stay together.

A few pairs of conjunctions are used together in the English language. These are a kind of coordinating conjunction called *correlative conjunctions*. They work like coordinating conjunctions. The correlatives are *either... or, neither... nor, not only ... but also*.

EXAMPLE   *Either* you *or* I must speak out.

EXERCISE 16   Number a sheet of paper 1–6. Next to each number, write each sentence. Circle the coordinating conjunction or correlative conjunction you find in the sentence.

EXAMPLE   Nat Love wore cowboy clothes and carried a gun.

Nat Love wore cowboy clothes (and) carried a gun.

1. There have been many famous cowboys, but only a few Black American ones are known today.

2. Nat Love was one who was good at riding and roping.
3. He was good not only as a cattle worker but also as a sharpshooter.
4. It is said he could shoot well with either a rifle or a revolver.
5. The story is told that some bandits tried to hold up a train, but Nat stopped them singlehandedly.
6. He neither went looking for trouble nor turned away from a challenge.

Subordinating Conjunctions

Certain conjunctions join word groups that are not equally important. Such conjunctions are called See Clauses, pp. 83–91 *subordinating conjunctions*. *Subordinate* means "less important."

Here is a list of common subordinating conjunctions:

after	because	though
although	before	unless
as	if	until
as if	since	when
as long as	so that	whenever
as soon as	than	wherever
as though		while

EXAMPLES An adult crocodile will eat baby crocodiles *when* it sees them.

The babies must hide *if* they are to stay alive.

The subordinating conjunction begins a group of words that needs other words to complete its statement. The subordinate word group may come in almost any position in a sentence.

EXAMPLES

LAST POSITION   Baby alligators scurry for cover *when* they break out of their shells.

FIRST POSITION   *When* they break out of the shells, baby alligators scurry for cover.

Hint: The group of words that follows the subordinating conjunction is never a complete thought or idea. Another group of words is needed to complete the sentence.

EXERCISE 17   Each of the following sentences contains a subordinating conjunction. Number a sheet of paper 1–10. Next to each number, write the subordinating conjunction.

EXAMPLE   Although she was tired, Pat kept running.

although

1. Pat would keep running as long as her legs held out.
2. The race would be over when she passed the middle of the grandstand.

3. Since Shirley Yuen and Janet Bedrosian were ahead of her, Pat felt the need to go faster.
4. There was less than half a lap to go until they reached the finish line.
5. Suddenly Pat spurted faster because she heard the other runners behind her.
6. When she did that, it seemed she was gaining on the leaders.
7. While they seemed to slow down, Pat speeded up.
8. Although her legs ached, she drove them harder.
9. She felt she could win if only her legs held up.
10. As the leaders approached the grandstand, Pat surged ahead of them to win.

INTERJECTIONS

2j   **An interjection is a word or group of words used to express strong feeling.**

> EXAMPLES   Whoopee! We get tomorrow off.
> Oops! I made a mistake.

An interjection or the sentence it appears in usually has an exclamation mark (!) after it. Commas may be used to set off an interjection in the middle of a sentence.

> EXAMPLE   The pump leaks, by golly, and water is running across the floor!

EXERCISE 18   On a separate sheet of paper, write six sentences. Use a different interjection in each sentence.

Goodness   Mercy
Wow   Oh
Help   Whew

WORDS AS DIFFERENT PARTS OF SPEECH

2k Many words can be used as different parts of speech.

Words such as *rope, glass, shine,* and *leaf* can work as different parts of speech in different sentences. Remember, it is the way a word is used in a sentence that tells you what part of speech it is.

EXERCISE 19 The following sentences have underlined words used as different parts of speech. Number a sheet of paper 1–8. Next to each number write what part of speech the underlined word is in the sentence.

EXAMPLE The cowboy <u>roped</u> the mustang.

verb

1. You can <u>wax</u> the car tomorrow.
2. Try not to break the <u>watch</u>.
3. <u>Watch</u> out for water.
4. It may hurt the <u>wax</u> surface.
5. The movers <u>tag</u> each piece of furniture.
6. Then they carefully <u>load</u> it all.
7. The truck will have a full <u>load</u>.
8. Sign the <u>paper</u> to release the shipment.

REVIEW EXERCISE A Kinds of Verbs

All of the verbs in the following sentences are underlined. Number a sheet of paper 1–10. Next to each number rewrite each underlined verb. Next to each verb write *A* if it is an action verb, *L* if it is a linking verb, and *Ax* if it is an auxiliary verb.

> EXAMPLE Windmills <u>seem</u> a good source of power.
>
> *L*

1. They <u>had</u> almost <u>disappeared</u>.
2. But when the cost of power <u>went</u> up, people <u>re-</u><u>membered</u> windmills.
3. Windmills <u>produce</u> energy.
4. Batteries <u>store</u> the energy.
5. When the wind <u>stops</u>, the batteries <u>provide</u> power.
6. Windmills <u>are</u> clean and smokeless.
7. They <u>do</u> not <u>produce</u> smog.
8. They <u>can pump</u> water.
9. You <u>must pay</u> for your windmill, but the wind <u>is</u> free.
10. Engineers <u>have worked</u> to bring the windmill up to date.

REVIEW EXERCISE B Tenses

Number a sheet of paper 1–10. Next to each number, write the simple past tense and the present perfect tense of each of the following verbs.

EXAMPLE   love

loved, have loved

1. win
2. drink
3. sing
4. go
5. fill

6. eat
7. jump
8. try
9. take
10. travel

REVIEW EXERCISE C   Adverbs

Each of the following sentences contains an adverb. Number a sheet of paper 1–10. Next to each number, write the adverb from the sentence. Then write the word the adverb modifies.

EXAMPLE   Worker honeybees fly tirelessly from flower to flower.

tirelessly, fly

1. They return to the nest frequently.
2. During the extremely busy summer season, a worker bee lives for six weeks.
3. Worker bees carefully guard their queen.
4. They know instantly if a strange bee comes to the hive.
5. Some workers constantly move their wings to fan fresh air into the hive.
6. Drones never work.
7. They eat eagerly.
8. Their lives must be dreadfully boring.

9. They spend their time inside.
10. They mate with the queen and starve to death later.

REVIEW EXERCISE D   Prepositions, Conjunctions, and Interjections

Each of the following sentences contains at least one preposition, conjunction, or interjection. Number a sheet of paper 1–10. Next to each number, write the preposition, conjunction, or interjection from each sentence. Then write *P* if the word you have written is a preposition, *C* if it is a conjunction, or *I* if it is an interjection.

EXAMPLE   Miguel and I were walking downtown.

and, C

1. Before we got very far, Miguel stopped me.
2. "Wow! Did you see that?" he asked.
3. We were standing in front of a bank.
4. Not only does Miguel have a good brain, but he also has a good imagination.
5. "Did I see what?" I asked, looking down the street.
6. "Did you see those two men run out of the bank?"
7. "They were carrying bags and they went that way!"
8. Because I know Miguel, it was difficult to believe him.

9. "Zounds!" I said, "If this is a wild goose chase, I'll get you!"
10. "It's not," said Miguel, "and if we don't hurry, we'll never catch them."

3

PHRASES

Noun Phrases, Verb Phrases, Prepositional Phrases, Participial Phrases

Most parts of speech are single words. However, groups of related words can work together as parts of speech. These groups of words are called *phrases.*

The kinds of phrases presented in this chapter are *noun phrases, verb phrases, prepositional phrases,* and *participial phrases.*

KINDS OF PHRASES

3a **A phrase is a group of related words used as a single part of speech.**

EXAMPLES *The grey and white pigeon* pecked the crumbs.
[*The grey and white pigeon* names a bird. These related words make a noun phrase.]

Its wings *were fluttering.*
[*Were fluttering* tells of the action
of the wings. These words make a
verb phrase.]

It hopped *on one foot.*
[*On one foot* tells how it hopped.
These words make a prepositional
phrase used as an adverb.]

Moving in circles, it ate all the
crumbs.
[*Moving in circles* describes what
the pigeon was doing when it ate.
These words make a participial
phrase.]

Hint: All the words in a phrase work together as a single part of speech.

Noun Phrases

See Noun,
p. 403 **3b A noun phrase is made up of a noun and
its modifiers.**

EXAMPLE   *The old pigeon* was *an odd bird.*
[*Pigeon* is a noun with its modifiers
the and *old.* Together, they make a
noun phrase. The noun *bird* and its
modifiers *an* and *odd* make another
noun phrase.]

See Pronoun,
p. 406   Almost any noun phrase can be replaced with a
pronoun.

EXAMPLE *An old man* spread the crumbs on the ground.
He spread crumbs on the ground.
[The pronoun *he* replaces the noun phrase *an old man.*]

EXERCISE 1 Copy the following sentences on a sheet of paper. Underline each noun phrase. Some sentences have more than one noun phrase. Be sure to underline all the related words that belong in each noun phrase.

EXAMPLE The old cow paths became crowded city streets.

The old cow paths became crowded city streets.

1. The city of Boston has many crooked streets.
2. Long ago many streets were meadow paths.
3. The big city was only a little town.
4. Domestic animals were allowed to graze freely.
5. The quiet animals and their owners used a common ground.
6. That common pasture is now called the Boston Common.
7. Tall buildings and busy streets now surround the park-like Common.
8. Any citizen may stroll through and enjoy this inner-city park.

Hint: The words in a noun phrase work together like a noun.

Verb Phrases

3c A verb phrase is made up of the main verb and its auxiliaries.

See Verbs, pp. 36–37
Main verbs are either action verbs or linking verbs. Auxiliary verbs may be used with either kind. The auxiliary verbs and their main verb make up a verb phrase. This phrase is also known as the *complete verb*.

EXAMPLES The dust *was blowing* yesterday.
The dust *has been blowing* all day today.
The dust *has covered* us.
Soon we *will be* dustbound.

All these examples show how main verbs and their auxiliary verbs combine to form verb phrases. The verb phrases tell of some action or condition.

Sometimes other words come between the main verb and its auxiliaries.

EXAMPLE The dust *had* already *drifted* around the house.
[The verb phrase is *had drifted*. The adverb *already* splits the phrase.]

EXERCISE 2 Number a sheet of paper 1–10. Next to each number, write the complete verb phrase from each of the following sentences.

EXAMPLE Cheese is made from milk.

is made

1. Cheese has been made since prehistoric times.
2. The milk of several animals has been used for the manufacture of cheese.
3. Milk is first heated in a container.
4. Then it is separated into curd and whey.
5. Sometimes the curd may be salted.
6. Certain cheeses are put under pressure.
7. The pressure will help in their curing and hardening.
8. Many cheeses are soaked in a salt bath.
9. People have been enjoying hundreds of kinds of cheeses for centuries.
10. What kinds do you enjoy?

Hint: The words in a verb phrase work together like a verb.

Prepositional Phrases

3d A prepositional phrase begins with a preposition and usually ends with a noun. See Preposition, p. 406

The prepositional phrase is made up of a preposition, the noun or pronoun that is its *object,* and any words that modify its object.

EXAMPLES   at the end
of the pencil
under the eraser
by noon
over it

Some prepositions are made up of more than one word.

EXAMPLES   according to   next to
           because of   on account of
           in spite of   out of
           instead of   up to

EXERCISE 3 Number a sheet of paper 1–12. Skip a line between each number. Next to each number, write the prepositional phrase from the sentence. Underline the preposition. Draw an arrow from it to its object.

EXAMPLE   Milo Pinchpenny lived in Mrs.
          Cortes's rooming house.

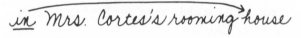

1. His mother owned a tiny cottage down the street.
2. Milo could walk there from the rooming house.
3. He used to walk there in the evening.
4. One night he failed to return to his room.
5. Mrs. Cortes had seen no one come into the rooming house.
6. She called Milo's mother after lunch.
7. "Have you seen Milo?" she asked in a worried voice.
8. "He left here before midnight," answered Milo's mother. "Is anything wrong?"
9. Two days later Milo returned to his quiet room.
10. He paid his bills, packed his bags, and moved to a Peoria suburb.
11. He got a new job in a week.
12. In another month he married a woman who owned a big house.

(1) A prepositional phrase may be used as an adjective.

Each prepositional phrase used as an adjective modifies a noun or a pronoun. The noun or the pronoun it modifies is not in the phrase. It is in some other part of the sentence. Usually the noun or the pronoun comes just before the phrase.

EXAMPLES The skirt *with the deep pleats* is upstairs.
[The prepositional phrase *with the deep pleats* modifies *skirt.*]

The rip *in the hem* needs mending.
[*In the hem* is a prepositional phrase. It works as an adjective by modifying the noun *rip.*]

EXERCISE 4 Each of the following sentences has a prepositional phrase used as an adjective. Copy each sentence on a sheet of paper. Skip a line between sentences. Underline each prepositional phrase. Draw an arrow from each phrase to the noun or pronoun it modifies.

EXAMPLE Human anatomy is the study of the human body.

Human anatomy is the study of the human body.

1. Its study reveals facts about your body.
2. The food in your diet influences your body's growth.
3. A lack of vitamins can cause illness.

4. Plenty of healthful exercise keeps you alert.
5. A reasonable amount of sleep is also necessary.
6. Cuts in the skin should be treated immediately.
7. The loss of too much blood will bring illness or even death.
8. The body of a human is an amazing organism, but it needs constant care.

(2) A prepositional phrase may be used as an adverb.

In most cases, the prepositional phrase used as an adverb modifies the verb. It tells *when, where, how long,* or *how much.*

EXAMPLES   Isobel lit the lights *at dusk.*
[This prepositional phrase tells when Isobel lit the lights.]

The lights had been placed *over the doorway.*
[This prepositional phrase tells where the lights had been placed.]

The lights burned *for three hours.*
[This prepositional phrase tells how long the lights burned.]

A prepositional phrase used as an adverb may also modify an adjective or another adverb.

Example of a prepositional phrase used as an adverb to modify an adjective:

Perhaps the elephants are too heavy *for the bridge.*
[This phrase modifies the adjective *heavy.*]

Example of a prepositional phrase used as an adverb to modify another adverb:

Students may have to leave earlier *in the morning.*
[This phrase modifies the adverb *earlier.*]

A few prepositional phrases end with an adverb instead of a noun or pronoun.

EXAMPLE   All the people stayed *up there.*
[This prepositional phrase serves as an adverb. It modifies the verb *stayed.* It tells where the people stayed.]

Hint: The words in a prepositional phrase work together like either an adjective or an adverb. They do *not* work like a preposition.

EXERCISE 5   Each of the following sentences has a prepositional phrase used as an adverb. Copy each sentence on a sheet of paper. Skip a line after each sentence. Underline each prepositional phrase. Draw an arrow from it to the word it modifies.

EXAMPLE   Salvatore Del Zampo spent the summer in the mountains.

Salvatore Del Zampo

spent the summer in the mountains.

1. He studied German for two months.
2. After one week he could say *"ja"* (yes).

3. In another week he had learned to say *"nein"* (no).
4. He gradually realized that German was hard for him.
5. If he studied for many years, he might learn only a few sentences.
6. He should have started earlier in his life.
7. He might have moved faster with his study.
8. He returned from the mountains to celebrate his one-hundredth birthday.

EXERCISE 6 Here are ten prepositional phrases. Use each in a sentence of your own. Underline each phrase. Draw an arrow from the prepositional phrase to the word it modifies.

EXAMPLES in the rain

She walked home in the rain.

by the riverbank

By the riverbank, we sang old songs.

1. after lunch
2. before the storm
3. with her friends
4. in his mind
5. from far away
6. between the two trees
7. without much anger
8. except for the cat
9. around the first turn
10. out of the flaming house

Participial Phrases

3e **A participial phrase is made up of a participle and its related words working like an adjective.**

See Participle, p. 404; Adjective, p. 387

EXAMPLES   *Pecking at the crumbs,* the bird was too busy to notice us.
[*Pecking* is the present participle. Its related words are *at the crumbs.* Together, these words make a participial phrase. It modifies the noun *bird.*]

Making little noises, it darted back and forth.
[*Making* is the present participle. Its related words are *little noises.* Together they make a participial phrase. It modifies the pronoun *it.*]

Scared by my step, it flew straight up.
[*Scared* is the past participle. *Scared by my step* is the participial phrase. The whole phrase modifies *it.*]

EXERCISE 7   Each of the following sentences contains a participial phrase. Number a sheet of paper 1–10. Next to each number, write the participial phrase. Next to that write the noun or pronoun it modifies.

EXAMPLE Running at the ball, Celinda hoped
to kick it.

Running at the ball

1. Racing after it, she almost fell.
2. Panting for breath, she swung her foot.
3. The ball, bounding into the air, sailed toward the net.
4. The goaltender, stretching her arms toward the ball, jumped too late.
5. Curving in an arch, the ball bounced into the goal.
6. Exhausted by the play, Celinda watched with a smile.
7. Celinda's teammates, roaring their approval, ran to her and hugged her.
8. Celinda, tired beyond words, knew she deserved their praise.
9. Tempted for a moment, she almost said the wrong words.
10. Then, catching herself in the act of speaking, she remained silent and happy.

REVIEW EXERCISE A Noun Phrases

Each of the following sentences has at least one noun phrase in it. Some sentences may have more than one. Number a sheet of paper 1–10. Beside each number write the complete noun phrase or noun phrases from each sentence.

EXAMPLE The Great Salt Lake in Utah is a
strange place.

The Great Salt Lake,
a strange place

1. It is a great inland sea.
2. Fresh-water streams and cool rain fill it.
3. Yet it is a salty lake.
4. It is saltier than the salty ocean.
5. This is because the fresh waters do not drain away.
6. They dry up and leave white, diamond-like salt.
7. Few fish can live in the Great Salt Lake.
8. Small brine shrimp live there.
9. The white shores are covered with hard salt.
10. Many tons of pure table salt are removed yearly.

REVIEW EXERCISE B   Verb Phrases

Number a sheet of paper 1–10. Beside each number write the verb phrase from each of the following sentences.

> EXAMPLE   No one knows when yeast was first discovered.
>
> *was discovered*

1. People have been using yeast in bread for over four thousand years.
2. Yeast is found almost anywhere.
3. The tiny plants are floating in the air around you now.
4. If you bake bread, you are probably using yeast.
5. The yeast will produce a gas.
6. The gas will form bubbles in the dough.
7. The dough will rise.

8. Then the dough will be baked in the oven.
9. The heat from the oven will have killed the yeast.
10. A light loaf of bread is left.

REVIEW EXERCISE C   Prepositional Phrases

Each following sentence contains one prepositional phrase. Number a sheet of paper 1–10. Next
to each number, write the prepositional phrase from
each sentence.

EXAMPLE   It was a quiet afternoon in the dusty
Western town.

in the dusty western town

1. The quiet was broken by a loud crash.
2. Big Clarence Jones had fallen through a hotel window.
3. A crowd gathered in the street.
4. They stood around the fallen man.
5. Everyone wondered what had happened to the big cowboy.
6. After a minute Big Clarence opened his eyes.
7. "I was standing by the window," he said.
8. "Someone hit me on the head."
9. "Now I'm lying here in the dust."
10. "By tonight, I'm going to find out who hit me."

REVIEW EXERCISE D   Participial Phrases

Each of the following sentences has one participial phrase. Number a sheet of paper 1–10. Beside
each number write the participial phrase.

EXAMPLE   Being a Black American, Daniel
Hale Williams faced many
hardships.

Being a Black American

1. Growing up as one of seven children, Williams found life hard.
2. Leaving Dan Williams to learn a trade, his mother moved away after his father died.
3. Working here and there, Williams made a little money.
4. A barber, allowing him to work part-time, helped him to go to school.
5. Studying hard, Daniel Hale Williams became a doctor.
6. Dr. Williams, seeing a need, founded the first hospital for Black Americans in 1891.
7. In 1893 a man, bleeding from an injury, became Dr. Williams's patient.
8. Taking a great chance, Dr. Williams operated on the man's heart.
9. Walking out of the hospital fifty-one days later, the man lived twenty more years.
10. Dr. Daniel Hale Williams, working without experience, had performed the world's first successful heart operation.

REVIEW EXERCISE E   Phrases

The following story contains noun phrases, verb phrases, prepositional phrases, and participial phrases. Find two of each kind of phrase. Write them on a separate sheet of paper. Next to each phrase, write whether it is a *noun phrase,* a *verb phrase,* a *prepositional phrase,* or a *participial phrase.*

EXAMPLE   Hearing a strange noise, Diana had jumped out of bed.

Hearing a strange noise, participial phrase

had jumped, verb phrase.

She had grabbed a warm bathrobe. Then she had tiptoed down the stairs. The cool, grey light of the moon was shining through the curtains. Her frightened heart was pounding. Holding her breath, Diana listened. The sound she had heard was coming from the kitchen. Thinking fast, Diana grabbed a heavy lamp. "I will see what is happening," Diana thought, "but I will take this along." Holding the big lamp, Diana walked toward the strange sound.

4

CLAUSES

Independent Clauses, Dependent Clauses

A *clause* is a group of words that acts as a sentence or as part of a sentence. A clause may stand by itself to express a complete thought. Or a clause may depend on some other statement to complete its meaning.

THE PARTS OF A CLAUSE

4a A clause is a group of related words containing a subject and a predicate.

The *complete subject* of a clause is the person or thing being talked about. The subject includes a noun or a pronoun or words that act as a noun or a pronoun. Other words may also belong to the complete subject.

See Noun, p. 403; Pronoun, p. 406

The *complete predicate* is made up of words that tell about the subject. The predicate includes a

See Verb,
p. 410 verb. Additional words may be part of the predicate as well.

Hint: A clause cannot have a subject without a predicate or a predicate without a subject.

EXAMPLES The lights burn all night.
[*The lights* is the subject of the clause. *Burn all night* tells what the lights do. It is the predicate.]

They waste electricity.
[*They* is the subject. *Waste electricity* is the predicate.]

EXERCISE 1 Eight of the following word groups are clauses. The others are not. Write each clause on a sheet of paper. Underline the complete subject once. Underline the complete predicate twice.

EXAMPLE Television offers much entertainment.

Television offers much entertainment.

1. You can see some educational television shows
2. Not everything funny
3. Too much violence
4. Critics argue about the quality of TV
5. A famous comedian makes a high salary
6. Laughing at the jokes

7. I heard one about a lost dog
8. The audience in the studio
9. Special movies are made for TV
10. Stunt people and the regular actors too
11. A woman fell from a window onto a huge sponge
12. Cushioned her fall without doing her any harm
13. An arrow stuck in his back
14. Under his shirt he wore a block of wood and under that a metal plate
15. The amazing tricks of TV shows

KINDS OF CLAUSES

There are two kinds of clauses: *independent* and *dependent*.

Independent Clauses

4b **An independent clause needs no other words to complete its thought.**

An independent clause may be either part of a sentence or a complete sentence in itself.

EXAMPLE The equator runs through the continent of Africa.
[This statement is complete. It needs no other words to finish its thought.]

An independent clause may be combined with another independent clause to make a longer sentence.

EXAMPLE *Libya is in the north,* and *Tanzania is in the south.*
[*Libya is in the north* is one independent clause; *Tanzania is in the south* is another clause.]

Dependent Clauses

4c   A dependent clause needs other words to complete its thought.

A dependent clause *depends* on other words to complete it. The other words a dependent clause needs often may be an independent clause.

EXAMPLES Just as they were beginning to settle down
[What happened as they were settling down? This is a dependent clause. It needs an independent clause to complete its thought.]

Just as they were beginning to settle down, the coyote howled.
[*The coyote howled* is an independent clause.]

If it howls again
[What will happen if there is another howl? An independent clause is needed to complete the thought of this dependent clause.]

If it howls again, you should cover your ears.
[The clause *you should cover your ears* is independent.]

Note that a dependent clause that comes before an independent clause is separated from it with a comma.

Hint: Most dependent clauses must be combined with independent clauses to make complete sentences.

EXERCISE 2 Six of the following clauses are independent. The others are dependent. Number a sheet of paper 1–12. Next to each number, write *I* if the clause is independent. Write *D* if the clause is dependent.

EXAMPLE If Chan-Ho Park gets off tomorrow

D

1. Chan-Ho knows all about riding the river
2. When we get there
3. We need a large rubber raft or two small ones
4. For safety everyone should have a life jacket
5. We can paddle the rafts
6. Whenever we reach calm water
7. In the white water the rafts turn too much
8. As soon as we bump into a rock
9. If the raft starts to tip
10. Your feet should be up and ahead of you
11. As you come near the edge
12. When we walk back along the shore with the rafts

EXERCISE 3 The following dependent clauses need independent clauses to complete them. Write each dependent clause on a sheet of paper. Include the comma. Add an independent clause to complete each dependent clause. Put punctuation at the end of each completed word group to show that it is a sentence.

EXAMPLE   When summer comes,

When summer comes, would you like to leave the city?

1. If you are thirsty,
2. When we run short of water,
3. As soon as water is available,
4. While a fire is spreading,
5. When gasoline is nearby,
6. Whenever you see an emergency,

Kinds of Dependent Clauses

Three kinds of dependent clauses are used in writing. Each kind works as a single part of speech. One kind is the *noun clause*. Another is the *adjective clause*. A third kind is the *adverb clause*.

(1) A noun clause is a dependent clause used as a noun.

EXAMPLES   You can have *whatever cereal is on the shelf.*
[*Whatever cereal is on the shelf* is the noun clause. *Cereal* is its subject. Its predicate is *is on the shelf.* This noun clause is part of the complete predicate of the sentence.]

```
       Subject              Predicate
      ╭──╮ ╭──────────────────────────────────╮
                     subject          predicate
```
You can have *whatever cereal is on the shelf.*

A noun or pronoun can replace the noun clause. For example, the whole sentence might read:

You can have the raisins.

Or it might read:

You can have them.

> *Whoever gets there first* should set up the tent.
> [*Whoever gets there first* is the noun clause. It acts as the subject of the sentence. *Whoever* is the subject of the noun clause. *Gets there first* is the predicate.]

```
            Subject                  Predicate
      ╭──────────────────╮ ╭──────────────────────╮
       subj.    predicate
```
Whoever gets there first should set up the tent.

A noun or a pronoun can replace the noun clause. For example, the whole sentence might read:

Julie should set up the tent.

She should set up the tent.

In most cases, a noun clause begins with one of the following pronouns:

that	who
what	whoever
whatever	whom
whichever	whomever

EXERCISE 4 Number a sheet of paper 1–10. Next to each number, write the noun clause from each sentence.

EXAMPLE We learn from history what
mistakes people make.

what mistakes people make

1. Historians agree that Julius Caesar was a great military leader.
2. What he did is partly recorded in his writings.
3. Whoever reads his writings will learn something about warfare.
4. However, what he wrote tells very little about anything else.
5. He wrote what happened away from Rome.
6. It was Rome that was then the center of the Western world.
7. What Caesar finally gained was power over Rome.
8. A group of political enemies planned what to do to take power from Caesar.
9. That he lived through foreign wars was a miracle.
10. What happened to him in the Roman senate was a tragedy.

(2) An adjective clause is a dependent clause used as an adjective.

See Adjective,
p. 387

An adjective clause modifies a noun or pronoun, just as an adjective does. An adjective clause is also called a *relative clause*. This is because it relates to a noun or a pronoun.

EXAMPLES There come the cattle *that will be put out on the range.*

[The adjective clause *that will be put out on the range* modifies the noun *cattle*. The clause tells which cattle will be put out on the range.]

Last night we heard the musicians play the song *that made them famous*.
[The adjective clause *that made them famous* modifies the noun *song*. The clause tells which song we heard them play.]

Everyone *who paid the admission* will get a refund.
[The adjective clause *who paid the admission* modifies the pronoun *everyone*. The clause tells which particular people will get a refund.]

Notice that in each example the adjective clause follows the noun or the pronoun it modifies.

Hint: The adjective clause always comes right after the word it modifies.

Most adjective clauses begin with one of the following pronouns:

that	who	whose
which	whom	

EXERCISE 5   Number a sheet of paper 1–6. Next to each number, write the adjective clause from the sentence.

EXAMPLE   An athlete who expects to do well
needs good equipment.

who expects to do well

1. A track runner who hopes to break records must
have the right shoes.
2. The shoes which a high jumper wears are not
the same as a runner's.
3. Runners have longer spikes in the shoes that
they wear.
4. A jumper who wears long spikes has trouble lift-
ing off in a jump.
5. Distance runners wear shoes that protect their
feet.
6. Some runners whose feet are tender wear extra
pads.

See Adverb,   **(3) An adverb clause is a dependent clause used**
p. 387   **as an adverb.**

Like an adverb, an adverb clause can modify
the action of a main verb. An adverb clause may
also modify an adjective or an adverb.

An adverb clause that modifies a verb tells
about its action. It usually tells *how, how much,
when, where,* or *why.*

EXAMPLES   Teresa directs traffic *when it gets
heavy.*
[When does Teresa direct traffic?
Answer: *when it gets heavy.*]

Teresa directs traffic *because it is
her job.*

[Why does Teresa direct traffic?
Answer: *because it is her job.*]

Teresa directs traffic *wherever it
will move the smoothest.*
[Where does Teresa direct traffic?
Answer: *wherever it will move the
smoothest.*]

Adverb clauses may tell more about adjectives
or adverbs in a sentence.

Example of an adverb clause that modifies an
adjective:

Tate was happy *that he had paid the money.*
[This adverb clause modifies the adjective
happy. It explains why Tate was happy.]

Example of an adverb clause that modifies an
adverb:

The geese arrived earlier *than they had the
year before.*
[This adverb clause modifies the adverb *earlier.*
It tells *how much* earlier the geese arrived.]

Adverb clauses begin with one of the subordinating conjunctions, such as *after, than, because,*   See
when, so that, or *that.*   Conjunction,
                                                          p. 392

EXERCISE 6   Number a sheet of paper 1–12. Next
to each number, write the adverb clause from the
sentence.

EXAMPLE   Everyone thought Ellen was the
          winner until Morey came forward.

until Morey came forward

1. Morey Wellenberger had never entered a contest before he signed up for the school's Kleverest Klutz Derby.
2. If he had known the outcome, he might not have signed up.
3. Even though he was awkward, he never thought he was clever at being klutzy.
4. When he entered, it was sort of a joke.
5. The judges made the contestants do several odd things after the entries were narrowed to six.
6. While the early contestants had only to sing and dance, the finalists were put through difficult tests.
7. They all had to walk on the edge of a board while they balanced books on their heads.
8. After they finished that, they had to keep hopping twice on one foot and once on the other for a full minute.
9. Each one then had to pat the stomach and rub the head for thirty seconds and then switch so that each one rubbed the stomach and patted the head.
10. Next, each one had to try to thread a needle while he or she was rolling on roller skates.
11. As soon as Morey tried that, he knew he would lose.
12. Although he was a loser, everyone did worse than he did.

REVIEW EXERCISE A   Clauses

Some of the following word groups are clauses and some are not. Number a sheet of paper 1–10.

Next to each number write *C* if the word group is a clause and *frag* if it is not.

EXAMPLE   On a Friday afternoon

frag

1. The *Titanic* left England for New York
2. On April 15, 1912
3. The ship steamed ahead
4. The crew sighted an iceberg
5. The solid crunch as the ship
6. Sailing too fast
7. The band was playing
8. While the ship sank
9. Women and children first
10. A great tragedy for an "unsinkable" ship

REVIEW EXERCISE B   Dependent and
**   Independent Clauses**

Some of the following clauses are dependent and some are independent. Number a sheet of paper 1–10. Next to each number, write *I* if the clause is independent and *D* if the clause is dependent.

EXAMPLE   If Douglas Corrigan's plane had been
          equipped with a radio

D

1. When he took off from New York in 1938
2. He was planning to go to California
3. There was a dense fog

4. As he flew over the ocean
5. No one could warn him
6. After the fog cleared
7. When he landed twenty-four hours later
8. The houses looked different
9. Corrigan went to Ireland by mistake
10. When people began calling him "Wrong-Way Corrigan"

REVIEW EXERCISE C   Noun Clauses and Adjective Clauses

Some of the following sentences contain noun clauses. Some contain adjective clauses. Number a sheet of paper 1–15. Next to each number, write the clause from the sentence. If it is a noun clause, write *NC* next to it. If it is an adjective clause, write *AC* and the word it modifies.

EXAMPLE   The courage that Micki King displayed in the 1968 Olympics was unnoticed by many.

that Micki King displayed in the 1968 Olympics
AC, courage

1. The silence that greeted her during her climb to the diving board was electric.
2. What Micki planned to do was a one-and-a-half layout dive.
3. The dive, which she had practiced over and over, was a very difficult one.

4. That Micki was nervous goes without saying.
5. Her coach knew that she would do her best.
6. Micki, who had a chance to win a gold medal, got ready.
7. But the dive that Micki did was too fast.
8. She had to do something that would slow her spin down.
9. What she did was to extend her arms, hoping to lose speed.
10. Some spectators heard the sound that her arm made hitting the diving board.
11. Pain that was like a thousand fiery needles shot through her.
12. Some of the judges did not realize that she was injured.
13. That she could drop out of the competition never entered Micki's head.
14. She went through with her next dive, but with a form that was not nearly as good as usual.
15. The doctors discovered that Micki had broken her arm.

REVIEW EXERCISE D   Adverb Clauses

Each of the following sentences contains an adverb clause. Number a sheet of paper 1–5. Next to each number, write the adverb clause and the word or words it modifies.

EXAMPLE   Before she stepped into the space ship, Gak had never left the planet Argyle.

before she stepped into the space ship, had left

1. Because it was home to her, she would miss its boiling mud lakes and purple sands.
2. She pulled in her feelers as the takeoff began.
3. The passengers were allowed to move around the cabin as soon as they were out in deep space.
4. She felt better when her three legs could stretch themselves.
5. While she strolled around the ship, she thought about the upcoming visit with the strange creatures from outer space.

5

SENTENCES

To make sense, a written group of words must express a complete thought. Thoughts come into your head all the time. Perhaps not all of them are complete. When you take the time to write your ideas down, however, you probably want to share them with someone else. Complete *sentences* make your thoughts clear and easy to understand. Learning to write complete sentences is a valuable skill of the English language.

THE SENTENCE

5a A sentence is a group of related words that expresses a complete thought.

A group of words that does not express a complete thought is not a sentence. An incomplete sentence is called a *fragment*.

See Sentence Problems, pp. 141–146

SENTENCES	FRAGMENTS
The world turns.	The world
The sun rises and sets.	Rises and sets
People are happy or sad.	People

The trouble with fragments is that they seem to say something. However, they do not complete what they begin. Other words are needed to make sense.

For example, *The world* names something, but the words fail to tell anything about that thing. More words, including an action or linking verb, are needed to complete the sentence.

> EXAMPLES The world + is a good place to live.
> The world + becomes smaller every year.

EXERCISE 1 Number a sheet of paper 1–10. Some of the following word groups are sentences. Some are fragments. Write *S* next to the number of each sentence. Add words to each fragment to make it a complete sentence.

> EXAMPLE Stories of mermaids.
>
> *Stories of mermaids have been known for hundreds of years.*

1. Far under the ocean
2. The mermaid lived there
3. She sang softly
4. Glittering scales on her fish tail
5. Splashed, swam, and played

6. The castle was made of shells
7. Sailors stared
8. A lonely but happy life
9. Who would believe this story
10. A real mermaid

5b A simple sentence must contain a subject and a predicate.

The Subject

(1) The subject of a sentence is what the sentence tells about.

Most sentences have a noun or a pronoun as a subject.

See Noun, p. 403; Pronoun, p. 406

EXAMPLES Bands marched up the street.
[Who or what is doing the action? Answer: *bands*. They are doing the action of marching.]

Flags were everywhere.
[Who or what is being talked about? Answer: *flags*. *Flags* is the subject. They are being talked about.]

Hint: To find the subject of a sentence, ask: *Who or what is doing the action?* If there is no action in the sentence, then ask: *Who or what is being talked about?*

The *simple subject* of a sentence is the person or thing that is doing the action or being talked about. The *complete subject* is the simple subject plus all the other words directly related to the simple subject.

EXAMPLES   simple subject

The silver and gold *coins* flash in the sun.

complete subject

simple subject

The uniformed *marchers* keep in step.

complete subject

The complete subject may also include a prepositional phrase

EXAMPLES   simple subject

The *smile* on her face broke the ice.

complete subject

[The simple subject is *smile*. The complete subject includes *the* and the prepositional phrase *on her face*.]

simple subject

The *crack* in the cup caught his eye.

complete subject

[The simple subject is *crack*. The complete subject includes *the* and the prepositional phrase *in the* cup.]

EXERCISE 2 Number a sheet of paper 1–10. Write the complete subject of each sentence. Underline the simple subject.

EXAMPLE Several kinds of entertainment
interest people.

Several kinds of
entertainment

1. The people in the desert town had no television sets.
2. Square dances on Wednesday nights took the place of television.
3. A cable TV company offered to bring television to the town.
4. A special machine would pick up stations from Las Vegas and Los Angeles.
5. Some of the people did not want television.
6. Loud commercials broke into their conversation.
7. The programs were soap operas and police stories.
8. Some of the children liked the game shows.
9. New television sets showed up all over town.
10. Many families still go to square dances.

The Predicate

(2) The predicate of a sentence is the verb and the related words that tell something about the subject.

See Verb, p. 410

The verb helps tell of the action of the subject or what the subject is. The *complete predicate* is made up of the verb and all the other words that go with it. The *simple predicate* is made up of the complete verb, which includes the main verb and its auxiliaries. The main verb and its auxiliaries may

See Phrases,
pp. 68–69

also be called the *verb phrase*.

EXAMPLES   Reggie Stamfutter collected a million bottle caps.
[What did the subject do? Answer: *collected a million bottle caps. Collected* is the verb or simple predicate. *Collected a million bottle caps* is the complete predicate.]

It had been his hobby for years.
[*Had been* is the verb or simple predicate. *Had been his hobby for years* is the complete predicate.]

The simple predicate can be a main verb or a main verb and its auxiliary verbs.

EXAMPLES   Freida Frier *was hurrying* today.
[*Was hurrying* is the simple predicate of this sentence.]

She *had been running* from the bus stop.
[*Had been running* is the simple predicate of this sentence.]

Hint: To find the predicate in a sentence, ask either of these questions: *What does (or did) the subject do?* or *What tells about the condition of the subject?*

EXERCISE 3   Number a sheet of paper 1–10. Next to each number, write out the complete predicate from each sentence. Underline the simple predicate.

> EXAMPLE   In India, people treat animals
> kindly.
>
> <u>*treat*</u> *animals kindly.*

1. A monkey in southern India rides the tour bus every day.
2. The monkey travels from the jungle to the city zoo.
3. Children feed it nuts at the zoo.
4. The monkey enjoys the attention.
5. It takes the bus back to the jungle every night.
6. This monkey is never late for its bus ride.
7. It sits on the hood of the bus or at the back.
8. The other riders are glad to see it.
9. The bus driver saves a place for it.
10. The bus-riding monkey is everybody's pet.

Hint: Every sentence must have at least one subject and one predicate.

In writing, you can add other words to help describe or modify both the simple subject and the simple predicate.

EXAMPLE

SIMPLE SUBJECT	SIMPLE PREDICATE
Whales	sing.

COMPLETE SUBJECT	COMPLETE PREDICATE
Even giant blue whales	sing in an unusual manner.

EXERCISE 4 Following are five sentences made up of simple subjects and simple predicates. On a sheet of paper, write your own five sentences by adding modifiers to each simple subject and simple predicate.

EXAMPLE Jets fly.

Needle-nosed jets fly between continents at speeds greater than the speed of sound.

1. Worms will crawl.
2. Lights burn.
3. Children had been listening.
4. Workers dig.
5. Students study.

Another way of building sentences is by having more than one subject and more than one predicate.

Compound Subject and Compound Predicate

(3)   A compound subject is made up of two or more complete subjects in a sentence.

See Conjunction, p. 392 A coordinating conjunction such as *and, or,* or *but* often connects the compound subjects.

EXAMPLES *Nickels* or *dimes* fit in the machine.

Two nickels and *one dime* will operate it.

Either *a juicy apple* or *a package of peanuts* will slide out.

Pennies, quarters, and *half dollars* will not work in the machine.

EXERCISE 5 Each of the following sentences has a compound subject. Number a sheet of paper 1–6. Next to each number, write out the two complete subjects in the sentence.

EXAMPLE The guards and the tackles will practice together.

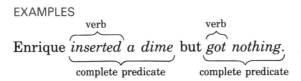

The guards, the tackles

1. Centers and quarterbacks should report at 3 o'clock.
2. The running backs and the backfield coach can work together.
3. Both the tight ends and wide receivers will run pass patterns the first half hour.
4. Punters and place kickers need extra footballs.
5. Defensive linemen and linebackers can work out their formations.
6. Cornerbacks and safeties practice running backward and sideways.

(4) **A compound predicate is made up of two or more verbs and their related words.**

EXAMPLES

Enrique *inserted a dime* but *got nothing*.

verb — *inserted*

verb — *got*

complete predicate — *inserted a dime*

complete predicate — *got nothing*

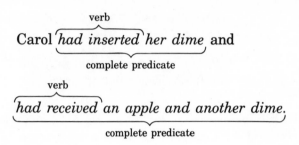

EXERCISE 6 Following are eight sentences with compound predicates. Number a sheet of paper 1–8. Write the two complete predicates in each sentence. Underline the verbs.

EXAMPLE   You probably have seen crazy stunts or have heard about them.

<u>have seen</u> crazy stunts,
<u>have heard</u> about them

1. Some people have fun and make themselves famous.
2. They do crazy things and get their names in record books.
3. A woman danced and read a book at the same time.
4. One man whistled tunes and gave bird imitations.
5. Another man stood on his head and drank from a glass.
6. Then he swallowed twelve eggs in fifty seconds and gulped sixty-two pancakes in six minutes.
7. Cindy Jano dived off a forty-foot platform and rode a horse at the same time.
8. She held her head down and gripped the horse with her legs.

EXERCISE 7 Some of the following sentences have compound subjects. Some have compound predicates. Some sentences have both a compound subject and a compound predicate. Write out each sentence on your paper. Underline each part of the complete subject once and each part of the complete predicate twice.

EXAMPLE People have been curious about flight and have tried many ways of flying.

People have been curious about flight and have tried many ways of flying.

1. Some men and women fly through the air without airplanes.
2. Young people and some older flyers hang from gliders and sail through the air.
3. The modern hang glider was invented by a man named Rogallo and is called the Rogallo Wing.
4. You can buy a Rogallo Wing or make your own from a kit.
5. The takeoff and landing are the hardest part of hang gliding.
6. Either a beginner or a veteran glider can plow headfirst into the ground or be pulled over backward.
7. Your skill and the wind currents will decide how long you stay up.
8. Serious injury or death can strike careless hang glider pilots.

Types of Sentences

Sentences are of four types: *simple, compound, complex,* and *compound-complex.*

5c   A simple sentence contains one independent clause.

EXAMPLES   The bolts tie into the beams.
The beams hold up the roof.

See Clause, pp. 389–390
Both a sentence and a clause must have a subject and a predicate. Only an independent clause can be a sentence, however. Its thought is complete. A dependent clause needs other words to complete its meaning. It is not a sentence. It is a fragment. Be careful not to use a dependent clause as a simple sentence.

EXAMPLES

INDEPENDENT CLAUSE OR SIMPLE SENTENCE
Jean went to the store.

DEPENDENT CLAUSE OR FRAGMENT
When she got there.

5d   A compound sentence contains two or more independent clauses.

EXAMPLES   *The foundation is laid in a hole in the ground,* or *the beams are solidly attached to a concrete slab.*

The upright stanchions must be absolutely vertical, and *the horizontal beams must be level.*

Two independent clauses in a compound sentence are usually joined by a comma and a coordinating conjunction. The examples above show this.

See Punctuation, pp. 291–292

Occasionally the comma and the coordinating conjunction are not used. Instead, a semicolon is used. The semicolon shows that the two independent clauses are closely related.

See Punctuation, p. 306

> EXAMPLES The stanchions are braced up; then the concrete is poured around them.
>
> All pieces are set with precision; there is no room for error.

Hint: Independent clauses in a compound sentence are joined as follows:
Independent clause, (**conjunction**) independent clause
or
Independent clause; independent clause.

Some compound sentences may have more than two independent clauses. In this case, the clauses are combined as follows:

> EXAMPLE *The trucks brought concrete, the men poured it,* and *the finishers troweled the surface smooth.*
> [Notice that the first independent clause is separated from the second by a comma. The second independent clause is separated from the third independent clause by a comma and a conjunction.]

EXERCISE 8   Some of the following sentences are simple sentences. Some are compound sentences. Number a sheet of paper 1–10. Next to each number, write *S* if the sentence is simple. Write *C* if the sentence is compound.

> EXAMPLE   We think of sewage as waste, but
> sometimes it is valuable.
>
> *C*

1. The sewage waste from a town in California is full of gold and silver.
2. The metals from factory chemicals end up in the sewage.
3. Nevada's Comstock lode was rich in silver and gold, but this town's sewage is richer still.
4. At today's prices, the sewage is worth $200 a ton.
5. This is bonanza ore by any standards.
6. The townspeople would like the gold, but it costs too much to get it out of the sewage.
7. Extracting the metals costs more money than the value of the metal.
8. No one has found a cheap way to get the metal out, but many people are trying.
9. You or your friends might invent a new way, and then you could try it in your town.
10. You could take home some sewage mud, or you could work on it at school.

5e   **A complex sentence is made up of one or more dependent clauses combined with an independent clause.**

EXAMPLES The building will lean if it is not
straight at the bottom.
[The independent clause is *the building will lean*. It could stand alone as a sentence. The dependent clause is *if it is not straight at the bottom*. This clause cannot stand alone.]

The floors will be slanted because the beams will not be level.
[The independent clause is *the floors will be slanted*. The dependent clause is *because the beams will not be level*. It needs the independent clause to complete its meaning.]

EXERCISE 9 The following sentences are simple, compound, or complex sentences. Number a sheet of paper 1–10. Next to the number of a complex sentence, write *Cx*. Next to the number of a compound sentence, write *C*. Next to the number of a simple sentence, write *S*.

EXAMPLE If you like food with flavor, you can add one of these spices.

Cx

1. If you like hamburgers or hot dogs, you probably like ketchup.
2. Ketchup came from the Orient, but the ancient Romans also ate something like ketchup.
3. Chinese ketchup was made from fish, vinegar, and spices.

4. Ketchup was brought to Europe by English sailors who went to China centuries ago.
5. People could not make Chinese ketchup in England.
6. English ketchup makers did not use fish, but they did use tomatoes.
7. After ketchup became popular in England, its use spread to America.
8. American families grew tomatoes so that they could make their own ketchup.
9. Some made ketchup with mushrooms or oysters, and some made ketchup with walnuts.
10. People in America and Europe have loved ketchup for hundreds of years.

5f A compound-complex sentence contains two or more independent clauses and one or more dependent clauses.

EXAMPLES   Architects can design skyscrapers and engineers can build them because the technology of construction has advanced so far. [*Architects can design skyscrapers* and *engineers can build them* are independent clauses; *because the technology of construction has advanced so far* is a dependent clause.]

The architects could design taller buildings and the engineers could build them if there were reason to increase the height of a skyscraper.

> [*The architects could design taller
> buildings* and *the engineers could
> build them* are independent
> clauses; *if there were reason to
> increase the height of a skyscraper*
> is a dependent clause.]

EXERCISE 10 Number a sheet of paper 1–12.
Next to each number, write one of the following
symbols to show what kind of sentence each is: *S*
(simple), *C* (compound), *Cx* (complex), *CCx* (compound-complex).

EXAMPLE Felicita Ferrer works in a market
during the day, but at night she
takes courses at the local college.

C

1. Felicita is a checker in a supermarket.
2. She is going to be a doctor, but she has to earn
   money for school.
3. After she stands up all day, her feet get tired.
4. She feels angry when customers say, "Hurry
   up!"
5. Felicita knows the price of every item in the
   store.
6. She looks at the price list each day, and she
   makes a note of any changes.
7. She likes her work as long as people are
   friendly.
8. Squalling babies and curious children sometimes make problems for Felicita.

9. If she works hard enough, she could become senior checker; then she would have to stay two more years.
10. When someone thanks her for her good work, Felicita is very pleased.
11. Whenever she feels tired, she thinks of the kindness shown to her; that makes her work easier to take.
12. It helps, too, to know she is making money.

EXERCISE 11   On a sheet of paper, write your own example of a simple sentence, a compound sentence, a complex sentence, and a compound-complex sentence. Label each example. You should have four sentences.

The Purposes of Sentences

Each sentence you write serves a purpose. There are four kinds of sentences to serve four different purposes. The four kinds of sentences are called *declarative, interrogative, imperative,* and *exclamatory.*

In some cases the structure and the punctuation of the sentences change to help show their purpose.

5g   A declarative sentence declares a fact, an opinion, or a feeling.

EXAMPLES   The earth shook.
The building swayed.
It was a miracle it stood up.

A declarative sentence ends with a period (.).

5h An interrogative sentence asks a question.

EXAMPLES   Was that an earthquake?
Did you feel the building move?

An interrogative sentence always ends with a question mark(?). Usually the verb comes before the subject of an interrogative sentence. This is the reverse of the normal subject-verb order of the declarative sentence.

EXAMPLES
DECLARATIVE SENTENCE   That was an earthquake.
INTERROGATIVE SENTENCE   Was that an earthquake?

5i An imperative sentence requests or orders something.

EXAMPLES   Please close the window.
Sweep up the bits of glass.
Get out as fast as you can.

The imperative sentence expresses a request or a demand to someone to whom you are speaking or writing. You may name the person.

EXAMPLE   Linda, lift up the rug.

Even if you do not name the person, it is understood you are talking or writing to someone.

EXAMPLE Sweep the steps.
[The subject of the sentence is *you*.
The actual word *you* is usually
omitted. Nevertheless, this is the
person or people being addressed.
You as the subject of the sentence is
said to be the *understood subject*.]

An imperative sentence usually ends with a
period (.).

5j   An exclamatory sentence expresses shock or surprise.

EXAMPLES Save yourself!
The quake is starting again!

An exclamatory sentence ends with an exclamation mark (!).

EXERCISE 12 Following are ten sentences.
Number a sheet of paper 1–10. After each number
tell what kind of sentence it is. Mark *D* for declarative, *I* for interrogative, *Im* for imperative, and *E*
for exclamatory. End punctuation has been omitted.

EXAMPLE Dolores Kayketer spends long hours
at the Stuphennys' restaurant

D

1. Who is the best worker in this restaurant
2. Dolores moves like a dancer when she carries
   her trays
3. What an incredible job she does
4. Please give me a rare steak, Dolores
5. She must get tired of standing up so long

6. What is the right tip to give
7. Go to the Golden Bowl next time
8. Dolores has worked there for fifteen years
9. What a fantastic salad this is
10. Thank Dolores and the cook when you leave

Completers

Often the complete predicate of a sentence will contain a word called a *completer* because it completes or makes clear what the subject and verb are telling about. Completers may be either *objects* or *subject completers*.

5k The direct object receives the action of the verb.

EXAMPLE Erik Kaiser raised his *hat.*
[*Hat* receives the action of the verb *raised*. It is the direct object in the sentence.]

Hint: Here are the steps to find the direct object of an action verb:
Find the verb. In the example above, the verb is *raised*.
Find the subject. Ask: *Who or what raised?*
Answer: Erik.
Find the direct object. Ask: *Who or what did Erik raise?*
Answer: his hat. *Hat* is the direct object of the action verb *raised*.

EXERCISE 13   Number a sheet of paper 1–5. Write the direct object of the action verb in each sentence.

EXAMPLE   Ms. Passmore spaded the garden.

garden

1. She mixed fertilizer into the soil.
2. She picked up the hoe.
3. Carefully she turned the ground.
4. At last she planted the seeds.
5. A few months later she ate fresh green peas.

5I   **The subject completer follows the linking verb and completes the meaning of the sentence.**

A subject completer may be a noun, a pronoun, an adjective, or an adverb. A subject completer that is a noun or a pronoun names the person or thing the sentence is talking about.

EXAMPLES   May Wu is my *friend*.
               The loser was *I*.

A subject completer that is an adjective describes or modifies the person or thing the sentence is talking about.

EXAMPLE   May was *tiny*.

A subject completer that is an adverb is a word such as *here* or *there*.

EXAMPLE   The trouble is *here*.

Hint: Here are the steps to follow to find the subject completer:
Find the linking verb. In the first example, the verb is *is*.
Find the subject. Ask: *Who or what is?*
The answer: May Wu.
Then ask: *May Wu is who or what?*
Answer: my friend. *Friend* is the subject completer.

EXERCISE 14   Number a sheet of paper 1–8. Next to each number write the subject completer in the sentence.

EXAMPLE   Jesse's father was angry at Jesse.

angry

1. He sounded stern as he spoke.
2. Jesse was nervous.
3. Outwardly he appeared calm, however.
4. Jesse grew quiet in front of his father.
5. His father was a giant alongside him.
6. But his father was not cruel.
7. His father was always fair.
8. "You are right after all," said his father as they relaxed.

Sentence Patterns

The pattern of a sentence is made by the order of its words and word groups. The English language has only a few basic sentence patterns. Every English sentence matches one of these patterns.

Sentence Pattern 1:   SUBJECT-VERB (S-V)

See
Intransitive
Verbs, p. 34 Sentence Pattern 1 is made up of a subject and an intransitive verb. The simple subject and the verb, or simple predicate, of Pattern 1 sentences may have modifiers. The subject and the verb may also be compound. The basic pattern remains the same.

EXAMPLES	SUBJECT	VERB
	The band	played.
	The stage	shook wildly.
	The people	yelled and clapped.

EXERCISE 15   All the following sentences are Pattern 1 sentences. Find the subject S and the verb V in each sentence. Number a sheet of paper 1–6. Next to each number, write the subject and mark it S. Next to the subject write the verb and mark it V. Do not write any modifiers.

EXAMPLE   The dance music played across the hall.

music, S   *played,* V

1. The loud drums boomed.
2. The clashing cymbals crashed.
3. Dancers swirled around the floor.
4. Bright lights played across the scene.
5. The long, fast dance ended in ten minutes.
6. The tired but happy dancers rested for a few minutes.

Sentence Pattern 2: SUBJECT-VERB-OBJECT
(S-V-O)

See Transitive
Verbs, p. 33

Sentence Pattern 2 is made up of a subject, a transitive verb, and an object. This pattern is used very often in English.

EXAMPLES

SUBJECT	VERB	DIRECT OBJECT
Nancy	ate	the pie.
The girls	will climb	the rope.
The band	polished	their instruments.

Sentence Pattern 2 may be made longer, as is true of other sentence patterns.

EXAMPLE In a rage, Warren violently slammed
the iron gate.

Hint: To find the key parts of a Pattern 2 Sentence, take the following steps:
Find the verb. Ask: *What is the action?*
In the example above, the answer is *slammed. Slammed* is the verb.
Find the subject. Ask: *Who or what does the action?*
Answer: *Warren. Warren* is the subject.
Find the object. Ask: *Who or what receives the action?*
Answer: *gate. Gate* is the object of the action verb *slammed.*

EXERCISE 16 Some of the following sentences are Pattern 2 sentences. Some are Pattern 1 sentences.

Number a sheet of paper 1–10. Next to each number, write the subject and *S* and the complete verb and *V*. If the sentence is Pattern 2, also write the object and *O*. Do not write any modifiers.

EXAMPLE   Freddie Biggerstomp cut the tree's bark.

Freddie Biggerstomp S,
cut V, bark O

1. Freddie's knife slipped in his hand.
2. The long blade folded suddenly.
3. It sliced his finger.
4. Blood appeared on his hand.
5. He dropped the knife to the ground.
6. Then he angrily kicked the trunk of the tree.
7. His toes hit the hard bark.
8. Furious, Freddie grabbed his fallen knife from the ground.
9. He stuck a bandage on his finger.
10. After that he cut no trees.

Sentence Pattern 2 has another form, which is given here.

**Sentence Pattern 2a: SUBJECT-VERB-INDIRECT
                          OBJECT-DIRECT OBJECT
                          (S-V-IO-DO)**

Sentence Pattern 2a is made up of a subject, a transitive verb, an indirect object, and a direct object. Sentence Pattern 2a is similar to Pattern 2. However, Pattern 2a has an indirect object. The indirect object comes between the verb and the direct object. The indirect object tells to whom or for whom something is done.

EXAMPLES
$$\overset{S}{\text{The clerk}} \overset{V}{\text{gave}} \overset{IO}{\text{Mr. Finbagger}}$$
$$\overset{DO}{\text{the package.}}$$
[*Mr. Finbagger* is the indirect object. He is the person to whom the package was given.]

$$\overset{S}{\text{Mr. Finbagger}} \overset{V}{\text{gave}} \overset{IO}{\text{his wife}} \overset{DO}{\text{a gift.}}$$
[*Wife* is the indirect object. She is the person to whom the gift was given.]

EXERCISE 17 Following are six Pattern 2a sentences. Write the numbers 1–6 on a sheet of paper. After each number write the subject in the sentence. Put *S* after the subject. Next to it write the complete verb and *V*. Then write the indirect object and put *IO* after it. Finally, write the direct object and *DO*.

EXAMPLE History books tell students some fascinating stories.

books S, *tell* V,
students IO, *stories* DO

1. Long ago, elephants brought Hannibal a victory.
2. The strange beasts gave this African general's enemies a shock.
3. Hannibal gave the Romans many hard fights.
4. His bravery caused his enemies much trouble.
5. His love of battle brought him difficulties.
6. Finally he gave his homeland his life.

The structures of Pattern 2 sentences and Pattern 2a sentences are very much alike. Look first at a Pattern 2 Sentence:

EXAMPLE Mrs. Finbagger gave a dollar to the
                  S   V   O
         butcher.

The prepositional phrase *to the butcher* tells who Mrs. Finbagger gave the dollar to, but it is not the direct object of the sentence.

However, by removing the word *to* and placing *the butcher* between the verb and the direct object, a Pattern 2 sentence becomes a Pattern 2a sentence:

EXAMPLE Mrs. Finbagger gave the butcher
                  S   V   IO
         a dollar.
         DO

The same sort of switch can work the other way. A Pattern 2a sentence can be made into a Pattern 2 sentence with a prepositional phrase instead of an indirect object.

EXAMPLE Mr. Brump bought Toni the flowers.
              S   V   IO   DO

         Mr. Brump bought the flowers for
              S   V   O
         Toni.

EXERCISE 18 Rewrite these Pattern 2a sentences on a sheet of paper. Make each sentence a Pattern 2 sentence.

EXAMPLE Spot threw Roger a stick.
         Spot threw a stick to Roger.

1. Roger brought Spot two sticks.
2. Spot gave Roger a pat on the head.
3. Roger gave Spot a big grin.
4. "I give Roger good training," Spot seemed to bark.
5. Spot gives Roger lots of practice in obedience.
6. Someday fate will give dogs the world, Spot thinks.

Sentence Pattern 3: SUBJECT-LINKING VERB-SUBJECT COMPLETER (S-LV-SC)

Sentence Pattern 3 is made up of a subject, a linking verb, and a subject completer. The completer of the subject follows the verb and completes what is being said about the subject. The completer may be a noun, an adjective, or an adverb.

EXAMPLES

NOUN COMPLETER

S LV SC
Willa is the leader.

ADJECTIVE COMPLETER

S LV SC
She is sincere.

ADVERB COMPLETER

S LV SC
Her followers were there.

Hint: To find the key parts of a Pattern 3 sentence, follow these steps:
Find the linking verb. In the first example, the verb is *is*.
Find the subject. Ask: *Who or what is?* Answer: *Willa. Willa* is the subject.
Find the subject completer. Ask: *What is Willa?* Answer: *leader. Leader* is the subject completer.

EXERCISE 19 Write the numbers 1–12 on a sheet of paper. For each of the following sentences, write the subject of the sentence and *S*. Then write the linking verb and *LV*. Finally, write the subject completer and *SC*.

EXAMPLE A gypsy's life is unusual.

life S, is LV, unusual SC

1. A modern gypsy's life is different from life in the old days.
2. Camping in a different place each night, gypsies were free.
3. In many countries today, laws against free camping are severe.
4. Legal camping places for gypsies are scarce.
5. Gypsies feel unhappy in paved trailer camps.
6. The open country is important to these people.
7. Many gypsies become unhappy in one place.
8. Odd jobs are enough for many gypsies.
9. Some people are openly critical of gypsies.
10. People's comments are often harsh.
11. Gypsies feel angry at the criticism.
12. Their way of life seems beautiful to them.

5m   Any sentence pattern that is a statement can be made into a question.

EXAMPLES
STATEMENT The band played.
QUESTION Did the band play?

STATEMENT Nancy ate the pie.
QUESTION Did Nancy eat the pie?

STATEMENT   Jonathan is the leader.
QUESTION   Is Jonathan the leader?

A statement can be made into a question by adding an auxiliary verb in front of the subject. Then the form of the main verb must be changed if the verb is past tense.

EXAMPLE
STATEMENT   The band played.
QUESTION   Did the band play?

The other way to change a statement into a question is by switching the positions of the subject and the verb.

EXAMPLE
STATEMENT   Jonathan is the leader.
QUESTION   Is Jonathan the leader?

EXERCISE 20   On a sheet of paper, rewrite each of the following sentences. Make each into a question by one of the methods shown earlier. Remember to end each question with a question mark.

EXAMPLE   Jazz is making a comeback.

Is jazz making a comeback?

1. Rock and roll gained popularity in England in the 1960's.
2. Its fame spread to America.
3. Europeans took a liking to it, also.
4. Country music has become a favorite among many.
5. Soul music has a large following.

6. Jazz still has a following.
7. Classical music has been loved by millions.
8. It can be said that music, in general, pleases people.

5n   Some sentence patterns can be reversed.

Sentence Pattern 2 can be reversed from S-V-O so that the object becomes the subject.

EXAMPLE

S-V-O Mr. Ossenhaus fixed the roof.
REVERSED The roof was fixed by Mr. Ossenhaus.

Roof becomes the subject of the reversed sentence pattern. In addition, the verb changes its form. In the regular Pattern 2 sentence, the verb states the action of the subject. The verb is said to be in the *active voice*.

In the reverse pattern, the new subject has the action done to it. In this form the verb is said to be in the *passive voice*.

Here are more examples of reversed Pattern 2 sentences, using the passive voice of verbs:

The runners were cheered by the crowd.
The animals were kept in cages.
The bottles were capped automatically.

Learn to revise sentences that use the passive voice in order to make them more interesting.

EXAMPLES

PASSIVE VOICE (weak) The ball was hurled
by the pitcher.

ACTIVE VOICE (stronger)   The pitcher hurled the ball.

PASSIVE VOICE (weak)   The table was cleared by the waiter.

ACTIVE VOICE (stronger)   The waiter cleared the table.

Hint: Too much use of passive voice leads to weak writing. In most cases, use the passive voice of the verb only when the person or thing doing the action in a Pattern 2 sentence is not known.

EXAMPLES   The baby was left on their doorstep early one morning.
[The person who left the baby is not known.]

The towels had been stolen.
[The person who stole the towels is not known.]

EXERCISE 21   The following sentences use the passive voice of verbs. On a sheet of paper, rewrite each sentence using the active voice of the verbs.

EXAMPLE   Ice cubes were melted by the heat.

The heat melted the ice cubes.

1. The flowers were wilted by the direct rays of the sun.
2. A mirror was angled at the sun by a young scientist.

3. The sun's reflected rays were directed at a target by the scientist.
4. The target was made hotter by the rays.
5. Additional mirrors were set up by the scientist.
6. Sunpower experiments were begun by the scientist.
7. The target was hit by reflections from several mirrors.
8. In a short time, the target was burned by the reflected rays.
9. A temperature of several hundred degrees above the boiling point of water was generated at the target by the rays.
10. Solar energy can be used by scientists to gain high heat.

Sentence Combining

5o Two or more sentences may sometimes be combined in a variety of ways.

The ideas in separate sentences often should be more closely related. *Sentence combining* is a valuable way of showing a closer relationship.

See Clause, p. 390 **(1) Combine one sentence with another by making one into a dependent clause.**

EXAMPLES   Harumi took down a glass.
           It slipped between her fingers.

           As Harumi took down the glass, it slipped between her fingers.

[The two sentences have become a
single complex sentence by turning
the first sentence into the
dependent clause *As Harumi took
down the glass.*]

See Complex
Sentence, p.
391

Two events told about in separate sentences
may be close in time. This is true of the examples
above. Two events told about in separate sentences
may have a cause-and-effect relationship. The two
sentences can be combined to show this relationship.

See Guidelines
for Writing,
pp. 188–189

EXAMPLES   Harumi's fingers were wet and
slippery.
The glass slid from her grip.

Because Harumi's fingers were wet
and slippery, the glass slid from her
grip.

EXERCISE 22   Each of the following pairs of sentences can be combined into one complex sentence
by making one of the pair into a dependent clause.
Rewrite the pairs of sentences as a single sentence.
Where possible, use either a relationship of time or
cause-and-effect.

EXAMPLE   Sam Trenton stepped onto the
platform.
He stopped for a moment to gain his
balance.

*As Sam Trenton stepped
onto the platform, he
stopped for a moment to
gain his balance.*

1. He hesitated.
   He felt unsteady.
2. He looked down at the water.
   He moved one foot a few inches.
3. His heart pounded more heavily.
   A strange fear took hold of his body.
4. "Why am I up here?" he thought.
   "It's what I have to do, I suppose," he murmured.
5. A puff of wind pushed gently at him.
   He gripped the metal railing more firmly.
6. He hated to feel afraid.
   He could not control his feeling.
7. The feeling washed over his body.
   His arms and legs went weak.
8. The day was not warm.
   He felt perspiration on his face.
9. His one choice was to leap ahead.
   His other choice was to climb back down.
10. He climbed down with trembling knees.
    He walked away from the diving platform at the edge of the swimming pool.

(2) Combine one sentence with another by making one into a phrase.

EXAMPLES The music echoed through the hall. The sound disturbed the students in their rooms.

The music, echoing in the hall, disturbed the students in their rooms.
[The idea of the first sentence has been included in the participial phrase *echoing through the hall*.]

The wind was gusty and cold.
It swept the leaves across the
brown field.

The wind, in cold gusts, swept the
leaves across the brown field.
[The idea of the first sentence has
been included in a prepositional
phrase *in cold gusts*.]

EXERCISE 23   Number a sheet of paper 1–10.
Combine each following pair of sentences by making one of the two sentences into a phrase.

EXAMPLE   Easter Island is sometimes called
Rapa Nui. The island is a very
strange place.

*Easter Island, sometimes
called Rapa Nui, is a very
strange place.*

1. Two groups of people once lived on Easter Island.
   The groups were doing different jobs.
2. The rulers were intelligent but lazy.
   They made the other people do all the work.
3. The slave people hated their life.
   They attacked and killed the rulers.
4. The slave people became free.
   They found they did not know how to take care
   of the island.
5. Two hundred years passed.
   Almost no one was left on the island.

6. The islanders had a picture language called rongorongo.
   It was carved on wooden boards.
7. Today no one can read the rongorongo boards.
   It does not matter whether a person is a native or a foreign scholar.
8. The islanders built gigantic statues of stone.
   They built them before their great battle.
9. People marvel today at these immense works of art.
   They try to guess how and why the statues were built.
10. Researchers have skill and patience.
    They are working to unravel the mysteries of Easter Island.

REVIEW EXERCISE A   Sentences and Fragments

Some of the following word groups form sentences. Some are only fragments. Number a sheet of paper 1–10. Next to each number, write out every complete sentence. Underline the complete subject once and the complete predicate twice. If the sentence is not complete, write *F* for fragment.

EXAMPLE   Native Americans built great cities in Mexico long before Columbus came to the Americas.

Native Americans built great cities in Mexico long before Columbus came to the Americas.

1. However, the natives had no gunpowder.
2. With the landing of the Spaniards.
3. The great cities fell.
4. The Spaniards took land everywhere.
5. The Native Americans helped build the missions in California.
6. Finally the Mexican people.
7. They won the battle against Spain after years of fighting.
8. Then the United States won a war with Mexico.
9. Texas, New Mexico, Utah, Arizona, California, and part of Colorado were once part of Mexico.
10. Mexican Americans or Chicanos.

REVIEW EXERCISE B   Simple and Compound Subjects and Predicates

Some of the following sentences have compound subjects. Some have compound predicates. Some sentences have both compound subjects and compound predicates. Number a sheet of paper 1–10. Write each sentence. Underline each part of the compound subject once and each part of the compound predicate twice.

EXAMPLES   Ulysses and his men met one of the first witches in the poet Homer's ancient tale, *The Odyssey*.

Ulysses and his men met one of the first witches in the poet Homer's ancient tale, The Odyssey.

This witch lived and practiced her magic on a beautiful island.

This <u>witch</u> <u>lived</u> and <u>practiced</u>, her magic on a beautiful island.

1. Tame wolves and tame lions lived in her house.
2. Circe had lured men to her house, drugged them with a magic potion, and turned them into beasts.
3. She could change peoples' shapes, work spells, and brew herbs for magic purposes.
4. Witches or witchlike creatures have been feared or worshipped for many centuries.
5. Witches could get rid of enemies or make them suffer through image magic.
6. Witches would make a doll, stick pins in it, or destroy it.
7. The enemy and the doll would suffer at the same time.
8. Powers for good and powers for evil were used by witches.
9. In later centuries witches were feared for their evil powers and were hunted.
10. Judges and their assistants would torture anyone accused of witchcraft and would burn that person to death.

REVIEW EXERCISE C Kinds of Sentences

The following sentences are either simple, compound, complex, or compound-complex. Number a sheet of paper 1–10. Next to each number, write *S* if the sentence is simple, *C* if it is compound, *Cx* if it is complex, and *CCx* if it is compound-complex.

EXAMPLE If you have never seen anyone ride a one-wheeled cycle, you might think no one could.

Cx

1. Unicycle riding is fun.
2. You must have confidence and you must practice.
3. Some people can learn to ride in a few hours, but this is the exception.
4. You must adjust the height, and you must adjust the saddle angle if you want to ride one.
5. If you have a partner, learning will be easier.
6. When you take your first ride, you should place a stop-block in back of the unicycle.
7. You should place one foot on the down pedal, unless it would feel better to use the other foot and you would rather reverse the pedals.
8. When you have found the position you like best, you can lock arms with your partner.
9. Begin your ride.
10. If you want to stop, you should step forward off the unicycle.

REVIEW EXERCISE D Purposes of Sentences

The following sentences are either declarative, interrogative, imperative, or exclamatory. Number a sheet of paper 1–10. Next to each number, write *D* if the sentence is declarative, *I* if it is interrogative, *Im* if it is imperative, and *E* if it is exclamatory.

> EXAMPLE   Rope spinners twirl a rope with the noose open.
>
> D

1. You can't use that old rope!
2. Take a fourteen-foot piece of braided sash cord.
3. Make a loop in front of your body.
4. Are you ready to do a "flat loop" spin?
5. The rope is spun by movements of your wrist.
6. A spinner stands outside the loop for this spin.
7. The rope spins a few feet off the ground.
8. Are other rope tricks considered harder?
9. The harder ones are called the "vertical spins."
10. Give yourself lots of room!

REVIEW EXERCISE E   Sentence Patterns

Identify the patterns of the following sentences. Number a sheet of paper 1–10. Write S-V next to each number if the sentence follows Sentence Pattern 1. Write S-V-O if the sentence follows Sentence Pattern 2. Write S-V-IO-DO if the sentence follows Sentence Pattern 2a. Write S-LV-SC if the sentence follows Sentence Pattern 3.

EXAMPLE   The universe may expand in all
directions.

S-V

1. Some say a "big bang" gave the universe its start.
2. Our home galaxy is the Milky Way.
3. Our sun will probably explode one day.
4. It will heat up the earth.
5. At one time the earth was heavier.
6. Lighter elements escaped.
7. These leaked out into space.
8. The earth still leaks some gases.
9. The earth may be only about five billion years old.
10. That is young for a planet.

6

SENTENCE PROBLEMS

Fragments, Run-on Sentences, Dangling and Misplaced Modifiers

Many problems in writing are found inside sentences. A correctly written sentence must say something about its subject. The sentence must tell what the subject does, or it must tell what the subject is. It must also follow a grammatical pattern. Therefore, if you make sure your sentences are working correctly, you will have fewer writing problems. This chapter deals with the most common kinds of problems that occur when you are writing sentences.

Most problems in sentence construction fall into three groups: *fragments, run-on sentences,* and *dangling* or *misplaced modifiers.* By studying these groups, you will learn ways of dealing with sentence problems.

SENTENCE FRAGMENTS

6a A sentence fragment is an incomplete sentence.

A part of a sentence sometimes seems like a complete sentence. When you think about it, however, you realize that something is missing—the thought is not complete. Incomplete sentences are called *fragments*.

EXAMPLES

FRAGMENT *The fast train that roared through town.*
[This fragment seems to be stating something about a fast train. However, the train is only identified. The group of words lacks a predicate that tells what the fast train did.]

See Predicate, p. 406

COMPLETE SENTENCE *The fast train that roared through town* dropped off two mail sacks.

FRAGMENT *When a freight train is on the siding.*
[This fragment has a subject and a predicate, but the thought is not yet complete.]

COMPLETE SENTENCE *When a freight train is on the siding,* the rail switch does not operate.

EXERCISE 1 Each of the following word groups is a sentence fragment. On a sheet of paper, write each word group as a complete sentence by adding whatever words are needed.

> EXAMPLE   If the FBI catches them

If the FBI catches them, they will be tried.

1. In the dark alley behind the bank
2. While he clutched a heavy suitcase
3. Heard running footsteps at midnight
4. When they·found the safe with a broken lock
5. Could have come through the window
6. An important clue on the floor
7. One of the twenty suspects
8. Since it was next to the shattered windows
9. Left the country on the next plane
10. "Wanted" posters all over town.

You will avoid fragments in your writing if you make certain each of your sentences has a subject and a predicate.

See Subject, p. 408

Hint: To check your sentences, ask these questions:
Does the group of words have a subject?
Does the group of words have a predicate?
Does the group of words express a complete thought?

See Phrase, p. 405

Sentence fragments may be phrases. The most common examples are prepositional phrases and participial phrases.

EXAMPLES

FRAGMENT *Under the old schoolhouse.*
[This fragment, which is a prepositional phrase, can be corrected by adding a subject and predicate.]

COMPLETE SENTENCE *Jimmy Chin found it* under the old schoolhouse.

FRAGMENT *Standing guard all night long.*
[This fragment, which is a participial phrase, can be corrected by adding a subject and a predicate.]

COMPLETE SENTENCE *The young soldier,* standing guard all night long, *was weary.*

Sentence fragments are sometimes dependent clauses. See Clause, pp. 389–390

EXAMPLES

FRAGMENTS *After Mel clamped down the lid.*
Until the last player is out.

To correct a dependent clause fragment, add an independent clause.

EXAMPLES

COMPLETE SENTENCES After Mel clamped down the lid, *he heard a loud squeal.*
We need to stay in the game until the last player is out.

Sometimes a sentence fragment occurs because the verb is not complete.

EXAMPLE *The woman feeling dizzy.*

To correct a fragment like this, make the verb complete.

EXAMPLE The woman *was feeling* dizzy.

A complete verb tells the action or condition of the subject. It also tells the tense, or *time,* of that action or condition. To correct a fragment with an incomplete verb, add the necessary verb form to show time.

Examples of incomplete verb form fragments:

The experiment being tried.
The old man having his dinner.
Cartoons shown the funny side of life.

Examples of verb forms completed to make sentences:

The experiments *were being tried.*
The old man *was having* his dinner.
Cartoons *have shown* the funny side of life.

EXERCISE 2   Each of the following word groups is a sentence fragment. On a sheet of paper, write each word group as a complete sentence. Add whatever words are needed.

EXAMPLE The clever dog showing off its tricks.

The clever dog was showing off its tricks.

The clever dog showing off its tricks was trained by Barbara.

1. Balancing on its hind legs.
2. Then switching to its front legs.
3. When the hurdles were in place.
4. A hoop flaming all over.
5. The dog leaping through the hoop.
6. Impressing the crowd.
7. A balancing act that amazed everyone.
8. More human than dog.

Occasionally a sentence fragment appears in writing because punctuation is incorrectly used.

EXAMPLE   We hoped for a ride. After the movie finished.

The first group of words is an independent clause. The second group of words is a dependent clause. The two clauses should be combined into a single sentence.

EXAMPLE   We hoped for a ride after the movie was finished.

EXERCISE 3   Each of the following dependent clauses is a fragment. Add an independent clause to each dependent clause and write the complete sentence on a sheet of paper.

EXAMPLE   While no one believes entirely in dreams

While no one believes entirely in dreams, the truth in some dreams cannot be ignored.

1. When you have a dream over and over
2. Although some say dreams foretell the future
3. While Lucia's dreams did not come true
4. As soon as you wake up
5. Until Paco wrote down all his dreams
6. Before Elsie dreamed about the monster
7. As if our dreams were trying to tell us something
8. When dreams seem to mean something unusual
9. As if it had turned into Cousin Nellie
10. If you wake up laughing

RUN-ON SENTENCES

6b A run-on sentence is two or more sentences incorrectly joined.

EXAMPLES   Ossie Laffer said he would come he did what he said.

The others left at once they knew they had to leave.

In general, there are four basic methods for correcting run-on sentences.

Method 1: The separate thoughts in a run-on sentence may be divided into separate sentences.

RUN-ON SENTENCE Tillie Savus stopped at the drug store then she drove straight home.

CORRECT SENTENCES Tillie Savus stopped at the drug store. Then she drove straight home.

Method 2: The separate thoughts in a run-on sentence may be correctly joined by adding a comma and a coordinating conjunction, such as *and, or, nor, for,* or *but.* A coordinating conjunction alone may sometimes be enough.

See Punctuation, p. 291; Conjunction, p. 392

RUN-ON SENTENCE She saw nothing unusual she kept her eyes on the road.

CORRECTED SENTENCE She saw nothing unusual, for she kept her eyes on the road.

Method 3: Some run-on sentences may be corrected by making one part into a dependent clause.

See Clause, pp. 389–390

RUN-ON SENTENCE She saw nothing frightening she looked straight ahead of her.

CORRECTED SENTENCE She saw nothing frightening because she looked straight ahead of her.

If you put the dependent clause first, remember to separate it from the main clause with a comma.

EXAMPLE Because she looked straight ahead, she saw nothing frightening.

Hint: Dependent clauses that begin a sentence are set off with a comma. Dependent clauses that end a sentence need no comma.

See
Punctuation,
p. 306 **Method 4:** Some run-on sentences may be corrected by means of a semicolon.

> RUN-ON SENTENCE The house was empty and still the windows looked blankly out at her.
>
> CORRECTED SENTENCE The house was empty and still; the windows looked blankly out at her.

EXERCISE 4 Rewrite correctly the following run-on sentences.

> EXAMPLE We have heard of people climbing a high mountain because it is there now we have a young man climbing a skyscraper for the same reason.

We have heard of people climbing a high mountain because it is there. Now we have a young man climbing a skyscraper for the same reason.

1. A mountain climber went up the outside of the world's second tallest building his name was George Willig.
2. He spent a year getting ready for his climb he made several trial runs at night.
3. He made special equipment for climbing buildings instead of mountains he knew exactly what he was doing.

4. He started his climb at 6:30 A.M. it took three hours.
5. Thousands of people watched him they must have thought he was Spider Man.
6. The police thought something else they thought he was crazy.
7. Willig wanted to finish his climb he stayed out of reach of the police.
8. At last Willig got to the top everybody clapped and cheered.
9. The police gave him a hand too then they arrested him.
10. He had to pay a fine of $1.10 that was one penny for every floor he had climbed.

DANGLING AND MISPLACED MODIFIERS

6c **A misplaced or dangling modifier is a phrase or clause that seems to modify the wrong person or thing.**

Be sure that modifiers refer to a named person or thing and are placed next to it.

EXAMPLE After running hard almost a block, the bus left without me.

This sentence seems to state that the bus ran hard for almost a block. That makes no sense. It was the writer who ran for almost a block. The writer should have written the sentence either one of two ways:

After I ran for almost a block, the bus left without me.

After running for almost a block, I still missed the bus.

Here are some examples of misplaced or dangling modifiers.

DANGLING   Sitting for hours in front of TV, boredom will result.
            [Is boredom doing the sitting?]
CORRECTED   Sitting for hours in front of TV, we will be bored.

            or

            Sitting for hours in front of TV will bore us.

DANGLING   At the age of two, her mother moved the family to Alabama.
            [Was her mother only two when they moved?]
CORRECTED   At the age of two, she moved with her family to Alabama.

DANGLING   Like weary warriors, our coach told us to lie down and rest.
            [Was our coach like weary warriors?]
CORRECTED   We were like weary warriors. Our coach told us to lie down and rest.

MISPLACED   Sara put the vase on the counter with the flowers in it.
CORRECTED   Sara put the vase with the flowers in it on the counter.

MISPLACED   He read about the car that was hit in the newspaper.

CORRECTED   He read in the newspaper about the car that was hit.

EXERCISE 5   On a sheet of paper, rewrite correctly each of the following sentences that has a misplaced or dangling modifier. Every sentence needs correcting.

EXAMPLE   A girl of seventeen, Joanie's poise is remarkable.

A girl of seventeen, Joanie shows remarkable poise.

1. While hoping for a sunny day, the rains kept coming down on us.
2. After failing to open the jar, the pickles were left on the shelf.
3. Weeping softly, the detective questioned the frightened old man.
4. Laughing uproariously, the third act delighted the audience.
5. Since he did not wish to be arrested, the police had trouble finding the suspect.
6. After climbing Mt. Everest, the class saw the picture of the Sherpas.
7. Brenda gave a dollar to her friend that was torn.
8. Jeb bought a motorcycle from a dealer without brakes.

REVIEW EXERCISE A   Sentence Fragments

Number a sheet of paper 1–10. Next to each number, write whatever words are needed to make each of the following fragments into a complete sentence.

> EXAMPLE   The battle between Miracle Man and the monster
>
> *The battle between Miracle Man and the monster was quite a sight.*

1. While the monster was twenty feet tall
2. Had eyes all over its head
3. Could the Man of Cast Iron
4. The monster, eyes rolling, tongue dripping acid
5. Hid behind a tree
6. Miracle Man being cowardly
7. The people of Peoria
8. But when Miracle Man turned a fire hose on the monster
9. Knocked out by a telephone pole
10. A miracle we weren't all killed

REVIEW EXERCISE B   Run-on Sentences

The following sentences are run-on sentences. Correct each of them using one of the methods on pages 146–148. Number a sheet of paper 1–10. Next to each number write the correct version of each sentence.

> EXAMPLE   Dot Wilkinson was the greatest of all women softball players she was named all-American nineteen times.

Dot Wilkinson was the greatest of all women softball players. She was named all-American nineteen times.

1. Dot Wilkinson was born in 1921 she played softball with the Phoenix Ramblers for thirty-three years.
2. She began playing second base she really came into her own as a catcher.
3. Her batting average was about .340 she batted left-handed.
4. The Ramblers won the World Championship in 1940 they won the championship again in 1948 and 1949.
5. Once a fan for another team came to the Ramblers' bleachers she began to heckle the Ramblers.
6. Dot put her finger over the dugout fountain then she aimed a stream of water at the heckler.
7. Dot retired from softball in 1965 she began to pay attention to another sport.
8. She had been bowling once or twice a week she won many honors.
9. Dot won the Women's International Bowling Congress Queens Championship it was a spectacular victory.
10. Dot Wilkinson became the first woman to be elected to the Arizona Sports Hall of Fame she has become a softball legend.

REVIEW EXERCISE C Dangling and Misplaced Modifiers

Each of the following sentences contains a misplaced or dangling modifier. Number a sheet of paper 1–10. Next to each number, rewrite the sentence correctly.

EXAMPLE Although they were once hunted ruthlessly, scientists have hoped for the future of elephant seals.

Although they were once hunted ruthlessly, elephant seals may have a hopeful future, scientists believe.

or

Although elephant seals were once hunted ruthlessly, scientists have hope for them.

1. Because they were not afraid of people, seal hunters caught and killed them easily.
2. After melting it down, the seal oil was valuable to people.
3. Although they almost died out completely, scientists say the elephant seal is coming back.
4. The seals have long faces and flippers with strange-looking noses.

5. At the age of three years, babies are born to female elephant seals.

6. You cannot find out about everything an elephant seal eats in a book.

7. Studying the seals, it is unknown how many kinds of food they eat.

8. Although happy because of the seals' comeback, full recovery is not yet certain.

9. Watching them carefully, the seals are protected by the Mexican and American governments.

10. The governments have given them complete protection from being killed by law.

UNIT TWO

COMPOSITION

Paragraphs
Guidelines for Writing
Letter Writing

7

PARAGRAPHS

Whenever you write several sentences about one idea, you should group these sentences into a *paragraph*. That paragraph is your way of showing a reader how you have organized your thoughts. Every paragraph should begin with an indented line. This is the signal that the sentences in it are organized around one idea.

As you study this chapter, you will learn ways to make your paragraphs stronger and better organized.

DEVELOPING PARAGRAPHS

7a   A paragraph is a series of sentences that tells about a single idea, description, or action.

A paragraph may have one of several purposes. It may tell of an event—something that has happened. It may describe a person or some activity. It may set forth an opinion.

Example of a paragraph telling of an event:

The great blizzard of 1888 brought life on the East Coast almost to a stop. Seven-meter-high snowdrifts trapped trains on their tracks. Ice-coated telephone and telegraph wires fell to the ground, taking with them all chance of communication between cities. Many people slept on factory floors because they could not go home. People in their homes shivered in the dark because the electric wires were down, along with the telegraph wires. Horses and people were injured or killed in the stricken cities. At last the snow stopped, and major cities like New York and Washington began to dig themselves out of the drifts. But many people would remember the terrible days of the blizzard for the rest of their lives.

Example of a paragraph describing a person:

Many cowboys of the Old West were Black, and Nat Love was one of the finest of them. He began breaking in wild horses while he was still a boy. Riding the cattle trails in Texas, he survived hailstones and buffalo stampedes. He could rope, tie, saddle, and mount a wild pony in nine minutes. In a shooting contest, Nat put twelve rifle shots in the bull's-eye of a target while his nearest rival only managed eight. Nat was a winner in every part of cowboy life.

Example of a paragraph stating an opinion:

Most young people who pin their career hopes on sports are wasting their time. Even sports heroes like Muhammad Ali and Arthur Ashe tell teenagers to spend time in the classroom, not in the gym. Only a small number of talented people ever make a living from sports. Fewer still make big money. And even these often have a career that lasts only a few years. In most sports, athletes of thirty-five years are old, and those forty are finished. Young people would be better off to train for jobs they can do all their lives.

In each of these paragraphs, the topic is stated in the first sentence. This is called the *topic sentence*. In many well-written paragraphs, the topic sentence is the first sentence.

7b   State the main idea of a paragraph in a topic sentence.

While thinking about what you plan to say in a paragraph, think how you can state your main idea in a topic sentence. Write the topic sentence. Then read it to yourself before going on to write the rest of the sentences in your paragraph. Check to see that your topic sentence expresses the main idea for your paragraph.

The following paragraph states an opinion of the writer. The opening sentence sets forth the opinion. This is the topic sentence. Every other sentence deals with that topic in some way.

Cats make much better pets than dogs. Cats are small, so they don't need a lot of space. They can do as well in a city apartment as in a house with a yard. They keep themselves clean. They are not as messy as dogs are. Most of the time they are quiet. Cats seem to be smarter than dogs. They are certainly more independent. Yet cats can be every bit as affectionate as dogs. Dogs often seem to love everybody, but cats are more choosy. When a cat loves you, you really feel as though you are somebody special.

EXERCISE 1 The following three paragraphs are missing topic sentences. Following the paragraphs are six possible topic sentences. Choose the best topic sentence for each paragraph. Write the numbers 1, 2, and 3 on a sheet of paper. Next to each number, write the topic sentence that belongs with that paragraph.

1. (Topic sentence missing.) In one place, people say that it always rains when the circus comes. In another, they believe that a cow with its tail in the air means a storm will soon arrive. Some people say that a red sky in the morning means rain before night. Others predict rain whenever their bones ache. In eastern Kentucky, some people will tell you how to change the weather: just drag a dishcloth across the floor. They say that will change the weather.

2. (Topic sentence missing.) Long ago, children in ancient Greece liked to play with tops, just as children do today. African children had tops

made out of bones. Very old tops have been found in the South Sea islands. They are made out of palm wood and volcanic ash. And at the other end of the world, Eskimos made their tops out of ice.

3.   (Topic sentence missing) Young blanket octopuses wind stinging jellyfish tentacles around their arms. These help the octopuses defend themselves when they are small. One kind of crab carries tiny sea anemones in its front claws. The stinging anemones let the crab give a "double whammy" to any enemy it meets. But the real sting-stealing prize goes to a sea slug that eats stinging animals called sea firs. The sea firs' stinging cells are harmless to the slug. Somehow the cells leave the slug's stomach and move to its skin—where they can still sting. The slug gets a meal and free "fire power" at the same time!

1. Sea animals are frightening.
2. There are as many ways of predicting rain as there are people for rain to fall on.
3. The Greeks played with tops.
4. Some sea animals protect themselves with stolen stingers.
5. Sun and rain come in unpredictable patterns.
6. All over the world children have played with spinning tops.

7c Keep every sentence in a paragraph on the topic.

A poorly-written paragraph often has sentences that do not deal with the topic of the paragraph. When you write, make every sentence in a paragraph tell about the topic in some way.

The following paragraph has a sentence that does not deal with the topic. As you read the paragraph, look for the sentence that should not be there. This will give you practice in looking over your own writing. The practice will help you keep out unwanted sentences.

(1) In Israel there is a place where things roll uphill by themselves. (2) It is in the middle of a road not far from a tiny village. (3) Israel is in the Middle East. (4) If people put their cars in neutral gear on that part of the road, the cars will start to roll uphill. (5) People have seen footballs and even water run uphill in this strange place. (6) Nobody seems to know what makes things break the law of gravity in this peculiar spot.

If you have read carefully, you can see that it is the third sentence that does not belong in the above paragraph: *Israel is in the Middle East.* The fact that Israel is in the Middle East, though true, does not tell about the topic: the strange place where things seem to roll uphill.

EXERCISE 2 Number a sheet of paper 1–3. Each of the following paragraphs contains a sentence that is not on the topic of the paragraph. Next to each number, write the sentence that does not belong in the paragraph.

1.   In 1855 a daring Frenchman named Blondin began doing stunts on a tightrope across Niagara Falls. One day he walked across with his

arms and head in a sack. Another time he rode across on a bicycle. Once he took a table and chair and ate a meal out there. Niagara Falls is over 300 meters across. Blondin even carried another man across the falls on his back. Day after day, people crowded around the falls to see what the French daredevil would do next.

2.   The main purpose of the beautiful designs on the banners and shields of the Middle Ages was to tell who someone was. A knight would ride into battle, or into the knightly sports contest called a tournament, with the face plate of his helmet closed. As soon as people saw the heraldic designs on his shield and banner, they knew exactly who he was. Knights sometimes tried to hit targets with long poles called lances. A heraldic design told people who the knight's mother and father were. It told whether he was their oldest son or a later arrival. It even suggested one or two important things about his family's history.

3.   A boy and his father found one of the largest diamonds in the United States while they were playing a game of horeseshoes. "Punch" Jones and his father were playing their game by Rich Creek in West Virginia in 1928. Suddenly Punch saw a big gray-green stone on the ground. "That's pretty," he said. "I think I'll keep it." Punch kept the stone for fifteen years. Then one day he had a professor test it and found out that his gray-green stone was a diamond. Diamonds are made of carbon. Punch's pretty stone is now in the Smithsonian Institution in Washington, D.C. It is still called the Punch Jones Diamond.

7d A paragraph may be developed with details, examples, or reasons.

Every sentence following the topic sentence in a paragraph adds more information about the topic. If the paragraph is describing someone or something, the sentences should add descriptive details. If the topic sentence states an opinion, the other sentences in the paragraph can supply examples or reasons to support the opinion.

Example of a paragraph developed with details:

A hot lava flow from an active volcano causes many unusual effects. The stream at first is an orange and red mass, moving like soft mud. Everything inflammable in its path burns. Even hard earth and some rocks will melt and flow with the lava. Oddly, however, very wet objects may be partly protected. Hit by the lava, they create steam. The expanding steam may push lava away, allowing the wet objects to survive the high heat. Sometimes a wet plant, covered by a lava stream, will live to grow again after the lava stream has cooled.

Example of a paragraph developed with examples:

The language of Citizens' Band radio slang has developed like a kind of funny poetry. Sometimes it even rhymes. A police helicopter is an "eye in the sky" or "bear in the air." Police are called "Smokey Bears" or just "Bears" in CB talk. "My toenails are on the front bumper" means "I'm going full speed ahead." Shelled corn is "Texas strawberries" to a CB operator. Even each kind of car and each big city has a special CB name. A Ford Thunderbird is a "Thunder Chicken." Hollywood, California, is "Tinsel Town." When the CB talk is coming in loud and clear, it's "wall to wall and ten feet tall."

Example of a paragraph developed with reasons:

Women in the police force are just as effective as men—maybe more so. If properly trained, women can run as fast and shoot as straight as men. Many women are more agile and have faster reflexes than men. Because they are often smaller than men, women sometimes can squeeze through narrow places more easily. They can handle powerfully built criminals by using karate and judo. They can be just as tough and fearless as their male counterparts, and they may be more gentle in helping crime victims. Many female crime victims would rather talk to a woman than to a man.

EXERCISE 3 Choose one of the following topics. Write a paragraph of at least 6 to 8 sentences about your topic. You may wish to find information about your topic by reading or by actual investigation. Develop your paragraph with details, examples, or reasons.

1. The condition of a nearby body of water
2. The condition of a nearby piece of land
3. The condition of the air

7e A paragraph may be developed through comparison or contrast.

When two things are compared, the main differences between them can often be stated in one paragraph. The description of one thing may be the main topic. The description of the other thing serves as a comparison.

Example of a paragraph developed by comparison and contrast:

Would you rather ride a meebong or a spraddlewhacket? Both beasts will carry you across the plains of Venus in style, it is true. But a meebong is so slow! It lumbers along on its four legs, while a spraddlewhacket gallops forward on eight. And the spraddlewhacket has two feet on each leg, at that. Both the meebong and the spraddlewhacket have pretty blue eyes. But only the spraddlewhacket has gold eyelashes. I love its shiny green fur, too. Its fur feels softer than that splotchy pink coat of the meebong. Yes, riding a spraddlewhacket is better than riding a meebong any day!

EXERCISE 4 Choose one of the following topics. On a sheet of paper, make a list of points about the two items mentioned in the topic. In your list, include points that show the comparison and contrast between the two items.

1. Hot dogs and hamburgers
2. Sailboats and powerboats
3. Lions and tigers

4. Fountain pens and ball-point pens
5. Clouds and fog
6. Stars and planets
7. Spaghetti and macaroni
8. Hard rock and soft rock
9. A topic of your choice

7f   A paragraph may be developed by showing causes and effects.

Anytime something happens, it may cause something else to happen. If you tell of an event in a paragraph, you can often tell of one or more effects of that event in the same paragraph.

Example of a paragraph developed by cause and effect:

Desert peoples all over the world have told stories about sand dunes that boom and "sing." It now seems that the stories are true. Even though the scientists have heard the sand dunes make their strange noises, they still do not know what causes them to do it. They know a dune must be big before it will boom. Also, the sand must be piled mostly on one side. Some scientists think that electrical changes in the sand make the noises. No one knows how electrical changes could make a sand dune sound like a railroad train, a tuba, or a barking seal. The sounds are so loud that they make the dune shake. Sand slides down its steep face. The vibrations can make other dunes nearby start "singing," too.

¶

EXERCISE 5 Choose one of the following topics and write a paragraph. Show cause and effect in your paragraph.

1. Colors in the sunset
2. The cricket's song
3. A photographic image on film
4. Mold
5. How a compass works
6. The electric light bulb
7. A topic of your choice

7g Events in a paragraph may be organized by time.

Telling about an event in a paragraph means that you are telling of things that happened in time. Perhaps everything happened at once. If this is so, make sure you state that fact. Usually, however, things you write about happen one after the other. As you write a paragraph, make sure you keep clear what happened first, then next, then later.

Example of a paragraph organized by time:

One snowy Saturday morning the Parsons family turned on their television. At 11:00 A.M. a commercial for a used car dealer came on. "If you come in today," the dealer announced, "I'll take a dollar off my prices for every snowball you bring me." The family agreed that this was a way to get a better car than their old one. Right away they went to work. By 11:30 A.M. they were piling snowballs next to their old car. As the day went on, neighbors joined the Parsons in manufacturing snowballs. Hour after hour the snowball pile grew. Four hours after they began, the tired Parsons loaded the snowballs into the back of their car and drove to the used car dealer's lot. The car dealer found that they had 1,834 snowballs. The Parsons wanted a car that cost $1,895. Mrs. Parsons gave the dealer $61 in cash because she said she was too tired to make any more snowballs. Finally, late in the day, the Parsons family drove home in their new used car.

It is clear in this paragraph that the events happened from morning until night. The writer keeps referring to the times of the day. Also, words like *after* and *finally* help to show in what order the things happened. The paragraph is organized by time.

EXERCISE 6   Only the first and last sentences in the following paragraph are in the right order in time. The other sentences are out of order. On a separate sheet of paper, write the numbers of the sentences in the order they belong.

(1) The beginning of a gold-mining boom town was just a few men sitting around a campfire. (2) If the gold strike looked good, "permanent" houses of wood replaced the tents. (3) In a year or two, the camp could be well on its way to being a real town. (4) In two or three weeks, tents sprang up, along with cabins made of brush or packing boxes. (5) After some months had passed, hotels and stores may

have appeared on the main street. (6) Or instead, many buildings could be empty, and the town could be sinking back into the wild land from which it had come.

7h A paragraph may be organized by space.

Any paragraph that describes a person, a thing, or a place needs to tell how parts are related in space. Words such as *next to, above,* and *around* help to do this.

Example of a paragraph organized by space:

Lila had never seen anything like this planet. Sheets of shimmering purple crystals covered the ground. On Lila's right, the crystals grew larger and in piles to make small, craggy hills. To her left and in front of her, the crystal plain stretched flat and bare as far as she could see. There seemed to be no life here except herself. And yet—just where the hills ended, out of the corner of her eye—had she just seen something move?

EXERCISE 7   Choose one of the following sentences as a topic sentence for a paragraph. Or think of one of your own. Write a paragraph of five or six sentences. Organize your paragraph by time or by space.

1. My driving test went better than I expected.
2. Breakfast was a disaster.
3. Last night I was scared.
4. That fishing trip gave me one moment of glory.

5. The best class period I remember came last year.
6. I have finally found out how to keep things in my locker.

7i   Link the sentences of a paragraph together by connecting words.

Certain words help to link the ideas of sentences together. You can use these words in your paragraphs to keep sentences on the topic. For example, in a paragraph organized by time, the following words are useful:

at first	next	then
after (that)	following this (that)	at last
afterward	finally	in time

In a paragraph organized by space, you can use some of the following words to tie sentences together:

around	next to	at the right (left)
above	over	inside
between	near	under

When showing comparison or contrast, you can use words like *however, compared with,* or *in contrast to.* All of these words help to link sentences together in a paragraph.

EXERCISE 8 The following paragraph has no connecting words to link its ideas together. The blank spaces and the numbers in parentheses show where connecting words could go. Number a sheet of paper 1–6. Next to each number, write the best choice of a connecting word.

Pouring a concrete foundation demands hard, careful work. __(1)__, the ground must be dug deep and level enough for a solid base. Around the edges goes a form that will shape the sides of the foundation. __(2)__, the concrete should harden flat. __(3)__, if the side form is weak, the weight of the concrete will push it out of shape. Before concrete goes in the form, a steel mesh can be laid to give extra strength. __(4)__, the fresh concrete fills the form to its edges. __(5)__, as the concrete begins to harden, it needs to be smoothed on top. __(6)__, the dried concrete holds firm and the form can be removed.

7j   Use a paragraph to show the words of a new speaker.

When you are writing a story that contains the actual words spoken by one or more individuals, begin the speech of each individual with a paragraph. The following example illustrates how speeches are set off by paragraphs.

"Anybody home?" Ratty thrust his head in through the open door.

"Ump." Wheeler turned away from the coffee table upon which he had been organizing a troop of lead soldiers.

Not at all surprised by this greeting, Ratty slid into the room and sat down in the green swivel rocker. From the window next to it he could see Joanna in the garden. She was picking strawberries.

"And she'll leave at least half of 'em," he said to himself. He thought for a moment about the dark-haired woman. "Proves she isn't greedy," he decided.

Wheeler looked up. While his hands rested lightly on the battered metal warriors, he gave his lanky visitor a thoughtful glance.

"Johnson's in town," he said. His light Irish eyes showed nothing more than mild interest.

Before he answered, Ratty thought, "Wheeler's always that way. Never one to fly off the handle." Then he nodded quickly. "That's why I'm here," he said.

He waited while Wheeler rose, crossed the small room to a rosewood cabinet, and unlocked it. From a small drawer he drew out a package wrapped in yellowing paper. The two men drew up to the coffee table on which Wheeler had placed the package. Their faces were suddenly grim.

REVIEW EXERCISE A   The Topic

Find the topic sentence in each of the following paragraphs. Then check and see that all the sentences deal with the topic. On a sheet of paper, write the topic sentence and any sentence you have found that does not tell something about the topic.

EXAMPLE   On April 18, 1906, at 5:13 A.M. a great earthquake hit San Francisco. Tall buildings crumbled. Water and gas lines broke. Everywhere fires broke out, causing more damage. Thousands of people were made homeless by the earthquake and had to sleep in the parks. San Francisco is one of the most popular cities for tourists in America. The earthquake and the fires left the city almost completely leveled.

On April 18, 1906, at 5:13 A.M., a great earthquake hit San Francisco. San Francisco is one of the most popular cities for tourists in America.

1. To make a good pie crust, you need good ingredients, patience, and the ability to let it alone when it is ready. Take chilled butter and cut it into flour and salt with two knives. You can also use a pastry blender if you have one. Peach is a favorite kind of pie. Keep at it until the mixture is like cornmeal. Then add cold water a little at a time until the dough sticks together and will form a ball. Don't handle the dough too much or the piecrust will be tough. Roll it out with short strokes, aiming away from your body. Make the pie crust an inch or two bigger than the pan.

2.   Watching football games on television is a
waste of time. You sit there, slumped in a chair,
on beautiful fall afternoons when you could be
playing football. The announcer screams at you.
Every fifteen minutes you listen to the same
commercials. The Super Bowl is the biggest
game of the year. You get fat from lack of exercise and too many snacks. You lose track of what
your friends are doing. You become a bore because you don't have anything to talk about except football.

3.   Many Puerto Rican-born athletes have become
famous in this country. Roberto Clemente and
Orlando Cepeda were outstanding baseball
players. Eddie Belmonte is a famous horse joc-
key. Puerto Rico is an island about 140 kilometers long and 80 kilometers wide. Juan "Chi Chi"
Rodriguez is a champion golfer. In the field of
boxing, three Puerto Ricans have won world
championships. Sixto Escobar won the World
Bantamweight Championship twice in the
1930's. José Torres became the World Light-
Heavyweight Boxing Champion in 1965, and
Carlos Ortiz has won the title of World Lightweight Boxing Champion five times.

REVIEW EXERCISE B   Points to Make

Following is a list of topics for paragraphs.
Choose two. Then, on a sheet of paper, write a list of
points you would make in a paragraph about one of
these topics. Do the same for the other topic. If you
don't choose from the list, you may choose two of
your own topics.

EXAMPLE   Swimming is good exercise.

Points to make: uses all the muscles, doesn't put particular stress on any given area; teaches breath control; expands lung capacity; is a useful skill.

TOPIC SENTENCES

1. Motorcycles should be banned.
2. I remember the best present I ever received.
3. Many people have claimed to see ghosts.
4. Chinese immigrants to America were often discriminated against.
5. Tea is a better drink than coffee.
6. Friday morning was really hectic!
7. It was an exciting football game.
8. Muhammad Ali had a spectacular career.
9. Ice skating and roller skating are similar in some ways.
10. Rainbows are caused by light shining through water droplets.

REVIEW EXERCISE C   Writing Paragraphs

Write two paragraphs of a few sentences each on two of the following topics. Make sure you have a topic sentence and that the other sentences relate to it. If you don't see a topic you like, make up one of your own.

TOPIC LIST

1. Steel-belted radial tires
2. A football game
3. A trip you took
4. How to make enchiladas
5. Your views on foreign aid
6. Wooden and aluminum tennis rackets
7. Hummingbirds
8. Why the sky is blue
9. How to find gold

8

GUIDELINES FOR WRITING

Putting your thoughts into words often means writing several paragraphs about a topic. When you organize your ideas on paper in this way, you are writing a *composition.*

This chapter deals with some basic ways to improve your writing of compositions. The first way is to begin writing about what you know. From this point, you can compose sentences and paragraphs aimed at a particular audience. You can organize your sentences and paragraphs to state your ideas more effectively.

Many more composition guidelines exist than are found in this chapter. Yet the ones included here are basic. You will gain much from following them. Study this chapter and try to put into practice its advice. You will find that what you want to say will become clearer in time.

CHOOSING YOUR TOPIC AND YOUR AUDIENCE

8a Write about what you know.

You may have trouble sometimes thinking of something to write about. When you feel this way, be careful not to choose just any topic. If you know nothing about a topic, you will probably have trouble writing a good composition.

What topics can you choose? Your experiences are well known to you. These make good topics for writing. Your thoughts and feelings, based on your experiences, can also become the source of worthwhile compositions.

Choosing the right topic is the first step to preparing an interesting composition. The best topic is the one you know best. After you choose a topic you know about, make a list of the most important items related to it.

EXERCISE 1 Choose one of the following topics for a composition. Make a list of the things that were involved in the experience.

1. The time I really tried and was successful
2. The time I really tried and was unsuccessful
3. Why did it have to happen to me?
4. It was a big gamble
5. It was a terrible mistake
6. Revenge can be sweet
7. Revenge can be sour
8. My cleverest moment
9. Was it all a bad dream?
10. My best dreams

EXERCISE 2   Write your own composition about the topic you chose in Exercise 1. Or choose another topic that is similar. Describe the events that happened. Group them into paragraphs. Your composition should be at least two paragraphs long.

8b   Choose a topic to suit your audience.

When you are planning your composition, think of your *audience*—the person or people who will probably read it. Then direct your writing toward your audience. Write almost as though you were speaking to that person or persons.

The topic you choose should be suited to your audience. The words you use should also be suited to your audience. Writing for your audience helps them to understand what you intend to say in your composition.

EXERCISE 3   Choose one of the following topics to write about. Think about how you would write about it to someone you know well who is your age. Then think how you would write about it to an adult you do not know well. Decide whether your audience will be someone your age or an adult.

On a sheet of paper, write who your audience is. Then write one or two paragraphs about the topic for that audience.

1. Two reasons why I like being my age
2. Two reasons why I wish I were some other age
3. The time I was called wrong but was right
4. The time no one knew I was wrong
5. How my secret goal can someday come true

6. Why my secret hope can never come true
7. The trouble I found from keeping a secret
8. The trouble I found from sharing a secret
9. A topic of your choice

EXERCISE 4   Write a new composition on the topic you chose in Exercise 3. This time, write it for the other audience, either a friend your age or an adult.

ORGANIZING YOUR WRITING

Many times a composition lacks organization. It starts out on a topic but soon wanders away from that topic. Or it lacks a clear beginning or a definite ending.

Good organization results from careful planning. Plan ahead how you will treat the topic you have chosen. Your first steps should be to choose a topic and an audience. Then plan how you will treat that topic.

Think of possible ways you can deal with your topic. For example, do you plan to treat it seriously? Possibly you can treat it humorously.

Next, you should make sure you can deal with the topic you have chosen.

8c   Limit the topic you choose to write about.

You will avoid difficulty in writing a composition if you keep your topic to the right size. For example, you may decide to write about automobiles because they interest you greatly. The topic "automobiles" is full of interesting ideas.

However, you will not be able to deal with all those ideas in a single composition. In fact, there are so many ideas it would take several books to cover them all. And even then you would probably miss some.

Instead of choosing the topic of "automobiles," limit the topic to a specific subtopic, such as hood ornaments or body shapes. Even writing about one particular car might require more time and space than you have. Therefore, plan a composition around a carefully limited topic.

EXERCISE 5 Assume you have had a number of different experiences with cars. You plan to write about one of them. You need to limit the topic so that your composition is no longer than four paragraphs. Which of the following topics are best limited to a composition of four paragraphs? Write these topics on a sheet of paper.

1. An embarrassing stall
2. The world's fastest racing cars
3. The safest car on the road
4. Antique cars
5. The automobile of the future
6. Fuel-efficient cars
7. A well-designed dashboard
8. A funny car

EXERCISE 6 The following list contains some topics that are too broad and some topics that are limited enough for a composition of three to five paragraphs. Make two columns on a separate sheet of paper, headed *Broad Topics* and *Limited Topics*. Under one heading list the topics that are too large.

Under the other heading list the topics that are limited.

The best milkshake	The four seasons
The damage caused	Fashions in clothing
by a drought	The importance of
How to dunk a basketball	Latin America
The dangers of motorcycle	Junk food
riding	The soccer dribble
A horseshoe contest	

8d Organize events under major subtopics.

After you have chosen a topic, list the most important points you want to tell about it. Often several of these major points, or subtopics, will belong together. Usually you will want to write a paragraph about each subtopic or each group of subtopics.

For example, if you choose the limited topic "The soccer dribble" from Exercise 6, you can probably describe the entire maneuver in a single paragraph. If you choose the limited topic "A horseshoe contest" from the same list, however, you may organize your description under three major subtopics: the contestants, the rules, and the action. You may also have a fourth subtopic, the winner. You may find you want to write a paragraph about each of these subtopics.

EXERCISE 7 For each of the following topics, think of two or three subtopics. Number a sheet of paper 1–4. Skip two or three lines between numbers. Next to each number, write two or three or more subtopics you would include in a composition about the topic.

1. Good ways to relax when nervous
2. My favorite steps for losing weight
3. How to deal with teasing
4. How I prove I'm not lazy

8e Relate events in the order they happen.

Events happen in a *sequence,* or order, in time. For instance, in driving a car you must insert the key in the ignition before starting the engine. You must put the engine in gear before the car will move. When the car begins to move, you must steer it. To bring the car to a halt, you must use the brakes.

These seem like simple events, and they are. But they illustrate the fact that events happen in a certain order. When you write about a series of events, make sure you relate their correct sequence. Then your reader can follow what happened.

To make sure the events you relate are in the order they happened, make a list of the events before you begin your composition.

As you look over this list, you can check it to be sure that each event is in order. If any event is out of order, you can rearrange it. You may want to divide the list of events into a *beginning,* a *middle,* and an *ending.* Listing events in order before you begin your writing will save you and your readers much trouble. It will also help you decide how many paragraphs to write to cover all the events.

EXERCISE 8 Following is a list of connected events. However, the events are out of order. Only the first and last events are in order. On a sheet of paper, write the letters of the events in the order they probably happened.

a. Someone saw smoke coming out of the side window of an empty warehouse.
b. The firefighters put out the fire.
c. The firefighters broke the side window and chopped a hole in the roof of the warehouse.
d. That person telephoned the fire department to report smoke.
e. Flames shot through the side window.
f. Firefighters hooked the long hoses to a hydrant.
g. The fire marshall in a red car was the first official on the scene.
h. Firefighters uncoiled their hoses.
i. The first fire truck arrived.
j. With hoses the firefighters sprayed water through the window and the hole in the roof.
k. The firefighters cleaned up their equipment.
l. The firefighters left the warehouse.

8f   Tell about the setting of events.

The *setting,* the place where events happen, is usually important for you to describe in a composition. Your description of the setting allows your readers to picture what you have in your mind.

When you describe a setting, do not try to tell about every feature. Instead pick out the important ones.

Imagine that you have seen the events listed in Exercise 8 and that you wish to write about these events in a composition. Some of the features of the setting are important.

For example, it is important to tell whether the warehouse is set off by itself or is close to other buildings. If it is close to other buildings, the danger of a spreading fire adds to the excitement of the event.

Even if the warehouse is set apart from other buildings, it might be in a field of high grass. Is the grass very dry? The fire may spread through the grass. Or has it been raining heavily so that the grass is wet? Wet grass is less likely to burn. Again, the difference in setting makes a difference in the excitement of your writing.

Describe the important features of the setting where events take place. Your reader will gain a better picture from your composition.

EXERCISE 9 Describe the place where you had a special experience. Tell how features of the place are situated in relation to one another. You can choose an experience from the following list. Or you might wish to choose one of your own.

1. A secret hiding place
2. Where the damage was worst
3. A perfect place for a (picnic, wedding, game)
4. The busiest place I know
5. The view from the window
6. Where the accident occurred
7. A place for laughs
8. A place for memories

8g Tie events together by causes and effects.

One event often causes another. For example, when someone rings a fire alarm, firefighters race to the fire. After firefighters pour water on a fire, it is important to tell what happens as a result.

Not all events are clearly related as causes and effects. Often you need to tell your audience how events are related. Where one event causes another, tell about that relationship.

EXERCISE 10   The following left-hand list includes causes. The right-hand list includes effects brought about by the causes. Number a sheet of paper 1–6. Next to each number, write the cause. Next to the cause, write the related effect that probably occurs.

CAUSES	EFFECTS
1. You accidentally hit your hand with a hammer	you slip
	a sleeping baby wakes up
2. A student does perfect work in class	you breathe fast
	the temperature goes down
3. You walk on ice in smooth-soled shoes	you yell
4. You make a loud noise	a grade of *A* is earned
5. Winter comes	
6. You jump high ten times in ten seconds.	

See Conjunction, p. 392; Adverb, p. 387; Preposition, p. 406   When you write about events that are closely related as causes and effects, you can use special words to show their relationship. These words are called *connectors*. Conjunctions, adverbs, and prepositions serve as connectors.

Here are some examples of connectors.

as a result	Teresa argued loud and long; *as a result,* Ada decided to go to the dance. [Cause: loud and long arguing. Effect: Ada decides to go to the dance.]
because	Dana smiled *because* he was happy. [Cause: happiness. Effect: a smile.]
since	Since we need eggs and milk, we can stop at Maxi's Market. [Cause: a need for milk and eggs. Effect: stop at Maxi's Market.]
therefore	The door was bolted inside; *therefore,* the police had to smash it. [Cause: a bolted door. Effect: the police smashing it.]
whenever	*Whenever* the siren goes off, the engine will start up. [Cause: the sound of the siren. Effect: the engine's starting.]

EXERCISE 11 Following are pairs of sentences that can be combined as causes and effects. Number a sheet of paper 1–5. Write each pair as one sentence. Use connectors to show the relationship of cause and effect. Underline the connectors you use.

EXAMPLE   June swerved the car to one side. A
          skunk had run into the road.

June swerved the car to one
side __because__ a skunk had
run into the road.

1. The pot boiled over on the stove. Greta had left
   the heat high.
2. Trixie's feet failed to clear the crossbar. It fell on
   top of her.
3. Dust lay on the furniture. No one had cleaned it
   in more than a month.
4. The boat slowly disappeared. The leak in its bottom had never been fixed.
5. The flag flapped loudly on the pole. The wind
   blew fiercely.

EXERCISE 12   Write a composition of two or three
paragraphs about an experience you had or an
event you know about. Show the relationship between at least two causes and two effects. Use connectors to show how the causes are related to the
effects.

CHOOSING YOUR WORDS

See Phrase,
p. 405   **8h   Use words and phrases that appeal to the
       senses.**

Words and phrases that appeal to the reader's
sense of sight, hearing, touch, taste, and smell help
to make your writing come alive.

Study the differences in the two following examples. The first one lacks words that appeal to the senses. The second one is more interesting to read because of its sensory appeal.

EXAMPLES   1. The point of the needle stuck Ella's finger and drew blood.
2. The point of the shiny needle stabbed like a dart into Ella's finger and drew a drop of dark red blood that grew larger on her pale skin.

Notice that the first sentence lacks words that appeal specially to the senses. The second sentence contains a number of such words. For example, the needle is described as *shiny*. The verb *stabbed* suggests more action than the verb *stuck*. The comparison of the point of the needle to a dart also adds to the liveliness of the description. Further sensory appeal comes from mention of the dark red blood on the pale skin.

In your own writing, think of words that appeal to the senses. Remember that the senses are sight, hearing, touch, taste, and smell.

EXERCISE 13 Following is a list of words that appeal to the five senses. Make five columns across the top of a sheet of paper. Write one of the senses as a heading for each column: *Sight, Hearing, Touch, Taste, Smell*. Under each heading write the words from the list that appeal to that sense. For example, the word *rasp* goes under *Hearing* because it appeals to the *ear*. Some words appeal to more than one sense. You may put them under either heading.

thud	sizzle	puckery
silky	licorice	thistly
patter	gravelly	crooked
rasp	chipped	warped
droning	sputter	mushy
bitter	mint	soaking

EXERCISE 14   Each of the following sentences lacks words that appeal to the senses. Rewrite each sentence on a sheet of paper. Add words that appeal to the senses. Underline each of the sensory words you add. Do not change the basic meanings.

EXAMPLE   The statue of the general seemed out of place in the middle of the traffic circle, with cars and trucks going around.

The <u>towering</u> statue of the <u>stern</u> general seemed out of place in the middle of the <u>bustling</u> traffic circle, with <u>smelly</u>, <u>honking</u> cars and <u>belching</u> trucks <u>roaring</u> around.

1. Flakes of snow fell against the window and collected in a small but growing mound on the sill.
2. The cat slipped through the opening in the fence and walked along the other side in safety.
3. The river flowed past the wharves and anchored ships.
4. The feather rose up on a gust of wind.

5. Many lights came on in the city below.
6. Ricardo wrote a line of words across his paper.
7. The garbage truck stopped near the dump to un-load its contents.
8. The youngster carried a portable radio along the street.

8i Use comparisons to improve your descriptions.

Your descriptions of people, places, or things will benefit from your use of comparisons to show how one thing is like another. For example, you might write about the way the sun casts shadows as its light shines through the branches of a tree. To improve the description, you can compare the motion of the shadows to dancers moving their bodies, arms, and legs.

EXAMPLE

SIMPLE DESCRIPTION   The shadows of the branches moved on the side of the building.

COMPARISON   The shadows of the branches seemed to dance a primitive ballet on the side of the building.

Often a comparison uses the word *like* or *as* to show how one thing is like another.

See Common Confusions, p. 266

EXAMPLE   The lightning shattered the night sky *like* jagged icicles hurled toward the earth.

The phrase *like jagged icicles* compares streaks of lightning to icicles. The two things are not the same. Yet the comparison of one to the other adds to the impression the reader gets.

To write effective comparisons, think how one person, place, or thing is like another. Then relate the two in your writing.

EXERCISE 15   List A contains objects or qualities. List B contains comparisons. Number a sheet of paper 1–5. Next to each number, write the item from List A. Next to it, write the best comparison from List B. The first one is done for you as an example.

EXAMPLE   *1. sharp as a snake's fang*

A	B
1. sharp	as a locked bank vault
2. a far-off train whistle	as a newborn calf
	as a snake's fang
3. a face	like the full moon
4. safe	like the wind moaning
5. unsteady	in a tall chimney

EXERCISE 16   The following items need comparisons to make their descriptions interesting. Write each item on a sheet of paper. Add your own comparison to each to make it more interesting.

EXAMPLE   helpless

helpless as a mummy

1. shiny   3. a waterfall
2. a trumpet's call   4. a bald head

5. the eye of a cat   8. still
6. loud   9. a pool of dark liquid
7. dishwater   10. flat

EXERCISE 17 Choose one of the following topics.
Or choose a topic from Exercise 1 on page 180. On a
sheet of paper, write a composition of two or three
paragraphs describing what you have chosen. Include comparisons in your description.

1. The best money I ever earned
2. The worst driver I have known
3. That fabulous holiday
4. This feeling might be love
5. This feeling is not love
6. A well-known person I like
7. My kind of car
8. I hope that never happens
9. Tomorrow's best athlete
10. The most overpaid player

8j   Support your ideas with specific details, examples, or reasons.

See
Paragraphs,
pp. 165–166

If you hear someone say "School is a waste of
time," you know generally what the speaker means.
The word *school* and the term *waste of time* can
mean many things, however. The broad statement
needs details, examples, or reasons to give it a
specific meaning. Without them, this statement is
only a *generalization.*

In most cases, a generalization without supporting details, examples, or reasons is a weak
statement. The way to strengthen a generalization
is by adding specific points.

Often the topic of a composition may be stated as a generalization which can be used as a topic sentence.

EXAMPLES   The art of letter writing is disappearing.
Students are a minority group in society.
Southern hospitality is still alive.

As you begin planning a composition whose topic sentence is a generalization, think of the specific details, examples, and reasons you need to include. Make a list of these specific points before you begin writing your composition. In this way you will make your topic understandable to your readers.

EXERCISE 18   The ideas in the following list are general statements. They need supporting details, examples, or reasons to make them stronger. Choose one of the generalizations. Write the complete statement on a sheet of paper. You may reword the statement. Write down at least four details, examples, or reasons to support the statement.

1. (name of a commercial) is the cleverest commercial on TV
2. (name of a song) is the best song I know
3. (name of an eating place) serves the best hamburgers around
4. (name of a teacher) is the strictest teacher in school
5. (name of a rule) is the worst rule in school
6. (name of a magazine) is the best magazine for young people.

EXERCISE 19   Write a short composition (100–250 words) about the topic you chose in Exercise 18. Use the supporting details, examples, or reasons you listed. Also remember to use words that appeal to the senses. Where you can, make comparisons.

8k   Show clearly how your ideas are linked together.

In your writing, use words and phrases that clearly link your ideas. To link your ideas more clearly, you can use *connectors* that tell your reader how your ideas are related. (Some of these connectors are listed earlier, on page 172.) Your ideas may be in sentences or they may be developed in full paragraphs. Wherever you express ideas that are related, show the relationships to your reader.

Here is a list of commonly used connecting terms. They may be useful to connect sentences. Many are useful to connect paragraphs.

after that (or *this*)—used to show what follows an event.

> The curtain came down. *After that,* the house lights came on.

as a result—used to tell of the effect of some action.

> As a result of her efforts, Shana was able to get the engine started.

at first, at last—used to begin or end a series of items related in time.

> *At last* the storm seemed harmless.

besides—used to introduce an additional point.

> I was late because the bus was late. *Besides,* traffic was very slow.

finally—similar to *at last.*

for example (or *for instance*)—used to introduce a specific point to support a general statement.

> Birds hunt for insects. *For example,* a ground robin scratches through dead leaves on the ground hoping to find bugs underneath.

furthermore—used to show another point is coming.

> You have extablished a new record. *Furthermore,* you have set a fine example for others to follow.

hence—used to show that something is a result of some action or thought.

> You and I have made the same points. *Hence,* we can agree.

however—used to tell of a contrast.

> The sofa was too big to fit in the trunk of the car. *However,* it fit easily in the back of Dan's truck.

in addition—used to show that more is coming.

> We have cleared up the argument. *In addition,* we have made new friends.

in conclusion—used to begin a final point.

> *In conclusion,* I would like to thank my sponsors.

instead—used to tell of a contrasting action or point.

> Teresa could have taken a chance. *Instead,* she used great care.

later—used to show a time relationship.

> Luis flung his clothes about the room. *Later* he would have time to put them away.

meanwhile—used to tell about something else that happens at the same time.

> Jan rode the bus into town. *Meanwhile,* Abe had driven to her home.

moreover—similar to *in addition.*

nevertheless—similar to *however.*

on the other hand—similar to *however.*

therefore—similar to *hence.*

thus—similar to *hence.*

EXERCISE 20 Each pair of sentences needs a connector to show how the ideas are related. On a sheet of paper, write each pair of sentences and include the best connecting term in its most suitable position.

> EXAMPLE The charges against him were dropped. He was really upset by the experience.

> *The charges against him were dropped. Nevertheless, he was really upset by the experience.*

1. Shaneen missed her train. She was forced to take a taxi.
2. Vandalism is increasing in this city. Last week someone smashed the windows in the back of City Hall.
3. Patsy will not eat in the lunchroom. She nibbles raw vegetables and fruit at her desk.

4. The flood waters rose three feet. The towns-people took to boats.
5. The roof of the house was steeply sloped. The snow slid off to the ground.

REVISING YOUR WRITING

8I   Revise your writing to improve its effectiveness.

Your first writing of a composition may result in something less than your best. In order to end up with your best ideas in writing, it will be necessary to revise your composition.

The process of revision requires almost as much care as the first writing. Sometimes, to make your writing even better, you may need to revise it several times.

If you can allow some time to pass between your first writing and your revising, you can notice ways to improve what you have written. This period of time—a kind of recess—lets you look at the writing with a fresh eye. You see errors you may have overlooked before. You find more effective ways of stating your ideas.

For further help in revising, try reading your composition aloud to a listener. The reading often helps you hear an unclear or uninteresting phrase or sentence or a disconnected series of supporting points. If you have no one who will listen to you read your composition, read it aloud to yourself.

When you revise your compositions, you may find it helpful to follow the Composition Checklist on page 201.

8m Check the mechanics of your writing.

After you have written and revised your composition, look it over for mechanical errors. See that you have spelled words correctly and that your punctuation is accurate. Have you used capital letters in the right places? Does your paper look neat and readable?

Again, check your composition against the Composition Checklist.

COMPOSITION CHECKLIST

1. Do you know enough about your topic?
2. Have you an audience clearly in your mind?
3. Does your topic suit your audience?
4. Is your topic limited so that you can deal with it?
5. Have you organized the events in time and place?
6. Have you used words and phrases that appeal to the audience?
7. Have you used comparisons?
8. Have you supported general ideas with specific points?
9. Have you used connecting terms clearly?
10. Does each paragraph develop an idea or an event?
11. Are your words, phrases, and sentences doing their best work?
12. Have you left any phrases or clauses separated from complete sentences?
13. Have you checked the mechanics to the best of your ability?

REVIEW EXERCISE A   Choosing Your Topic and Your Audience

Following is a list of topics for compositions. Suppose you are going to read a composition to your school class. Which topics would *not* suit you and your audience? On a sheet of paper, write down all the topics from the list that do *not* suit you or your audience.

EXAMPLE   *My fortieth birthday party*

TOPICS

My fortieth birthday party
My favorite record
A good football play
When the children leave home
A really interesting fact
If I could do anything
Why I am a millionaire today
One thing I am good at
One thing I cannot stand
Working for the railroad for ten years
A silly thing that I am afraid of
The best kind of tires to buy

REVIEW EXERCISE B   Organization in Writing

On a sheet of paper, write one or two paragraphs on one of the following topics or choose your own topic. After you have written the composition, tell what the setting is. Write down at least one place where you have used cause and effect.

TOPICS

One of my life's small mysteries
An embarrassing moment
The best kind of day
A visit with someone I like
An interesting store
A beautiful place

EXAMPLE

The Department of Motor Vehicles was a grim and airless place lighted by bleak fluorescent lights. Isobel stood waiting to take the driving test. Nervousness overtook her like a disease, making her palms sweat. Finally, her turn came. A man in uniform holding a clipboard called her name. Together they walked over to her car and got in.

"Drive down to the end of the block and turn right," the man ordered. Isobel turned on the ignition and put her foot on the accelerator. Nothing happened. She tried again, but still the car made no sound. Her mind raced frantically as she tried to think of what she had done wrong. She sat there feeling numb.

"I think the battery's dead," said the driving instructor, after what seemed an eternity.

setting: the grim Department of Motor Vehicles
cause and effect: nervousness caused her palms to sweat

REVIEW EXERCISE C   Choosing Your Words

Following is a list of words. Number a sheet of paper 1–10. Next to each number, write a complete sentence using each word. Include in each sentence either a comparison or a group of words that appeal to the senses.

EXAMPLE   boat

The boat sailed out of the harbor in a flutter of white, like an angry bride.

1. lemon
2. crow
3. rug
4. pastry
5. clothes

6. taste
7. hammer
8. rain
9. motorcycle
10. steak

REVIEW EXERCISE D   Using Details and Examples

Choose one of the topics that follow or use one of your own. On a sheet of paper, list at least five specific examples, details, or reasons that you would use if you were writing a composition on the topic.

TOPICS

Why I hate to babysit
My least favorite television personality
I like electric trains

The most interesting place I know
My idea of a good politician
How women are discriminated against
How men are discriminated against

EXAMPLE

*Why working in an ice cream
store is a hard job.*

*1. You have to bend over a lot and
scoop hard ice cream.*

*2. You have to stand there and
wait while people make up their
minds about the flavor they want.*

*3. Children drip ice cream on the
floor, and you have to clean it up.*

*4. Some people buy one scoop of
ice cream and sit there all
afternoon, taking up space.*

*5. Three people told me what
they wanted and then changed
their minds just as I was
fixing it.*

REVIEW EXERCISE E   Revising

On a sheet of paper, neatly revise the following
composition. You should refer to the Composition

Checklist on page 201 for points to cover in your revision.

A FRUSTRATING BEGINNING

Today was my most frustrating experience in a long time. The local transit system is a mess. It happened because I decided to ride the bus to go downtown instead of walk.

I waited for twenty-five minutes. Three buses went past me. They were too full for me to squeeze on. I did get a seat on a local bus that stopped at every other corner and took forever. By the time I reached my stop it was jammed, too. I took a breath of fresh air gratefully when I stepped off. Next time I'll walk.

9

LETTER WRITING

Every letter you write represents you. The *content* and *form* of the letter say something about you. The content is what you write. The form is how your letter appears.

The two main kinds of letters are *personal,* or friendly, *letters* and *business letters.* You need to be concerned with content and form when writing both kinds. Your letters should say what you mean in the best form possible.

This chapter gives guidelines for writing both personal and business letters.

PREPARING THE LETTER

9a Follow the five guides for letter writing.

(1) Think ahead before you write.

What points do you intend to make in your letter? Are you telling about your experiences? Are you trying to get some information? Think before you write. Make sure you include in your letter the points you have in mind.

(2) Use the best paper and writing equipment.

Your stationery represents you to your reader. If you write on neat, clean paper, you create one kind of impression. If you use smudged or torn paper, you give a different kind of impression altogether.

The kind of pen or typewriter you use will also make a difference. Clean, straight letters look better than letters that are scratched or blurred.

Do not use a pencil for writing business letters. It gives a poor appearance.

(3) Follow standard form.

Standard form in letters is expected in the business world. Follow the form illustrated on page 210. A personal letter is also usually written in a standard way.

Write names and addresses correctly and clearly. Be sure you have written your return address so that a return letter can reach you. Remember to sign your name in the closing of your letter.

(4) Use standard grammar, spelling, and punctuation.

The rules of good writing apply to letters just as they do to other kinds of compositions. Successful communication in letter writing depends upon following the rules.

(5) Read over your letter before you send it.

Once you have sealed and sent a letter, you cannot call it back to correct mistakes. Take care, therefore, to find and correct your mistakes before you mail the letter.

Often you can spot an error in a letter if you read it aloud. Do this as though you were the person receiving the letter. Try to look at the letter and listen to yourself read it as though it were for the first time.

If you have only one or two minor errors in a letter, they may be corrected directly on the page. Make a correction by putting a single, clean line through the error. Then write the correction just above the error you have marked. If you have made several mistakes—or if the letter is extremely important and has an error—rewrite the whole page.

THE BUSINESS LETTER

9b   Use the standard form in a business letter.

Business letters require special attention, mostly because of the form. Study the example of a standard business letter on page 210. Notice its six parts.

Business letters are generally of three different kinds: the *request letter,* the *order letter,* and the *letter of adjustment* or *complaint.*

HEADING

                           15 Red Keg Highway

                           Edenville, Michigan 48620

                           May 1, 1979

INSIDE ADDRESS

The Manager
Broken Arrow Dude Ranch
Quincy, California 95971

SALUTATION

Dear Sir or Madam:
   I am writing to ask you if it would be
possible to work at your dude ranch this summer.
   I am fifteen years old. I will finish school
on May 26 and will be available for work
immediately after that date.
   Last summer I worked at the Edenville Day
Camp as an assistant counselor for five-
to-eight-year-old children. I have been a

BODY

member of different scouting groups for
five years, and I enjoy outdoor activities.
I like to cook and I have other household skills.
   I would be especially interested in a job
involving horses, but I am willing to
consider any other job you have available.
My parents support my interest. I can
supply you with references if you wish.
   Thank you for your consideration.

CLOSING
                     Sincerely,

SIGNATURE
                     Francine Wixom

                     Francine Wixom

The Request Letter

You use this kind of business letter to request
something you want. You may want only free information. However, asking for free material or in-

formation requires that you use care in preparing your letter.

You will probably get better attention to a request letter if you enclose a stamped, addressed return envelope. If you do not enclose a return envelope, at least be sure you have your name and address on both the envelope and at the top of your letter.

Following is an example of a request letter.

```
                              1028 Hydra Street
                              Cleveland, Ohio 44140
                              January 28, 1979

Tookey, Tailor & Co.
Cleveland, Ohio 44103

Mail Order Department:
   Please send me your most recent catalog
showing your line of hiking boots and
camping equipment.
   If there is a charge for the catalog or
postage, please let me know in advance.
   Thank you.
                              Sincerely,

                              Jack Winward
                              Jack Winward
```

EXERCISE 1   Write a letter requesting information. Ask for any catalogs or other printed material.
Do not send the letter unless you really need the
information.

The Order Letter

It is common practice to order goods by mail.
Following are two examples of order letters:

```
                               3145 High Road
                               Brooklyn, N.Y. 11201
                               March 18, 1979

Autotech Division
Scorefire Corporation
P.O. Box 179
Neward, N.H. 07110

Dear Sirs:
  Please send me six (6) "Thunderbolt"
spark plugs @ $8.00 each, as advertised
in your latest catalog.  I need them
for my 1967 Chevrolet two-door coupe
with the standard straight-six engine.
  I enclose a money order in the
amount of $48.00.

                   Sincerely,

                   Marie W. Baretti
                   Marie W. Baretti
```

128 River Road
Forestville, PA 15301
August 10, 1980

Order Department
Terwilliger's
P.O. Box 7888
San Francisco, CA 94120

Dear Manager:
   Please ship me the following latch
hook rug kits:
1 "Tree Silhouette", size 24" x 36",
Catalog # 54a...................$24.40
1 "Inca" by Bernat, size 21" x 22",
Catalog #54g.................... 16.80

                                $43.20

   My personal check for $43.20
is enclosed.

                   Yours truly,

                   Jeff D. Masters

                   Jeff D. Masters

Some companies that sell by mail carry several
different items that are alike. Confusion about the
item you want will result if you do not clearly state
which item you are ordering. Ask yourself the following questions when you write an order letter:

1. Do I have the right name of each item and its
   catalog number?
2. Are the prices and totals correct?

3. If I must prepay, have I included the correct amount in a check or money order?
4. If the postage is required, have I included it?
5. Is my correct return address included?
6. If a choice of shipping is requested, have I stated how I want material sent?

EXERCISE 2   Write a business letter ordering the following items:

2 tubes of Deeptan Suntan Cream, 6 oz. size, at $2.25 each.

1 jar of Deeptan Skin Moisturizer, 10 oz. size, at $3.75.

1 Catchray visor cap, medium size, at $4.50.

The company is Sunray Products, 5300 N.W. 167th St., Hialeah, Florida 33014. You enclose a money order or a check for the total amount of $12.75.

The Letter of Adjustment or Complaint

When something has gone wrong and you want it corrected, you write a letter of adjustment or complaint. The adjustment letter is intended to adjust an error. The error might be in the materials you have ordered or the amount of money you are charged by a company.

The letter of complaint is used to call attention to something you believe is wrong. Such a letter must be written with great care, for complaints do not usually make people happy. Such a letter has a better chance of making its point if it is written in a considerate way.

Here is an example of an adjustment letter:

128 River Road
Forestville, PA 15301
September 3, 1979

Order Department
Terwilliger's
P.O. Box 7888
San Francisco, CA 94120

Dear Manager:
On August 10 of this year, I ordered two hooked rug kits. I have so far received only one kit.

The kit I ordered but have not received is as follows: 1 "Inca" by Bernat, size 21" x 22", catalog #54g @ $16.80.

Please send me this kit or refund my money.

Yours truly,

Jeff D. Masters

Jeff D. Masters

On the following page is an example of a letter of complaint calling attention to a concern of the writer.

14012 San Jacinto Rd.
Anytown, Texas 00102
October 12, 1980

President
The Power & Light Co.
Number One Downtown Mall
Anytown, Texas 00102

Dear Sir or Madam:
  As part of an energy conservation program
at Crockett High School, I have been survey-
ing the amount of electrical energy used in
homes in our neighborhood. I have found
that a family that has reduced its
consumption of electricity by more than
30 percent over the same month last year must
now pay 20 percent more per kilowatt hour.
  By contrast, the family that reduces its
consumption by less than 30 percent pays only
10 percent more than last year.
  You seem to be charging more per kilowatt
hour for the family using less electricity.
This seems unfair. I hope you will change
the rates to make them fair. Possibly you
can explain why the charges are different.
  Thank you for your cooperation.

                              Sincerely yours,

                              Melinda Waters
                              Melinda Waters

EXERCISE 3   Write a letter of complaint or a letter of adjustment regarding some matter that you
believe an organization should correct. Some examples are as follows:

1. You ordered a subscription to a monthly magazine (choose one you like to read). Three issues

have been published since you sent in your order. However, you have received no magazines from the publisher.

2. You bought a transistor radio from a mail-order company. However, you have received only a set of headphones from the company.

3. A manufacturing company near you is dumping a strange-looking liquid into an open pit in the ground. You believe the company should cover the pit. You wonder if the liquid is harmful to living things.

4. The local authorities in your area have closed a nearby drag strip and refused to permit any other strip to open up. You believe the authorities should allow drag racing in your area.

MAILING THE LETTER

9c   **Use standard form in addressing an envelope.**

The following form is standard for addressing a business envelope:

```
Francine Wixom
15 Red Keg Highway
Edenville, MI 48620


                    The Manager
                    Broken Arrow Dude Ranch
                    Quincy, CA 95971

```

EXERCISE 4   Prepare a piece of paper as though it were the front of an envelope. Write the correct form for an envelope for one of the model business letters on pages 210–216.

REVIEW EXERCISE A   Letters

The following is a true-or-false exercise. Number a sheet of paper 1–10. Next to each number, write T if the statement is true and F if it is false.

> EXAMPLE   You should always use blue ink and yellow paper when writing a personal letter.
>
> F

1. Standard form in letters is expected in the business world.
2. You do not need to sign a business letter.
3. One type of business letter is the sympathy card.
4. Always include your return address on a letter.
5. Three of the most common types of business letters are the request letter, the order letter, and the letter of adjustment or complaint.
6. Rules of punctuation and spelling for letter writing differ from rules for other kinds of compositions.
7. Never read over a letter before you send it— you might change your mind about mailing it.
8. Include the right name of each item, the catalog number, and the price with an order letter.

9. The company from which you order always pays the postage or shipping.
10. Letters of complaint are a waste of time.

REVIEW EXERCISE B Personal Letters

On a sheet of paper, write someone you know a personal letter. Be sure that you follow the five guides for letter writing.

REVIEW EXERCISE C Business Letters

Write a business letter. Make sure it follows the standard form and is written correctly. If you have no reason to write a business letter of your own, choose one of the following reasons.

1. Water is scarce in your area. You notice that a water faucet in the rest room of the library runs constantly and cannot be shut off. You feel that it should be fixed, since water is being wasted.
2. You wish to order: 1 coonskin cap, size 7, catalog #73A in Daniel Boone Brown at $5.99; 2 pairs of Frontier Sox, size medium, in Rooster Red at $2.50 a pair; and 2 pounds of Trail Food, catalog #121f, at $1.95 per pound. Shipping and handling will be $2.75 extra. You enclose a check for the full amount. The company is Western Wonders, 222 Rope-A-Steer Road, Philadelphia, PA 19117.
3. You would like some brochures about bus tours to New England from Galaxy Travel, 133 West Oak St., Dallas, TX 75218.

4. Three months ago you sent $7.99 to Television Station RTVU, Channel 123, 77 Main St., Peoria, IL 61611. You ordered an album they had advertised called "Great Hits from the Seventies." So far you have received nothing but a catalog of record titles.

5. You would like to find out what a certain congressional representative's stand has been on strip-mining. You write to her at the New Senate Office Building, Washington, D.C.

6. You want to order two dwarf fruit trees at $4.50 each from Happy Dell Nursery, RFD #7, Ringling, OK 73456. The ones you want are a flowering peach called Mighty Wonder and a flowering plum called Big Blue. Enclose a check for the correct amount. Shipping by private parcel service will cost $3.25; by airmail special delivery, the cost will be $4.80.

UNIT THREE

USAGE

Using Parts of Speech
Common Confusions

10

USING PARTS OF SPEECH

Speaking and writing are useful only for those people who follow the same basic rules. The rules make language the same for everyone. In a sense, language is like a game. Everyone who plays the game must follow the rules.

Language can be carried on at different levels. *Usage* in language means the level of strictness of rules. Usage can be formal or informal. When you are in an informal situation, as when writing a friendly letter, you can use informal language. When you are in a formal situation, as when writing to apply for a job, it is good to know how to use formal language.

This chapter presents the main features of formal usage. These features are compared with those of informal usage. From this comparison you can learn important differences in usage. You can also learn more about choices in language usage.

AGREEMENT OF SUBJECTS AND VERBS

10a A verb must agree with its subject in number.

See Verb, p. 410; Subject, p. 408

Most verbs in the present tense add **s** or **es** in the third person singular.

EXAMPLES   Mary walk**s**.
She move**s** fast.

Solly ride**s**.
He cruise**s** slowly.

The owl hoot**s**.
It screech**es** loudly.

When one person or thing is being talked about, it is the third person singular. *Mary, Solly,* and *the owl* are noun examples. *He, she,* and *it* are pronoun examples.

In the first and second persons singular and all the persons plural of the present tense, **s** or **es** is not used. Instead, the *infinitive* form of the verb is used. The ending of the verb indicates that it agrees with the number of the subject.

Hint: If the plural noun ends in **s**, the verb usually does not end in **s**.

The following list shows how the ending of a plural verb changes in the present tense.

	SINGULAR	PLURAL
FIRST PERSON	I hope	we hope
SECOND PERSON	you hope	you hope
THIRD PERSON	she ⎫	
	he ⎬ hopes	they hope
	it ⎭	

EXERCISE 1 Number a sheet of paper 1–10. Choose the correct verb for each sentence. Write the correct verb on the paper next to the number of each sentence.

> EXAMPLE   A job (become/becomes) more
> important every year.
>
> *becomes*

1. A college graduate (get/gets) some jobs easily.
2. Companies (look/looks) for qualified people.
3. The best person (get/gets) the most work.
4. Women sometimes (begin/begins) new jobs after raising a family.
5. A job in a factory often (pay/pays) well.
6. New workers (need/needs) training.
7. Business schools (help/helps) some people.
8. Bosses usually (try/tries) to be fair.
9. A union (tell/tells) the company what the workers think.
10. A big paycheck (make/makes) most people feel good.

See Subject, p. 408
10b A linking verb agrees with its subject.

See Completer, p. 390
A linking verb joins together its subject and a subject completer that refers back to the subject. Be

careful to make the verb agree with the subject, not the completer.

EXAMPLES

INCORRECT AGREEMENT Fall *are* colorful leaves and the smell of winter.

CORRECT AGREEMENT Fall *is* colorful leaves and the smell of winter.

INCORRECT AGREEMENT The scariest times *is* in your childhood.

CORRECT AGREEMENT The scariest times *are* in your childhood.

INCORRECT AGREEMENT There *is* the notes we took.

CORRECT AGREEMENT There *are* the notes we took.

Hint: In sentences beginning with *There is/There are* or *Here is/Here are,* the subject follows the linking verb. Make the verb agree with the following subject.

EXERCISE 2 Number a sheet of paper 1–10. Next to each number, write the correct verb form from the parentheses.

EXAMPLE They (is/are) here now.

are

1. Tidepools (is/are) like little fish tanks.
2. The pools always (seem/seems) to be filled with strange things.

3. Sometimes there (is/are) beautiful animal flowers in them.
4. A sea anemone (seem/seems) to be a delicate flower.
5. But an anemone (is/are) an animal that lives in salt water.
6. There (is/are) stingers on anemones.
7. These beautiful animals (is/are) related to jelly fish and coral.
8. They (is/are) able to live by eating other sea animals.
9. There (is/are) many fascinating creatures in tidepools.
10. In a tidepool (is/are) strange and wonderful things.

10c The verb *be* has special forms to agree with its subjects.

The forms of the verb *be* do not follow a regular pattern. Care needs to be taken to match the forms with the subjects. *Be* has three forms in the present tense and two forms in the past.

	PRESENT TENSE		PAST TENSE	
	Singular	Plural	Singular	Plural
First Person	I am	we are	I was	we were
Second Person	you are	you are	you were	you were
Third Person	he is she is it is	they are	he was she was it was	they were

The forms of the verb *be* are used a great deal. Practice using the correct form to maintain agreement between subject and verb.

EXERCISE 3 Number a sheet of paper 1–8. Next to each number, write the subject and the correct form of the verb from the parentheses. Make sure the subject and the verb agree.

EXAMPLE The giraffe (am/is) one of Africa's unusual creatures.

The giraffe is

1. Galloping giraffes (is/are) an amazing sight.
2. These odd animals (is/are) fast runners.
3. Their heads (is/are) steady while their legs gallop.
4. People used to think a giraffe (was/were) unreal, like a dragon or a unicorn.
5. Julius Caesar (was/were) the first person to bring a giraffe to Europe.
6. People thought it (was/were) a cross between a camel and a leopard.
7. European zoos in the nineteenth century (was/ were) the first to keep giraffes in captivity.
8. Today giraffes (is/are) seen all over the world.

**10d A compound subject joined by *and*
    usually takes a plural verb.**

EXAMPLES The governor and the mayor *are* friends.

Estelle and Jimmy *go* together.

The Whammy, the Shore Boys, and
the Delites *play* songs I like.

Two things that are thought of as one can take
a singular verb.

EXAMPLE   Ham and cheese *is* a tasty filler for a
sandwich.

EXERCISE 4   Some of the following sentences
have compound subjects. Some have simple subjects. Number a sheet of paper 1–10. After each
number write the correct choice of the verb in parentheses.

EXAMPLE   News and entertainment
(come/comes) to us on airwaves.

come

1. Radio and television (need/needs) new broadcasters today.
2. Both men and women (have/has) good oppor-
   tunities.
3. A wise beginner (look/looks) for a job in a small
   local station.
4. Few people (break/breaks) into the business at
   a big station.
5. College journalism and broadcasting courses
   (help/helps) a radio or TV career get started.
6. Newspaper work and magazine writing
   (doesn't/don't) hurt, either.
7. News stations and music stations (fill/fills)
   most of the radio bands.
8. A TV channel (show/shows) many different
   kinds of programs.

9. Children and adults (watch/watches) more TV than ever before.
10. Commercials and violence (hurt/hurts) the quality of some programs.

10e **When a compound subject is joined by** *or, nor, either . . . or,* **or** *neither . . . nor,* **the verb agrees in number with the nearer subject.**

EXAMPLES   The school or a local service club *sponsors* the Youth League each year.
[Two groups are in the compound subject. The subject nearer to the verb is singular. The verb is the third person singular form.]

Neither Missy nor her classmates *like* the food.
[The subject nearer the verb is plural. Therefore, the verb shows the third person plural form.]

EXERCISE 5 Look at each pair of verbs in parentheses. Choose the one which agrees with the subject of the sentence. Number a sheet of paper 1–10 and write the correct verb by each number.

EXAMPLE   Either a car or a motorcycle (provide/provides) transportation for young people.

provides

1. Either a Road Hog or a Champion (is/are) a popular motorcycle.
2. Either a track or open roads (make/makes) a good place to ride.
3. Clubs or schools (have/has) special jacket emblems.
4. The smell or noise of motorcycle exhaust (bother/bothers) some people.
5. Neither a helmet nor a jacket (give/gives) complete protection.
6. Either speed or inexperience (put/puts) a rider in danger.
7. Neither parents nor the average citizen quite (trust/trusts) motorcycles.
8. Gas savings or small size (speak/speaks) in favor of motorcycles, though.
9. Either an auto clinic or repair shops (check/checks) motorcycles.
10. A boy or a girl (enjoy/enjoys) riding a motorcycle.

10f When a group of words comes between the subject and the verb, the verb still agrees with the subject.

Whenever extra words come between the subject and its verb in a sentence, make the verb agree with its subject. Do not make the verb agree with any of the extra words.

EXAMPLES

INCORRECT AGREEMENT	The tools in the green box *is* mine.

CORRECT AGREEMENT   The tools in the green box *are* mine.

INCORRECT AGREEMENT   Either Mrs. Drayfoot or the girl with the yellow hair ribbons *are* to be at the head of the line.

CORRECT AGREEMENT   Either Mrs. Drayfoot or the girl with the yellow hair ribbons *is* to be at the head of the line.

Be sure you can identify the subject in a sentence in order to make the verb agreement with it in number.

EXERCISE 6 In the following sentences, choose the correct form of the verb in parentheses. Number a sheet of paper 1–10. Next to each number, write the correct form.

EXAMPLE   Mountain climbers who challenge a heavy storm (need/needs) to be prepared.

need

1. It has been reported that three teenaged boys, missing for sixteen days, (is/are) safe on Mount Hood.
2. A blizzard with all its dangers (has/have) slowed rescue efforts.
3. The first morning after the weather has cleared (bring/brings) good news.
4. The operator of a snow tractor (is/are) the first to find the boys.

5. Caves of snow (shelters/shelter) the boys.
6. The mother of one of the boys (say/says) she is crying for joy.
7. One of the boys (has/have) a frostbitten foot.
8. Food for eight days (need/needs) to be stretched thinly to last for sixteen.
9. The boys say that a calm attitude in a bad situation (help/helps) people to survive.
10. The boys, still talking of their love for the mountain, (plan/plans) another climb soon.

10g Certain nouns and phrases that name a quantity may appear to be plural, but they take a singular verb.

EXAMPLES The *news comes* at 7 o'clock in the morning.

A *dollar and twenty-nine cents sounds* like a high price for that little mouse.

10h Collective nouns are singular in form but may be singular or plural in meaning.

Examples of collective nouns:

class, club, crowd, family, flock, legislature, group, herd, mass, public, school, swarm, team

Examples of agreement of a collective noun and a verb:

The *crowd was moved* by the play.
[This means the audience reacted as one person.]

The crowd were struggling among themselves
to seize the balloons.
[Different people in the crowd were
struggling.]

EXERCISE 7 Number a sheet of paper 1–8. After
each number, write the correct form of the verb in
parentheses.

EXAMPLE   The public (hear/hears) a lot about
killer bees these days.

hears

1. The news (bring/brings) stories of killer bees
every few months.
2. A swarm of the bees (terrorize/terrorizes) a little
town in South America.
3. A crowd (flee/flees) from the angry stingers.
4. A herd of cattle (is/are) panicked when the bees
attack.
5. A mass of bee stings (cover/covers) an unlucky
victim.
6. A team of scientists (search/searches) for a way
to tame the bees.
7. An insecticide company (want/wants) to kill the
killers.
8. Our family (hope/hopes) we never meet any killer bees.

**10i Indefinite pronouns that are singular in
meaning take the singular form of the
verb.**

EXAMPLES   *Everyone holds* some responsibility as a citizen.

Neither of the baskets *is* filled to the top.

Everybody likes to eat some sweet foods.

Occasionally, extra words will come between the indefinite pronoun and the verb. Do not let any extra words change the agreement of the verb with the indefinite pronoun subject.

EXAMPLE

CORRECT AGREEMENT   *Everyone* out for sports *is* expected to have a signed release.

Somebody who likes to leave crumbs *has* been eating at this table.

EXERCISE 8   Number a sheet of paper 1–6. After each number, write the correct form of the verb in parentheses.

EXAMPLE   Each of us (has/have) to do a project for sewing class.

has

1. Everybody (choose/chooses) something different.
2. No one (think/thinks) of a patchwork quilt, so I decide to try that.
3. Either of the two patterns I pick (look/looks) beautiful on paper.

4. But when I sew them, neither (come/comes) out right.
5. Nobody (see/sees) a pattern in my quilt at all.
6. "I think people call that a crazy quilt," somebody (say/says).

10j The indefinite pronouns *all, any, most, none,* and *some* take either a singular or plural verb depending on the reference.

EXAMPLES   *All* the coins *were* on the counter.
[The coins are plural.]

All the money *is* in the bag.
[The money is singular.]

None of the flock *was* disturbed.
[Not a single bird was disturbed.]

EXERCISE 9 Number a sheet of paper 1–6. After each number, write the correct form of the verb in parentheses.

EXAMPLE   All the cowboys (is/are) ready for the big trail drive.

are

1. Some of them (has/have) never been on a long trail drive before.
2. None of the cattle (want/wants) to go on the long march.
3. Still, most of the herd (cooperate/cooperates) with the cowboys.

4. Many of the cowboys (get/gets) tired on the long drive.
5. All of the cowboys' work (is/are) well rewarded.
6. Most of their pay (is/are) spent in a hurry at the end of the drive.

SPECIAL VERB PROBLEMS

Active and Passive Verbs

10k An active verb tells of action done *by* the subject of a sentence. A passive verb tells of action done *to* the subject.

Examples of active verbs:

Agatha Hogg *painted* an ugly picture.
[Ms. Hogg did the painting.]
She *slashed* her canvas in disgust.
[She did the slashing.]

Examples of passive verbs:

An ugly picture *was painted* by Agatha Hogg.
[The picture had the action done to it.]
The canvas *was slashed* by her in disgust.
[The canvas had the action done to it.]

Hint: The passive form of the main verb takes a helping verb.

EXAMPLES *were* seen
                   was angered

EXERCISE 10 Five of the following sentences have active verbs. The others have passive verbs. Number a sheet of paper 1–10. After each number write the complete verb. Next to the verb, write the word *active* or *passive* to tell which it is.

> EXAMPLE On October 1, 1847, a new comet was spotted in the sky.
>
> *was spotted, passive*

1. Maria Mitchell saw it through her telescope.
2. This new comet was found first by this young woman.
3. A medal was given to Ms. Mitchell for her discovery.
4. Soon people all over the world knew about this young astronomer.
5. Maria Mitchell devoted most of her life to astronomy.
6. Through her telescope, she studied the stars, planets, and comets.
7. Many new stars were discovered by her.
8. Accurate maps of the nighttime sky were drawn by her.
9. As a teacher, Maria Mitchell taught many students about the stars.
10. She is remembered by scientists as a hard worker.

Irregular Verbs

Unlike regular verbs, irregular verbs do not add **d** or **ed** to the infinitive to show simple past tense. Instead, irregular verbs change form to show their past tense in special ways.

10I Irregular verbs form their past tense in special ways, without adding *d* or *ed*.

EXAMPLES	PRESENT TENSE	SIMPLE PAST
	eat	ate
	grow	grew
	lose	lost

Hint: You can practice using the present and simple past forms of irregular verbs by using standard sentence beginnings:

PRESENT Now you (give) . . .

SIMPLE PAST   Yesterday you (gave) . . .

In addition to the simple past, most irregular verbs change form to show action completed in the past. This form is called the *present perfect*. It is used with a present tense form of the auxiliary verb *have* and the past participle form of the main verb.

EXAMPLE

PRESENT Now he *swims* twenty laps of the pool.

SIMPLE PAST Last week he *swam* ten laps.

PRESENT PERFECT He *has swum* the length of the pool many times.

The present perfect form of the verb helps tell of action completed in the past. The following list of irregular verb forms includes the present perfect.

COMMON IRREGULAR VERBS

Infinitive	Simple Past	Present Perfect
bear	bore	has borne
begin	began	has begun
bind	bound	has bound
blow	blew	has blown
break	broke	has broken
bring	brought	has brought
buy	bought	has bought
catch	caught	has caught
choose	chose	has chosen
come	came	has come
dive	dived, dove	has dived
do	did	has done
draw	drew	has drawn
drink	drank	has drunk
drive	drove	has driven
eat	ate	has eaten
fall	fell	has fallen
fight	fought	has fought
flee	fled	has fled
fly	flew	has flown
freeze	froze	has frozen
give	gave	has given
go	went	has gone
grow	grew	has grown
hang	hung	has hung
keep	kept	has kept
know	knew	has known
lay	laid	has laid
lead	led	has led
lie	lay	has lain
lose	lost	has lost
make	made	has made

mean	meant	has meant
ride	rode	has ridden
ring	rang	has rung
rise	rose	has risen
run	ran	has run
see	saw	has seen
seek	sought	has sought
send	sent	has sent
shake	shook	has shaken
shine	shone, shined	has shone, has shined
sing	sang	has sung
sleep	slept	has slept
speak	spoke	has spoken
spin	spun	has spun
spread	spread	has spread
steal	stole	has stolen
swear	swore	has sworn
swim	swam	has swum
swing	swung	has swung
take	took	has taken
teach	taught	has taught
tear	tore	has torn
throw	threw	has thrown
wear	wore	has worn
write	wrote	has written

EXERCISE 11 Number a sheet of paper 1–10. Next to each number write the correct form of the verb.

EXAMPLE The rights of minority groups have (lead/led) courageous people to struggle.

led

1. Vilma Martinez has (knew/known) for a long time that she wanted to make life better for other Spanish-speaking Americans.
2. As a lawyer, she has (took/taken) many civil rights cases involving Mexican Americans.
3. After she finished law school, she (threw/thrown) herself into her work.
4. She (saw/seen) that there were many injustices in the way Mexican Americans were treated.
5. She (fight/fought) old, mistaken ideas about Mexican Americans.
6. She has (wrote/written) about the problems Mexican Americans face.
7. She (break/broke) the image of the quiet Latino woman who stays home and doesn't answer back.
8. Martinez has (chose/chosen) to go on working, raising a child at the same time.
9. She says that work to correct Mexican Americans' problems has barely (began/begun).
10. Few people have worked as hard for Mexican American rights as Vilma Martinez has (did/done).

SPECIAL PRONOUN PROBLEMS

Personal Pronouns

See Pronouns, pp. 12–13

Some of the personal pronouns change form depending on the way they are used in sentences. The pronoun *she,* for example, serves as the subject of a sentence. If it is the object of a verb or a preposition, it takes the form *her.*

EXAMPLES

SUBJECT   *She* carried water in a pail.

OBJECT   Vinnie saw *her.*

OBJECT   He took *it* from *her.*

10m   A personal pronoun is in the subjective case when used as a subject and in the objective case when used as the object.

EXAMPLES

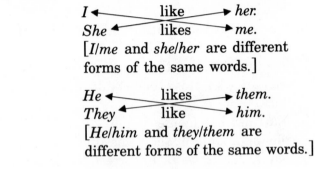

SUBJECT   OBJECT

I   like   *her.*
She   likes   *me.*
[*I/me* and *she/her* are different forms of the same words.]

He   likes   *them.*
They   like   *him.*
[*He/him* and *they/them* are different forms of the same words.]

It   likes   *you.*
You   like   *it.*
[Notice that *it* and *you* are two personal pronouns that keep the same form no matter what sentence position they are in.]

The objective case form of the pronoun is the same whether it is the object of a sentence or the object of a preposition.

EXAMPLES   Give *me* the cash.

Come with *me.*

Sell *her* the car.

Leave the money for *her.*

Take *them* to the bank.

We can go nearer to *them.*

pro
10m

Here is a list of the subjective and objective case forms of the personal pronouns:

PERSONAL PRONOUNS

	Subjective Case		Objective Case	
	Singular	Plural	Singular	Plural
First Person	I	we	me	us
Second Person	you	you	you	you
Third Person	he, she, it	they	him, her, it	them

When two subjects or objects appear in one sentence and one or both are pronouns, be sure the pronouns are in the correct form.

EXAMPLES

INCORRECT Dell brought lunches for Artero and *I*.

CORRECT Dell brought lunches for Artero and *me*.

INCORRECT Artero and *me* ate all but the salad.

CORRECT Artero and *I* ate all but the salad.

EXERCISE 12 Number a sheet of paper 1–12. Next to each number, write the correct form or forms of the pronouns in parentheses.

EXAMPLE **Jodie and (I/me) saw (they/them).**

I, them

1. Riding a subway was a new experience for (I/ me).
2. Sheila and (I/me) rode one yesterday.

3. The woman in the change booth told (we/us) to give (she/her) a dollar.
4. (We/Us) girls gave the money to (she/her).
5. (She/Her) gave Sheila and (I/me) two tokens.
6. The tokens looked like quarters with holes in (they/them).
7. She and (I/me) put (they/them) in slots at the gate.
8. A crowd of other people joined Sheila and (I/me) waiting for the train.
9. (We/Us) were pushed onto the crowded train when it came.
10. Sheila and (I/me) were worried (we/us) would lose each other.
11. It was impossible for (she/her) or (I/me) to move in the packed train.
12. At least (we/us) need not have worried about getting separated.

10n A pronoun must agree in number and sex with the noun or pronoun to which it refers.

A pronoun must be singular if the noun or pronoun to which it refers, the *antecedent,* is singular.

EXAMPLES   Any *man* who goes through that door risks *his* life.
[*Man* is a singular noun. It is the antecedent of *his.* Therefore, *his,* which refers to *man,* is singular also.]

Men who step through that door
risk *their* lives.
[*Men* is plural. Therefore, *their* is
plural also.]

In informal speech, Rule 10n is often relaxed.

Example of informal speech:

"*Someone* was foolish enough to try *their* luck
in that game," the gambler said.

In formal English, the pronouns listed below
are used as antecedents. Other pronouns that refer
to them should be in the singular.

anybody	nobody
anyone	no one
each	one
everybody	somebody
everyone	someone

EXAMPLES   When *anyone* tries to call in, *he* or
she hears a buzzing sound.

Each must have *his* permit with
him.
or
Each must have *her* permit with
her.

Reflexive Pronouns

A reflexive pronoun is a form of a personal
pronoun combined with the word *self* or *selves*. See Pronouns, p. 17

EXAMPLES   *your*self, *them* selves

SINGULAR	PLURAL
myself	ourselves
yourself	yourselves
herself ⎤	
himself ⎬	themselves
itself ⎦	

Do not use the form *hisself.* This was used several hundred years ago, but it is not considered acceptable today.

CORRECT   She hurt herself with the knife.

Relative Pronouns *Who* and *Whom*

See Pronouns, p. 15   These two forms are sometimes confused. Use *who* as you would use *he* or *she.* Use *whom* as you would use *him* or *her. Who* is in the subjective case. *Whom* is in the objective case.

EXAMPLES   *Who* brought the cider?
[*Who* is the subject of the sentence.]

Ned gave it to *whom?*
[*Whom* is the object of the preposition *to.*]

The words *whoever* and *whomever* are used in the same way as *who* and *whom.*

EXAMPLES   *Whoever* would believe such a story?
Tell it to *whomever* you think will listen.

EXERCISE 13   Write the following sentences on a sheet of paper. Fill in the blanks with the form *he/she, him/her, who, whom, whoever,* or *whomever.*

EXAMPLE   _____ saves money will have money on a rainy day.

Whoever saves money will have money on a rainy day.

1. A sound proverb means more to _____ who needs it.
2. _____ wants to succeed in the world should plan for failure.
3. _____ who fears to suffer, suffers from fear.
4. _____ follows his or her own advice must take the results.
5. Rich food is poor to _____ has overeaten.

PROBLEMS WITH ADJECTIVES AND ADVERBS

10o Use an adjective after a linking verb to refer back to the subject.

See Adjective, p. 387; Linking Verb, p. 401; Subject, p. 408

Do not confuse an adjective with an adverb. Only an adjective describes a noun or a pronoun. An adverb modifies a verb.

EXAMPLES   He seemed *happy*.
[*Happy* is an adjective that modifies *he*.]

Reginald Hamstringer folded the paper *carefully*.
[*Carefully* is an adverb that tells how he folded the paper.]

His plans had worked *well*.
[*Well* is an adverb that modifies the
verb *had worked*.]

Hint: Be especially careful not to confuse
the adjective *good* with the word *well*.
Well can be used either as an adjective or
as an adverb. *Good* can only be an adjective.

INCORRECT She sings *good*.
CORRECT She sings *well*.

EXERCISE 14   On a sheet of paper, rewrite any
sentence in which an adjective or adverb is incorrectly used.

EXAMPLE   Karl Klutzenheimer does not seem
to be a real good ping-pong player.

> *Karl Klutzenheimer does
> not seem to be a really
> good ping-pong player.*

1. He gives a good imitation of someone who has
   never played ping-pong before in his life.
2. Karl is a "nut" at the ping-pong table.
3. Karl can be counted on to make a bad serve.
4. The other players grin happy whenever Karl
   makes one of his real bad mistakes.
5. When Karl plays good it seems like an accident.
6. It seems strange that Karl wins almost every
   ping-pong game he plays.

The Double Negative

10p Avoid using a double negative.

Negatives are *no, not, never, none, nothing, no one,* and *hardly.* When one of these is used in a sentence, another should not be used.

EXAMPLES
INCORRECT They hardly need no help from us.
CORRECT They hardly need help from us.
CORRECT They need no help from us.

INCORRECT No one does nothing right.
CORRECT No one does anything right.

EXERCISE 15 On a sheet of paper, rewrite any sentence in which negative terms are incorrectly used.

EXAMPLE Suzie doesn't buy no records except ones by the Grateful Grape.

Suzie doesn't buy any records except ones by the Grateful Grape.

1. This group needs no introduction to its loyal fans.
2. The Grateful Grape doesn't hardly have to advertise its concerts.
3. No tickets never remain unsold.
4. No one understands any of the words to the Grateful Grape's songs.

5. But none of the group's fans can hear no words anyhow.
6. The Grateful Grape will never have to worry about its future as long as it plays loudly.

REVIEW EXERCISE A Usage of Verbs

Number a sheet of paper 1–10. Next to each number, write the correct form of the verb in parentheses.

> EXAMPLE Peanut butter and jelly _____ the most popular kind of sandwich in America. (is/are)
>
> *is*

1. Jars of peanut butter _____ the supermarket shelves. (line/lines)
2. Either crunchy or smooth peanut butter _____ available. (is/are)
3. Protein and other healthful substances _____ found in peanut butter. (is/are)
4. The information on the jar label _____ whether or not the peanut butter is pure. (tells/tell)
5. The best type of peanut butter _____ closest to being 100 percent peanuts. (comes/come)
6. In this type, peanuts and salt _____ the only ingredients. (is/are)
7. Natural oils in the jar _____ to the top. (rises/rise)
8. Either turning the jar upside down or stirring _____ all you need to do. (is/are)

9. Sugar and other ingredients sometimes _____ on jar labels. (appears/appear)
10. It is best if you _____ the label before you buy. (reads/read)

REVIEW EXERCISE B   Irregular Verbs

The verbs in the following parentheses are irregular. Number a sheet of paper 1–10. Next to each number, write the correct form of the verb in parentheses.

> EXAMPLE   The morning was so cold that the paper had _____ to the doorstep. (freeze)
>
> *frozen*

1. LaVonne _____ it would be hard to get the car started. (know)
2. "I have _____ it before and I'll do it again!" she thought. (do)
3. First she _____ a shovel and shoveled cold ashes from the fireplace into a paper bag. (take)
4. Then she _____ them on the sidewalk. (spread)
5. The sun _____ on the snow and glittered while she worked. (shine)
6. When she got to her car, she was glad she had _____ heavy gloves. (wear)
7. She _____ open the trunk of the car. (swing)
8. She found the tire chains she _____. (seek)

9. Picking up the jack, she _____ to work its handle. (begin)
10. Before long, she had gotten the chains on and had _____ away. (drive)

REVIEW EXERCISE C   Collective Nouns

Each of the following sentences has a collective noun in it. Decide whether the noun takes a singular verb or a plural verb. Number a sheet of paper 1–10. Next to each number write the correct form of the verb.

> EXAMPLE   It is 1870, and a group of cowboys _____ 3,000 cattle on a cattle drive. (leads/lead)
>
> *leads*

1. Each one of the herd _____ "road branded" before the long walk. (is/are)
2. The herd _____ to move. (begins/begin)
3. The herd _____ among themselves for the lead. (struggles/struggle)
4. The huge crowd of steers _____ from ten to fifteen miles a day. (travels/travel)
5. A band of antelope _____. (passes/pass)
6. A flock of buzzards _____ in the sky, watching for a dying cow. (wheels/wheel)
7. A team of night herders _____ around the cattle at night. (rides/ride)
8. The team _____ to each other once in a while during the long night. (calls/call)

9. When a mass of animals _____ this big, there is always danger of a stampede. (is/are)
10. If the herd of cattle _____ water, the weak ones may be trampled to death. (sees/see)

REVIEW EXERCISE D   Usage of Pronouns

Look at each of the following numbered sentences. Each sentence contains one or more pronouns. Number a sheet of paper 1–10. If the sentence is correctly written with the correct form of the pronoun, write *C* (for *correct*) next to the number. If the sentence is incorrectly written, rewrite it correctly.

> EXAMPLE   "Something is wrong," Reuben said to hisself.
>
> *"Something is wrong," Reuben said to himself.*

1. "Joan and me always lock the door when we go out, but there it is standing open."
2. "Whomever left it that way was up to no good."
3. He tiptoed through the open door and listened.
4. What he heard was a sound like a person humming to theirself.
5. "Who's there?" Reuben called.
6. "It is me," said a small voice.
7. "Whom are you?" asked Reuben, staring in astonishment at a strangely-dressed person about two feet tall.
8. "I have been living in your attic for quite a few years," answered the person.

9. "You still haven't said whom you are," said Reuben.
10. But the little man began singing to himself and didn't answer.

REVIEW EXERCISE E   Usage of Adjectives and Adverbs

Number a sheet of paper 1–5. Next to each number, write the correct word from the choices in parentheses.

> EXAMPLE   James A. Bland was (poor/poorly) when he died.
>
> *poor*

1. The Black singer did not get (no/any) credit for the songs he wrote.
2. One of his songs, "Carry Me Back to Old Virginny," became so (popular/popularly) it was declared the official Virginia state song.
3. Many of the songs that Bland wrote so (happy/happily) were pirated by others.
4. When he returned to America, there (was/wasn't) hardly any recognition for Bland.
5. He sang (good/well) but never was paid (good/well).

11

COMMON CONFUSIONS

Perhaps you have been confused about which term to use in speaking or writing English. This chapter lists in alphabetical order some terms that are often confused. It gives examples of their correct forms. In some cases, incorrect forms are given to show you what to avoid.

Several of the terms most often confused have practice sentences following them. Practicing the correct terms will help you avoid confusion in the future.

ALPHABETICAL LISTING

Accept/except: *Accept* is a verb that means "to receive or acknowledge."

EXAMPLES   We will *accept* the prize.
Try to *accept* defeat like a good sport.

Except is usually a preposition that means "leaving out."

EXAMPLES   Everyone *except* Juanita caught a cold.
I like most sports *except* basketball.

EXERCISE 1   Write the following sentences on a sheet of paper. Fill each blank with either *accept* or *except*.

1. We were glad to _____ the invitation to the president's ball.
2. Everyone was at the ball _____ the president.
3. He can go out any night _____ Saturday.
4. On that night he has to _____ a visit from all of his relatives.

Advice/advise: *Advice* is a noun meaning "an opinion or suggestion."

EXAMPLES   The *advice* came too late to do any good.
What is your *advice?*

Advise is a verb that means "to give an opinion."

EXAMPLES   Can you *advise* me in this matter?
A lawyer *advises* a client.

EXERCISE 2   Write the following sentences on a sheet of paper. Fill each blank with a form of either *advice* or *advise*.

1. I'd _____ you not to put your hand in the Glubalum's mouth.
2. You'd have more fingers now if you'd taken my _____ .
3. That sort of _____ we can do without.
4. Why didn't you _____ us to stay home?

Affect/effect: *Affect* is a verb meaning "to influence."

> EXAMPLES Did the weather *affect* you?
> Try not to let the heat *affect* you.

Effect is a noun that means "the result." It is sometimes used as a verb meaning "to bring about."

> EXAMPLES What *effect* will this have on our district?
> Can you *effect* any change in our system?

EXERCISE 3 Write the following sentences on a sheet of paper. Choose the correct form of the word in parentheses.

1. Don't let those strange things on your plate (affect/effect) your appetite.
2. What (affect/effect) are they supposed to have?
3. Can we (affect/effect) an improvement in the dinner menu?

All right: *All right* should always be written as two words. English has no such written word as *alright*. When you say, "All right," the two words often sound like one word. However, they are really two words.

Almost/most: *Almost* means "nearly" or "all but."

> EXAMPLES   We are *almost* ready.
> *Almost* all the food was eaten.

Most can mean "more than anything else."

> EXAMPLE   Toshima likes the *most* expensive clothing.

Most can also mean "the greatest amount."

> EXAMPLE   *Most* of the time we work.

Most may sometimes mean "almost all."

> EXAMPLE   Beth eats *most* foods.

Do not use *most* as a short form of *almost*.

> WRITE   The food is *almost* gone.
> not
> The food is *most* gone.
> WRITE   The cashier had counted *almost* all the money.
> not
> The cashier had counted *most* all the money.

EXERCISE 4   Write the following sentences on a sheet of paper. Correct errors in the use of *almost* or *most*. Put in *almost* where it belongs. Some sentences do not need correcting.

1. When Dan was three hours late, his mother most fainted.
2. Most of the time, Dan was a prompt son.
3. Most all of the others had come home late, too.
4. Dan didn't get home until most midnight.

Already/all ready: *Already* means "before now."

> EXAMPLES She has finished the book *already*.
> We *already* know the schedule.

All ready are two words meaning "completely ready."

> EXAMPLES The team was *all ready* to play.
> Each row in the field was *all ready* for the seeds.

Be sure to write the two words *all* and *ready* when you mean someone or something is fully ready.

> WRITE The canvas was *all ready* for painting.
> not
> The canvas was *already* for painting.

EXERCISE 5 Write the following sentences on a sheet of paper. Fill each blank with either *already* or *all ready*.

1. Fernando was _____ to call the fire department.
2. By then, the cat was _____ out of the pine tree.
3. He had _____ decided the tree was no place for a cat to be.
4. The cat was _____ to give up tree climbing for good.

Am not, are not, is not/ain't: *Ain't* is a contraction used in casual talk for *am not, are not,* and *is not*. *Ain't* has been used for a hundred years in English, but it still should be avoided in standard or formal usage.

Among/between: The meaning of these two words is very close. *Among* means "together with others" or "in the company of others." *Among* is used when you are talking about more than two things.

EXAMPLES   He is *among* his friends.
           They say there is no honor *among* thieves.

Between sometimes means "the space or time that separates two things."

EXAMPLES   The time *between* being seated and the raising of the curtain really seems to drag.
           You must stay *between* the two lines.

Between can also mean "something shared by *two* people or things."

EXAMPLES   *Between* us, Peggy and I have $25.00.
           Just *between* you and me, I don't believe it.

Use *among* when you are talking about three or more. Use *between* when you are talking about only two.

WRITE   There's not a loser *among* all of us.
        not
        There's not a loser *between* all of us.
WRITE   What's a dollar *among* four friends?
        not
        What's a dollar *between* four friends?

EXERCISE 6 Decide whether to fill each blank with *among* or *between*. Write each sentence on a sheet of paper.

1. One flower stood out _____ the others in the garden.
2. It was _____ a rose and a lily.
3. A jewel-like drop of honey lay _____ its many petals.
4. _____ you and me, it was the loveliest flower I have ever seen.

Beside/besides: *Beside* means "next to."

> EXAMPLES The rake is *beside* the shovel.
> The tanker steamed along *beside* the destroyer.

Besides as a preposition means *in addition to.*

> EXAMPLES *Besides* the rain, we had some hail.
> We expect punch *besides* the food.

Besides as an adverb means "as well."

> EXAMPLE You can lose weight. *Besides,* you will feel better.

EXERCISE 7 Write the following sentences on a sheet of paper. Put in *beside* or *besides* in each blank.

1. Willie didn't want to spend a day _____ the sea.
2. _____, he didn't bring his bathing suit.
3. He sat _____ the campfire and sniffled.
4. He had a stomach ache and a cold _____.

Burst/bust: *Burst* is the standard verb meaning "to break open." *Bust* is a slang verb and should not be used in formal speech or writing.

> WRITE The balloon *burst.*
> not
> The balloon *busted.*

Can/may: *Can* means "to be able."

> EXAMPLES Pellie *can* climb the highest trees
> in town.
> This bottle *can* hold enough water.

May means "to have permission."

> EXAMPLES Winona *may* stay out until
> 11:00 P.M.
> You *may* go with her.

Can hardly/can't hardly: Hardly means "barely."
Can hardly means "can barely."

> EXAMPLE She *can hardly* reach that shelf.
> [Reaching is hard.]

Do not use *can't hardly*.

> WRITE I *can hardly* hear you.
> not
> I *can't hardly* hear you.

Could have/could of: *Could of* makes no sense.
Some people write it by mistake. If you say *could
have* quickly, it sounds the same as saying the contraction *could've*. This sounds like *could of*, and so it
is sometimes written that way.

> WRITE I *could have* gone.
> not
> I *could of* gone.

Drowned/drownded: *Drown* is the verb meaning
"to die in the water." Its past tense adds **ed** only.
There is no such word as *drownded*.

> WRITE Liz dreamed she *drowned* in motor oil.
> not
> Liz dreamed she *drownded* in motor oil.

Good/well: *Good* is an adjective that means "better than usual."

>   EXAMPLE It was a *good* day for swimming.

Well as an adverb means "in a fine manner."

>   EXAMPLE She paints *well.*

>   WRITE She reads *well.*
>   not
>   She reads *good.*

EXERCISE 8 Write the following sentences on a sheet of paper. Fill the blanks with *good* or *well.*

1. It is a _____ thing that Murray can mend his own clothes.
2. He climbs fences _____, and he does it all the time.
3. His idea of a _____ fence to climb is a barbed wire fence.
4. His pants never look very _____ afterward.

Its/it's: *Its* and *it's* are *homonyms*—words that are pronounced the same. *Its* is one word, a possessive pronoun. It means that what follows is a part of it.

>   EXAMPLE The horse swished *its* tail.

It's is a contraction for *it is.*

>   EXAMPLE *It's* late in the day.

EXERCISE 9 Write the following sentences on a sheet of paper. Put *its* or *it's* in each blank.

1. _____ a glorious moonlit night.
2. Each ice-covered tree waves _____ glittering branches.

3. _____ a shame to stay inside.
4. Let's let the moon shower _____ light on our hair.

Lead/led: These two spellings can be homonyms. When they are homonyms, *l-e-a-d* is a word that names a metal.

> EXAMPLE　They mined the *lead.*

And *l-e-d,* which is pronounced the same way, describes an action that happened in the past.

> EXAMPLE　Long ago Harriet Tubman *led* the slaves to safety.

Remember that *l-e-d* always describes an action in the past. *L-e-a-d* is said like *l-e-d* only when it is the name of the metal.

EXERCISE 10　Write these sentences on a sheet of paper. Fill in the blanks with *led* or *lead.*

1. Some of the workers were sick with _____ poisoning.
2. Their friends _____ the fight against unsafe conditions in the factory.
3. Their concern for safety _____ all other worries.
4. They even wrote letters to the company that mined the _____ .

Learn/teach: *Learn* is a verb that means "to gain knowledge."

> EXAMPLE　I could *learn* about magic.

Teach is a verb that means "to give knowledge to someone."

EXAMPLE   Will that friendly magician *teach* me?

Leave/let: *Leave* means "to go away."

EXAMPLE   Juanita will *leave* home tomorrow.

Let means "to allow."

EXAMPLE   Please *let* her come with us.

Lend/loan: *Lend* and *loan* are verbs that mean the same thing. Either one is correct. *Loan* is also a noun meaning "the thing given for a while."

Lie/lay: *Lie* and *lay* are verbs that may become confused. *Lie* has two meanings. One is "to rest in a horizontal position." The other is "to tell an untruth."

EXAMPLES   She planned to *lie* down for a nap.

Aaron didn't want to *lie* to his aunt, but he knew the truth would hurt her.

Lay means "to put something down."

EXAMPLE   *Lay* the tools down.

People get confused about the two verbs because the past tense of *lie* is *lay*.

PRESENT TENSE   We *lie* around most of the morning because there is nothing to do.

PAST TENSE   Yesterday we *lay* around the house in the morning.

WRITE   A warm dog will *lie* in the shade.
not
A warm dog will *lay* in the shade.

Like/as: *Like* is a preposition that takes an object.

> EXAMPLES He flew *like* a bird.
> His arms flapped *like* wings.

As is a conjunction. It joins a dependent clause to an independent clause.

> EXAMPLES He stumbled *as* he stepped across
> the rug.
> Her arms caught him *as* he fell.

As may also be used as a preposition.

> EXAMPLE He came dressed *as* a ragpicker.

Like is sometimes used informally as a conjunction. Its use as a conjunction is not, however, recommended in formal speech or writing.

> WRITE She uses words *as* she should.
> not
> She used words *like* she should.

OK, O.K., Okay/all right: All of the three spellings of *okay* are common. Usually in writing it is better to use *all right* instead of *okay*.

Real/really: *Real* is an adjective.

> EXAMPLE This is a *real* diamond.

Really is an adverb.

> EXAMPLE He looked *really* tired.
> [The adverb *really* modifies the
> adjective *tired*.]

Do not use *real* as an adverb in formal speech or writing.

WRITE   He drove *really* fast.

not

He drove *real* fast.

Set/sit: *Set* as a verb means "to put something down." It also tells a bird's action on a nest of eggs. It does not tell of the action of a person on a chair.

EXAMPLES   The waiter *set* the table.

The hen *sets* on the nest nearly all the time.

Sit means "to be seated." People and animals sit.

EXAMPLE   The judge *sits* on the bench.

WRITE   Let's all *sit* down.

not

Let's all *set* down.

EXERCISE 11   Write the following sentences on a sheet of paper. Fill each blank with the correct form of *set* or *sit*.

1. Our dog likes to _____ his bone on Dad's chair.
2. Dad finds out about it when he _____ down.
3. Whenever our hen stops _____ on her nest, Rover puts a bone in there, too.
4. That dog will _____ his bones anywhere.

Shall/will: A tradition began about two hundred years ago in formal English that *shall* should be used in the first person to show simple future and in the second and third person to show serious intention. Tradition also says *will* should be used just the other way around. Most people do not follow the tradition today. Either *shall* or *will* is correct. *Shall* is less common and therefore more formal.

Should have/should of: *Should of* makes no sense. Some people write it by mistake. If you say *should have* quickly, it sounds the same as the contraction *should've*. This sounds like *should of,* and so it is sometimes written that way.

> WRITE   We *should have* stayed.
>   not
>   We *should of* stayed.

Their/there/they're: These three words sound alike in speech. They are homonyms. However, they are spelled differently and mean different things. *Their* is a possessive pronoun meaning "belonging to them."

> EXAMPLE   *Their* house is on the corner.

There points out a place. It also is used in the subject position in a clause.

> EXAMPLE   The cat sleeps *there.*
>   [place]
>
>   *There* are some mice in the barn.
>   [subject position]

They're is a contraction of the words *they* and *are.*

> EXAMPLE   *They're* all coming over tonight.

EXERCISE 12 Write the following sentences on a sheet of paper. Put in the correct form of *there, their,* or *they're.*

1. _____ go the big balloons!
2. _____ going to fly across the country.
3. _____ brightly-colored gas bags can be seen for miles.
4. _____ silent and beautiful as moons.

This/this here: Use only *this:* The added word *here* is not needed. The same is true for *that/that there.*

> WRITE   Do you see *this* mark?
>   not
>   Do you see *this here* mark?
> WRITE   It came from *that* knife.
>   not
>   It came from *that there* knife.

Those/them (there): *Them* and *them there* are not substitutes for *those.*

> WRITE   Give me *those* peanuts.
>   not
>   Give me *them* peanuts.
>   or
>   Give me *them there* peanuts.

To/too/two: These short words get confused in writing. They are homonyms.

To is a preposition.

> EXAMPLE   Give the artichokes *to* him.

Too is an adverb. It means "also" or "more than enough."

> EXAMPLES   She will eat lunch, *too.*
>   She may eat *too* much.

Two means "one plus one."

> EXAMPLE   The hen laid *two* eggs.

EXERCISE 13   Write the following sentences on a sheet of paper. Fill each blank with *to, too,* or *two.*

1. _____ years ago, we thought we would never grow our hair long.
2. Long hair looked messy, and our parents disliked it, _____.
3. But when we found out what haircuts cost, we decided we'd never go _____ the barber again.
4. We no longer want _____ change our hair styles.
5. We will let our hair grow _____ inches below our collars, but we will keep it neat.

Try to/try and: You should usually use *try to* in speech and writing.

> WRITE *Try to* open this jar.
> not
> *Try and* open this jar.

Note that it is correct to say or write, "People will *try and* try to do something too hard. Many people *try and* fail."

We/us: Some people make the mistake of saying "Us people" in a sentence such as, "We people know what's good for us." The pronoun *us* should not be used as part of the subject of a verb.

> WRITE *We* band members need to practice.
> not
> *Us* band members need to practice.

Who/whom: *Who* and *whom* are different forms of the same word. *Who* is in the subjective case. *Whom* is in the objective case.

> EXAMPLES *Who* seems happier?
> *Who* likes swimming?
> *Who* got the ticket?
> *Whom* did you see?

Whom should be used after a word like *to, from, by, of,* or *for.*

> WRITE to *whom*, for *whom*, from *whom*
> not
> to *who*, for *who*, from *who*

Whose/who's: These two words are homonyms. *Whose* is a form of *who* that shows ownership or possession.

> EXAMPLES *Whose* coat is that?
> Can you tell *whose* voice that is?

Who's is a form of *who* and *is*. The apostrophe (') takes the place of the *i* in *is*.

> EXAMPLES *Who's* afraid of Bigfoot?
> We know *who's* coming tomorrow.

Remember to use *who's* only when you mean *who is*.

EXERCISE 14 Rewrite each of the following sentences that has a *whose/who's* error in it.

1. Who's bright idea is that?
2. It belongs to the boy whose hiding under the sofa.
3. He's the one who's going to get the booby prize.
4. I don't know anyone who's ideas are brighter than his.

Your/you're: These two words are homonyms. *Your* is the possessive form of *you*. It shows ownership.

> EXAMPLES It's *your* day to do whatever you want.
> Let's go to *your* place.

You're means *you + are.*

> EXAMPLES   *You're* right.
> I think *you're* mean!
> Are you sure *you're* going?

EXERCISE 15 Rewrite each sentence that has a *your/you're* error in it.

1. You're poem about Peter Pumpkin Seed is sure to be the best.
2. Your going to get a lot of pumpkin seeds if you win first prize.
3. Have you decided what you're going to do with three thousand seeds?
4. You can decorate you're Christmas tree with them, I guess.

REVIEW EXERCISE A   The Right Word

In the following story, the underlined words are used incorrectly. On a sheet of paper, rewrite each sentence with an underlined word. Replace the word with the right one.

> EXAMPLE   When Carla received a strange
> invitation in the mail, she called her
> friend Maria for <u>advise</u>.
>
> *When Carla received a strange invitation in the mail, she called her friend Maria for advice.*

"This invitation has nothing on it accept a big black spot," Carla said. "Inside it says, come to this address."

"Don't except it," said Maria. "Just hearing about it has a funny affect on me. How does it effect you? I advice you not to go."

Carla most hung up when she heard this. "I see what you mean alright," she said. "But don't you even wonder about it? I'm already to go. Thank you for the advise, but I think I all ready knew I was going."

"Well just among the two of us," Maria said, "I don't hardly blame you. I hope, when you're between all those strange people, you don't get into trouble."

REVIEW EXERCISE B Correct Usage

Number a sheet of paper 1–10. After each number, write the correct form of the word in parentheses that should go in the blank.

> EXAMPLE During the Revolutionary War, American women not only took care of things at home, but often served in other ways _____ .
> (besides/beside)
>
> *besides*

1. It is a hot afternoon in 1778, and Mary Ludwig McCauley is standing _____ her husband. (beside/besides)

2. The battle of Monmouth is being fought, and many of the soldiers _____ _____ stand up because of the heat. (can hardly/can't hardly)
3. Mary does what she _____ to help. (may/can)
4. She carries pitchers of water to the soldiers _____ they fight and earns the name "Molly Pitcher." (like/as)
5. Suddenly the cannon Mary's husband has been firing stops _____ noise. (it's/its)
6. He has fought _____, but has fainted from the heat. (good/well)
7. Mary feels as if her heart will _____. (bust/burst)
8. She drags him into the shade and leaves him _____. (their/there)
9. Then she takes his place at the cannon and fights _____ the other soldiers have been fighting. (like/as)
10. Women like Molly Pitcher have left _____ mark on American history. (their/there)

REVIEW EXERCISE C   Some Common Confusions

The following words in parentheses sound alike but have different meanings. Number a sheet of paper 1–5. Next to each number, write the correct choice from the parentheses.

1. (It's/Its) too bad (they're/their/there) seems (to/too/two) be so few who like both rock and classical music.
2. Rock has (all ready/already) become one of music's most popular forms.

3. Everyone should (try and/try to) understand (that/that there) music.
4. (Between/Among) the lovers of classical music (there/their/they're) are some (who's/whose) interest includes jazz.
5. (Beside/Besides) classical music, (leave/let) (you're/your) listening time include jazz, rock, or light popular music.

UNIT FOUR

MECHANICS

Capitalization
Punctuation

12

CAPITALIZATION

Capitals are used to make letters stand out. A large letter among small letters attracts the eye. For this reason, a capital letter is used at the beginning of every sentence. The capital is a signal that an important group of words begins there. Other important words also begin with capital letters.

This chapter presents the ways capital letters are used as signals of special parts of writing.

CAPITAL LETTERS

12a Capitalize the first word in a sentence and the first word in a direct quotation.

The first word in every sentence begins with a capital letter. Even in a quotation, the first word in a sentence is capitalized.

EXAMPLES Fashions for women are often
invented by men.
Then André called out to Clarice,
"Put an ugly bug on the dress."

12b Capitalize the pronoun *I*.

EXAMPLE You and I finished the test together.

Do not capitalize other pronouns except when they begin sentences.

EXAMPLE We delayed their escape, but we
must report you to the captain
at once.

12c Capitalize proper nouns and proper adjectives.

See Nouns,
p. 5

Proper nouns are the names of particular persons, places, or things. A proper adjective is formed from a proper noun.

EXAMPLES
PROPER NOUNS Africa, Asia, Aaron Burr,
Andrew Young
PROPER ADJECTIVES American, Asian

(1) Capitalize the names of particular people and animals.

EXAMPLES It was Clyde Beatty who trained a
lion named Simba.

(2)   Capitalize the names of particular places.

EXAMPLES

Cities, Towns	Jacksonville, Seattle, Clinton
States, Counties	Rhode Island, Rockland County
Countries	Zaire, Peru
Continents	South America, Australia
Special regions	the South, the Milky Way (but not the word *the*)
Bodies of water, Islands, Points of land	the Sulu Sea, Nantucket, Santa Catalina, Aleutians Cape Hatteras
Parks	Grand Teton National Park, Central Park
Roadways, Waterways	Broadway, the Suez Canal

Do not capitalize directions.

EXAMPLE   When we traveled in the spring, we met a man who told us to go south into Arizona and then west to reach Los Angeles.

EXERCISE 1   The following sentences need capital letters. Number a sheet of paper 1–5. Next to each number, write the words that need capitals. Capitalize the words.

EXAMPLE   the history of rome in italy is centuries old.

The, Rome, Italy

1. at one time roman power reached westward to morocco and spain.
2. to the north it controlled what is now france, england, and belgium.
3. in europe and parts of asia, roman soldiers were in charge.
4. leaders like julius caesar crossed the mediterranean sea into north africa.
5. such famous people as cleopatra and spartacus are linked to roman history.

(3) Capitalize important words in the names of organizations, institutions, businesses, and branches of government.

EXAMPLES

Organizations	Federal Bureau of Investigation (**FBI**), National Association for the Advancement of Colored People (**NAACP**)
Institutions	Ford Foundation, Washington High School
Businesses and their products	General Electric, Toastmaster, Carnation, Pet milk
Branches of government	Department of Health, Education, and Welfare (**HEW**), the Senate

(4) Capitalize subjects taught in school when they name particular courses.

EXAMPLES Right after lunch we have American History I.

We learn about the history of
Europe in European History II.

Do not capitalize the name of a general field of
study.

EXAMPLE   I like math, but not science and
history.

**(5) Capitalize the names of nationalities, races,
and religions.**

EXAMPLES   Protestant, Mongoloid, Peruvians,
Canadians, Judaism

**(6) Capitalize the name of God and other beings
worshipped by people.**

EXAMPLES   Jehovah, Zeus, the Almighty,
Allah

EXERCISE 2   Write the following items on a sheet
of paper. Capitalize the words where necessary.

1. national labor relations board
2. lincoln high school
3. the carnegie foundation
4. general motors cars
5. carpentry and english at continuation high
6. africans
7. the first national bank for zambians
8. the department of agriculture in washington
9. the greek goddess hera
10. wilson's fish sticks

**(7) Capitalize the names of historical events,
periods of time, or other special events.**

EXAMPLES Thanksgiving, World War I,
Hanukkah

Do not capitalize seasons of the year, for example,
fall, winter.

**(8) Capitalize the first word and every important
word in the titles of people, books,
magazines, newspapers, movies, TV shows,
and other works people produce.**

EXAMPLES

People	Governor Grasso, Sergeant Kimna, Aunt Maria
Books, stories, poems	*The Way West* (book), "The Adventure of the Speckled Band" (story), "Stopping by Woods on a Snowy Evening" (poem)
Magazines	*Time, TV Guide, Seventeen*
Newspapers	the *Denver Post,* the *Los Angeles Times*
Movies, TV shows	*It Happened One Night,* "Search for Tomorrow"
Works in music, art, architecture	the Brooklyn Bridge, the Mona Lisa

EXERCISE 3 Write the following six sentences on
a sheet of paper. Capitalize the words where necessary.

1. The easter holiday comes in the spring.
2. It was president franklin roosevelt who suggested changing the date for thanksgiving.
3. In world war II, general omar bradley led the
   American troops into Europe.

4. The new york *times* newspaper carried a review of the movie *star wars*.
5. The magazine *time* supported general chiang Kai-shek in China.
6. The television show named "evening" showed pictures of the golden gate bridge.

REVIEW EXERCISE A Words to Capitalize

Each of the following sentences has at least one word that needs a capital letter. Some sentences have more than one word. Number a sheet of paper 1–10. Next to each number, write the word or words that need capitals.

EXAMPLE in 1977, carlos and i went to a professional soccer game.

In, Carlos, I

1. we were lucky because we saw pelé, the famous soccer star.
2. he was playing for the new york cosmos.
3. that year, they were the eastern division champions of the north american soccer league.
4. soccer has become the most popular sport in the world.
5. it has really caught on in the united states.
6. pelé is a brazilian who speaks mostly portuguese.
7. you can read about the soccer team standings in the sports page of most papers, like the *detroit news*.
8. many students take soccer in physical education 2c here at school.

9. i like it better than football.
10. we're going to travel in the west next year, and i want to see the san jose earthquakes play soccer.

REVIEW EXERCISE B   Words Not to Capitalize

Each of the following sentences contains at least one word that should *not* be capitalized. Find that word in each sentence. Then number a sheet of paper 1–10 and write the word in small letters.

EXAMPLE   A Cuban Baseball player named Roberto Ortiz played for the Charlotte Hornets in North Carolina in 1941.

baseball

1. He traveled South from Washington, D.C., after playing for the Washington Senators.
2. He loved Baseball and was a good outfielder.
3. He was lonely that Summer, since he could hardly speak English.
4. Ortiz was a stranger in The South and had almost no friends but a small yellow dog.
5. While Ortiz played with the Hornets, the Dog would wait quietly.
6. Here is how the dog became a star of The Piedmont League.
7. It was the Ninth inning and Ortiz was at bat.
8. He got a Hit and began to run.
9. Suddenly there was a yellow blur, and the dog raced out, ran the Bases with Ortiz, and even slid with him into third base.

10. The next day in The Charlotte *News* the dog was listed as a pinch runner who ran with Ortiz in the ninth inning.

REVIEW EXERCISE C Using Capitals

On a sheet of paper, write the words in the following story that should be capitalized. Put in capitals where they are needed.

EXAMPLE　i recently read a book called *japan today* by richard j. miller and lynn katoh.

I, Japan Today, Richard J. Miller, Lynn Katoh

it gave interesting facts about japan, a country made up of four large islands. the main island is called honshu. the island of hokkaido lies to the north and shikoku and kyushu to the south and west. among the world's hardest languages to learn, japanese is written in three different forms. one of these forms uses chinese characters. japanese students might take a course called japanese poets of the seventeenth century and learn about matsuo basho, one of japan's greatest poets. many japanese people belong to the shinto or buddhist religions. since world war II, government and ways of living have changed. japan now plays a large part in world affairs and is an active participant in the united nations.

13

PUNCTUATION

End Punctuation, Commas

Most marks of *punctuation* help to show how sentences should be read. For example, a question mark (?) means that a sentence is asking a question. A period (.) means only that a statement has been made. Consider the difference between the first and the second sentence below:

The light is on.
The light is on?

The first sentence states a simple fact about the light. It ends with a period. The second sentence is asking whether the light is on. It ends with a question mark.

End marks of punctuation are not the only marks to think about. Punctuation that comes inside sentences also affects meaning. And punctuation that encloses sentences or groups of words also helps determine meaning. This chapter deals with some of the various kinds of punctuation you need to use in your writing.

END PUNCTUATION

Every sentence you write must end with a mark of punctuation. There are three different marks of end punctuation: the *period (.)*, the *question mark* (?), and the *exclamation mark* (!). Each mark serves a purpose in showing how a sentence is to be read.

The Period

13a A period is used to mark the end of a statement or a request.

EXAMPLES The balloon began to fill with hot air.
Ziggy leaped into the basket.
Please get out.

13b A period is used after some abbreviations.

EXAMPLES   Forest St.   Ms.
Aug.   M.D.

13c A period is usually used after an initial.

EXAMPLES   Mr. F. W. Schwartz sent his taxes to the U.S. government in Washington, D.C.

Certain sets of initials that are used often together do not usually use periods.

EXAMPLES   GM (General Motors)
UFW (United Farm Workers)
USA (United States of America)

EXERCISE 1   Write the following sentences on a sheet of paper. Put in periods where they belong and circle them.

EXAMPLE   The US Weather Service and NASA use balloons for science

The U₀S₀ Weather Service and NASA use balloons for science₀

1. On Nov 21, 1783, J F Pilâtre de Rozier, a Frenchman, went up 78 ft in a hot-air balloon
2. On Aug 27, 1783, a hydrogen balloon without a passenger traveled 60 ft but was destroyed on landing
3. In 1785 John Jeffries, MD, of the USA sent balloons higher than they had gone before
4. In Philadelphia, Penn, Gen George Washington watched a balloon ascend on Jan 9, 1793
5. In Washington, DC, Pres Lincoln received a telegraph message from a balloon a mile away

The Question Mark

13d A question mark is used at the end of a sentence that asks a question.

EXAMPLES   How much money do you have?
Who wants to know?

EXERCISE 2   Copy the following sentences on a
sheet of paper. Put a period after each statement or
request. Put a question mark after each question.

1. How can I get to Plainfield
2. You take this road straight through
3. Do I keep going
4. You turn right at the first light
5. Is that the first traffic light
6. Tell me what other landmark there is
7. The courthouse is ahead on the hill
8. What if I miss the turn at the light
9. Ask a policeman
10. I could end up in the courthouse

The Exclamation Mark

**13e An exclamation mark is used at the end
of a sentence that shows shock or
surprise.**

Sometimes an exclamation mark comes right

See
Interjection, p.
401

after an interjection. In either place, the exclamation mark gives special emphasis to the word or
words it follows.

EXAMPLES   I can't believe it!
The world has come to a stop!
Nonsense! It's only that you're
running the wrong way so fast!

EXERCISE 3   Number a sheet of paper 1–10. After
each number, put the mark of end punctuation that
goes with each of the following sentences.

1. The leaves of a prayer plant seem to pray at night
2. I know of a house that was built around a large oak tree
3. How many plants grow in your house
4. Ivy readily grows up walls
5. A Venus's-flytrap eats meat
6. Those marigolds are brilliant
7. Is light an important factor in the growth of plants
8. Plants require sufficient amounts of water and light to grow
9. Climbing plants will grow around artistically tied wicker canes
10. What an attractive bottle garden

INSIDE PUNCTUATION

Certain marks of punctuation are used inside sentences to help keep meaning clear. Among these marks are *commas* (,), *semicolons* (;), and *colons* (:). By far the most common is the comma.

The following section presents the basic uses of the comma. Your study of this section will help you become more accurate in the use of this mark of punctuation.

The Comma

13f A comma is used between items in a series.

The items in a series may be words, phrases, or clauses. Or they may be letters or numerals. A

series of three or more of these items calls for commas between them.

EXAMPLES

WORDS   The station offered comedy, drama,
            and news.

PHRASES   Lois flipped on the switch, adjusted
            the picture, and turned up the
            volume.

CLAUSES   Doc Hadley's smile beamed out at us,
            then we saw Shannon's Dancers, and
            finally Chef Dupont was telling us
            how to prepare an omelette.

LETTERS   Across the room were the rows of
AND   huge letters: *A, B, C, D,* and the
NUMBERS   rest of the alphabet.

Some styles of punctuation do not require the
comma between the last two items in a series. Follow your teacher's instructions.

EXERCISE 4   The following sentences have commas missing. On a sheet of paper, write the words
just before and after a missing comma. Put a
comma between them.

EXAMPLE   Luis sang danced and played the
            trumpet for the talent show.

            sang, danced

1. Cotton wool and silk are natural fibers.
2. Rayon nylon and polyester are artificial fibers.

3. Knitting crocheting needlepoint and embroidering take patience and skill.

4. He sews skirts blouses dresses and suits.

5. Different fabrics smoke melt or catch on fire when placed near a flame.

6. Cotton grows on plants wool grows on sheep and silk is made from cocoons.

7. My jacket is cotton my raincoat is nylon and my dress coat is wool.

8. Do you want your pants made of cotton wool or leather?

9. Is that mink-type coat made from real mink rabbit or some fake fur?

10. Fabrics are made from alpaca vicuña and mohair.

13g Commas are used to set off items that interrupt a sentence.

EXAMPLES   That last explosion, *the bright red one*, came from a special rocket.

It would be, *well*, downright unfair to the rest of them.

Could you, *nevertheless*, try to be a little more serious?

(1) Commas are used to set off appositives.

An *appositive* is a word or group of words that repeats the meaning of the noun or pronoun it follows. An appositive interrupts the sentence. It is, therefore, set off with commas.

See Noun, p. 403; Pronoun, p. 406

EXAMPLE Ecology, *the study of interrelationships in nature*, is now a popular science.

(2) Commas are used to set off words like *yes, no,* and *well* when they interrupt a sentence.

EXAMPLES If you want me to go with you, *yes*, I will.

Can we, *for example*, bring friends on campus?

(3) Commas are used to set off transitional terms.

A number of words in English are useful in showing how ideas continue from one point to the next. These words are called *transitional terms*. Among the most common are *however, nevertheless,* and *moreover.*

EXAMPLES Bart tried to lift the giant crate. It would not budge, *however.* *Nevertheless*, Bart gave an extra push. He felt a sharp pain in his stomach.

(4) Commas are used to set off names used in direct address.

EXAMPLES "Well now, *Deadeye*, I don't think you've got a right to step on this land " drawled Ted Talltree.
"I'm coming over anyway, *Teddie boy*," taunted Deadeye.
"All right, *you varmint*, but leave your pea shooter behind."

> Hint: A comma usually comes in a sentence where your voice pauses and drops in tone as you read the sentence aloud.

EXERCISE 5 Number a sheet of paper 1–10. The following sentences are lacking commas. Next to the number for each sentence, write the words just before and after a missing comma. Put the comma between them.

EXAMPLE What is it I wonder that makes me fall in love?

it, I wonder, that

1. I like that person better now I think.
2. I know however it would be bad if we were married.
3. In fact one needs to realize that marriage will not make life perfect.
4. Getting married in my opinion would probably add to the problems.
5. On the other hand marriage may provide some security.
6. That may be a false security I suppose.
7. To tell the truth love is one of the hardest emotions to deal with.
8. In the first place it exposes you to pain.
9. After all there should be more to life than being in love.
10. There are other fish in the sea I guess.

EXERCISE 6 Number a sheet of paper 1–10. The following sentences are lacking commas. Next to each number write the words just before and after a missing comma. Put the comma between them.

> EXAMPLE   Mrs. Summer your daughter appears ill.
>
> *Mrs. Summer, your*

1. The first movie a silly comedy had no plot.
2. The second feature was to put it mildly a bore.
3. Nevertheless we sat through both pictures.
4. The popcorn you see was delicious.
5. During the first movie for starters we ate over two boxes.
6. The intermission a ten-minute break gave us a chance to count our money.
7. We were short of cash however.
8. Then I found quite by chance a quarter on the floor.
9. That money a gift from the heavens paid for another box.
10. I should perhaps start saving to buy a popcorn machine.

(5)   Commas are used to set off nonessential phrases or clauses.

A nonessential phrase or clause is one that is not necessary for the meaning of a sentence to be clear.

> EXAMPLES   Conrad Klopstock, *the fattest man in town*, runs a superb restaurant.
> [The fact that he is the fattest man

in town is not essential to the full
meaning of the sentence.]

Juanita Juarez, *who won the
cooking contest last year,* now
manages Conrad's kitchen.
[The clause *who won the cooking
contest last year* is not essential to
the meaning of the sentence.]

Hint: To tell whether or not commas
should be used to set off an inserted
phrase or clause, ask: *Are these words
necessary for me to know which particular
person or thing is meant?*
If your answer is no, you don't need the
phrase or clause. Set off the unnecessary
phrase or clause with commas.

Following are some examples of essential and
nonessential phrases:

ESSENTIAL
PHRASE
The vegetables *bought at
Sloan's market* were not
fresh.

NONESSENTIAL
PHRASE
The entire batch of
vegetables, *bought at
Sloan's market,* had to
be thrown out because
they were not fresh.
[The phrase *bought at
Sloan's market* is not
essential to the
meaning of the sentence.]

EXERCISE 7 Some of the following sentences contain nonessential clauses or phrases. On a sheet of paper rewrite each sentence with a nonessential phrase or clause. Add commas where they belong and circle them.

> EXAMPLE The telephone which is found everywhere uses plastic.
>
> *The telephone, which is found everywhere, uses plastic.*

1. The plastics that are used today have an interesting history.
2. Celluloid a chemical compound was invented by an Albany printer in 1869.
3. The work that was done later by several European chemists brought us rayon and cellophane.
4. Bakelite which is also a chemical compound came into use in 1909.
5. All these plastic materials that were manufactured became the forerunners of modern plastics.
6. The branch of chemistry which specializes in plastics is all-important in industry.
7. Fibers of plastic spun as thin as silk are used in clothing.
8. Plastic string made much the same way is used for fishing line and other sports equipment.
9. Some plastic string that is made this way is tougher than steel.
10. The world of plastics a little more than a hundred years old surrounds us now.

13h A comma is used to separate adjectives not joined by the conjunction *and*.

See
Conjunction,
p. 392

EXAMPLES Pernella gasped at the sight of Lynn's wet, slimy hands. "You'll get rough, old-looking hands if you don't wear rubber gloves while washing," said Pernella.

Sometimes the second of two adjectives together is closely related in meaning to the noun it modifies. In this case, no comma is needed to separate the two adjectives.

EXAMPLE The rough red brick had been scarred by years of wear.

EXERCISE 8 The following sentences need commas. Number a sheet of paper 1–6. Next to each number write the word before and after a comma that belongs in the sentence. Put in the missing comma.

EXAMPLE Early bicycles were stiff unsteady vehicles.

stiff, unsteady

1. The "boneshaker" gave its rider a rough dangerous ride.
2. In the 1870's a high metal-rimmed front wheel made the "penny-farthing" look unbalanced.
3. Dunlop developed the first soft air-filled rubber tire before 1890.
4. Tandem bicycles became popular in the 1890's when women wore heavy puffy clothes.

5. By 1900 America had more than three hundred busy industrious bicycle factories.
6. In today's energy-short clean-air times, bicycles are more popular than ever.

See Clause,
pp. 389–390;
Complex
Sentence, p.
391

13i A comma is used to set off a dependent clause at the beginning of a complex sentence.

EXAMPLES Whenever Sandra Kang came back to visit, she brought little presents for the children. While they opened the presents, Sandra visited with the old people. After visiting for a while, Sandra would then go out for a walk alone.

EXERCISE 9 Each of the following sentences needs a comma. Number a sheet of paper 1–10. After each number write the words before and after the place for a comma. Write in the comma.

EXAMPLE Before the Chinese invented paper in A.D. 105 people wrote on clay, bark, or animal skin.

A.D. 105, people

1. After several Chinese papermakers were captured in battles the Arabs learned how to make paper.
2. As a result of the Crusades in the Middle Ages papermaking spread throughout Europe.

3. Even though the manufacturing process was slow handmade paper continued in use for hundreds of years.

4. When a Dutch citizen invented a rag-processing machine in 1750 the manufacture of paper was speeded up a great deal.

5. While this process was faster than hand manufacture the need for more paper caused a continuing search for improved paper manufacture.

6. Although rags made good paper a cheaper substance was needed for mass production.

7. After much experimentation investigators found that wood pulp made a good base for paper.

8. When in 1882 wood processing was perfected the paper "explosion" hit the world.

9. If you try to think of all the uses for paper the list grows long.

10. After listing several dozen uses it will be necessary to get more paper to write them on.

13j **A comma is usually used before a coordinating conjunction joining the independent clauses in a compound sentence.**

See
Conjunction,
p. 392

EXAMPLES Gloria Kokesh tried on the coat, *but* it seemed to hang too far down in the back. She draped it over the hanger on the rack, *and* the salesperson gave a grunt of disapproval.

A compound sentence with very short clauses may not need a comma before the conjunction. Follow your teacher's direction.

> EXAMPLE Some people like one style of coat but others like another.

EXERCISE 10 Each of the following sentences needs a comma. Number a sheet of paper 1–8. After each number write the words before and after the place for a comma. Write in the comma.

> EXAMPLE Most paper is made from wood pulp but some special kinds use rags.
>
> *pulp, but*

1. Lumberjacks cut fresh trees in a thick forest and then they trim the branches to leave clean logs.
2. A trucker hauls the logs to the mill or they are floated there on a stream.
3. One machine at the mill cuts the logs into short sections and another removes the bark.
4. The short logs are not yet ready for processing for they must be chopped into chips less than an inch across.
5. The chips are then cooked in a chemical and then they are washed clean.
6. The clean pulp must next be screened or some wood knots and chunks might be left in it.
7. The next treatment is a beating and mixing but even then the material must be dried and pressed.
8. Drying machines remove moisture and rollers press and even cut the paper as it completes its manufacturing process.

13k Commas are used in certain standard ways.

Sometimes commas are used in standard ways to show a separation of items. Their use is not so much to clarify meaning as it is to make reading easier.

(1) Commas are used before the quotation marks around the words of a speaker.

> EXAMPLE Kurt shouted, "Cut the power," in the general direction of the control room.

Put a comma in front of quotation marks. Commas help to show where the words about someone are separated from the exact words said by someone.

> EXAMPLE The woman at the wheel answered, "Yes, sir."

EXERCISE 11 Number a sheet of paper 1–15. Next to each number write each sentence. Insert commas where they belong. Circle the commas you add.

> EXAMPLE "Check the space compass" ordered Ardee Won.
>
> *"Check the space compass⊙"*
> *ordered Ardee Won.*

1. "Watch our course" Ardee Won called.
2. He said "We can't drift off course."
3. He added "Give me the heading now."

4. "Star 4 plus two degrees sunside" came the response.

5. Ardee Won barked out the command "Bring it back!"

6. "I'm trying, commander" answered the steerman.

7. Entu Foor came on the line and said "What's our speed?"

8. "One quarter light speed less 18,000" responded the engineer.

9. Entu Foor demanded to know "Can you get any more speed?"

10. "We're losing speed" was the answer.

11. "We can't hold course" muttered Ardee Won "and we're losing speed."

12. Entu Foor cut in again, saying "We've got to get on track."

13. "The power is failing" said Ardee Won in a lower and quieter voice.

14. "Switch on emergency power" called Entu Foor.

15. "I'm too weak" whispered Won, and then there was silence.

(2)   Commas are used to separate items in dates and geographical names.

> EXAMPLES   It was in A.D. 1066 that the battle of Hastings, England, changed the course of history in the Western world. June 13, 1922, came on a Friday

EXERCISE 12   Number a sheet of paper 1–4. Next to each number, write each part of the following items that need commas. Add commas where they belong.

EXAMPLE In the Bay of Tokyo Japan on September 2 1945 the surrender was signed that ended World War II.

Tokyo, Japan
September 2, 1945, the

1. Japan's unconditional surrender had been demanded in the Potsdam Declaration on July 26 1945.
2. General Douglas MacArthur directed Japan's affairs from September 2 1945 to April 28 1952.
3. Fully normal relations between Japan and America came April 28 1952 with the treaty of peace.
4. The treaty was signed in San Francisco California on September 8 1951.

(3) **A comma is used after the greeting and the closing in a friendly letter.**

EXAMPLES Dear Willa,   Very truly yours,
Dear Friends,   Sincerely yours,

REVIEW EXERCISES for Punctuation will be found at the end of Chapter 14.

14

PUNCTUATION

Semicolons, Colons, Hyphens, Apostrophes, Dashes, Italics, Quotation Marks, Parentheses

This chapter presents the uses of the remaining marks of inside punctuation—*semicolons, colons, hyphens, dashes, apostrophes,* and *underlining (italics)*. Several marks of enclosing punctuation —*quotation marks* and *parentheses*—are also discussed.

INSIDE PUNCTUATION

The Semicolon

See Compound Sentence, p. 391; Conjunction, p. 392

14a A semicolon is used between the clauses in a compound sentence that are not joined by a conjunction.

The semicolon that is used between two independent clauses serves as a strong comma.

EXAMPLES Most science fiction films are a waste of time; *The Planet Pirates* is another example.

Its plot is predictable; its dull characters act like robots.

14b A semicolon is used between the clauses of a compound sentence when either clause has a comma in it.

EXAMPLES Nessie Wuden, an awkward actor, played the commander of the space squadron; and Truk Hangten played the part of his assistant.

Neither one seemed to be awake; and, in fact, the other actors looked pretty sleepy.

14c A semicolon is used to separate items in a series having inside punctuation.

EXAMPLES The space squadron of two ships, based on Mars, took off safely enough; but soon they ran into trouble; and, as anyone could have guessed, one trouble led to more trouble.

One ship's power supply mysteriously shut down; the lead ship, trying to help, bumped and damaged the powerless ship; and just then a space pirate ship came into view.

14d A semicolon following a quotation goes outside the quotation marks.

EXAMPLE   Wuden radioed to Mars base, "We're under attack"; but the pirate ship, which had powerful radio equipment, interfered with the transmission.

EXERCISE 1 The following sentences are missing semicolons. Number a sheet of paper 1–12. Next to each number, write the words before and after the place where a semicolon belongs. Put in a semicolon.

EXAMPLE   Og Lee Go Rilla, the leader of the pirates, had sighted the space squadron and, thinking to gain a victory, put his crew on war alert.

squadron; and

1. Rilla had a spy, Sneek E. Ratt, aboard a squadron ship and it was Ratt who cut the power supply.
2. Seeing his chance, Rilla and the pirates moved toward the squadron but they did so cautiously.
3. Rilla barked an order to his radio room, "Turn on the jammer" and then he listened to the squadron's radio.
4. A garbled transmission, full of crackles and buzzes, came across for Rilla's jammer was working well.
5. Aboard the squadron command ship Wuden, the commander, sounded an alarm he shouted orders to his crew, who seemed confused and,

without any clear plan, they ran back and forth
yelling at each other.

6. As I watched this unfold, I had to laugh but the
movie was not supposed to be a comedy.

7. Rilla and his pirates, obviously getting bolder,
moved closer and, when they reached the firing
range, let loose a laser blast at a squadron ship.

8. This put the command ship out of action or at
least, in some unexplained way, it made them
unable to defend themselves.

9. Rilla, who by now had the upper hand, ordered
the command ship to prepare for docking or he,
Rilla, would destroy the squadron completely.

10. Hangten told Wuden, "I guess we're trapped"
but Wuden whispered something and then
radioed Og Lee Go Rilla to come aboard.

11. Rilla did but there followed an unbelievable
series of events including a long fist fight, a
wrecking of the ships's instruments, the final
victory by Wuden, and a safe return to Mars
with the pirate ship towing the squadron ships.

12. This silly movie, supposedly a space epic, could
have been a Western or it could have been a
cops-and-robbers thriller or maybe it just never
should have been made at all.

The Colon

**14e A colon is used to introduce a list of
items.**

EXAMPLES The sports catalog showed pages of
camping equipment: tents,
cookstoves, sleeping bags, and
utensils.

Exercise and body-building
materials are on the following
pages: 24–26, 31–45, and 47.

14f A colon is used in numerals expressing time.

EXAMPLES   The radio came on at 6:25 A.M. I
thought I had set it for 7:45.

14g A colon is used after the greeting in a business letter.

EXAMPLES   Dear Sir:
Dear Ms. Hoyle:
Dear Antonio:

EXERCISE 2 Number a sheet of paper 1–5. After
the number, write the following sentences. Put in
colons where they belong. Circle the colons you add.

EXAMPLE   The radio section of the newspaper
listed for 630 A.M. the following
programs "Daily Exercise," "Wake
Up America," and "Early News."

*The radio section of the
newspaper listed for
6⊙30 A.M. the following
programs⊙ "Daily Exercise,"
"Wake Up America,"
and "Early News."*

1. I listened until 645.
2. I heard about the following bits of news the price of gold in London, a local robbery, and the weather.
3. Then came three commercials one for hair soap, the next for an airline, and the next for lawn food.
4. At 648 I shut off the radio and turned on TV.
5. In between commercials I watched these shows "Body Trim," "Come Awake," and "Morning News."

The Hyphen

14h A hyphen is used to connect the parts of certain compound words and word numbers from twenty-one to ninety-nine.

EXAMPLE   sister-in-law
a well-oiled machine
thirty-three

Word numbers greater than ninety-nine do not take hyphens.

EXAMPLE   one hundred and four

If the word number is a fraction used as an adjective, use a hyphen.

EXAMPLES   a one-quarter cup of milk
[*One-quarter* is an adjective that modifies *cup*.]

one quarter of the hour
[*One quarter* is used as a noun.]

14i A hyphen is used to divide a word between syllables at the end of a line.

EXAMPLES   Harriet Kickbush went on a disas-
trous trip.
She rode a mule the long distance from Maine to Florida.

WRONG   The heavy trucks and the fast automobiles on the roads made it difficult to travel.

RIGHT   The heavy trucks and the fast automobiles on the road made it difficult to travel.

EXERCISE 3   Number a sheet of paper 1–15. Copy each of the following items. For each single word, write the syllables separately. Put hyphens between the syllables to show how to break each word at the end of a line. You may use a dictionary.

EXAMPLE   industry

in - dus - try

1. intricate
2. uniform
3. celebrate
4. forty three
5. mother in law
6. underwear
7. excursion
8. convenience
9. original
10. orchestra
11. two thirds of a kilo
12. one hundred and twenty one
13. a one third piece of the lot
14. stationery
15. a well trained dog

The Dash

14j The dash is used to set off certain interrupters in a sentence, especially those with inside punctuation.

EXAMPLE   Our struggle for our rights—even if it takes us to Washington, D.C.—must not be allowed to weaken.

The Apostrophe

14k An apostrophe is used with nouns to show possession or close relationship.   See Nouns, pp. 8–10

EXAMPLES   Hilda's brother takes the neighbor's dogs for walks.
The plane's engine nearly fell off.
Jolenna's cat drank Rex's milk.

(1) Most singular nouns form the possessive with an apostrophe and s.

EXAMPLES   a dog's life
Berta's phone number
one sailor's view

(2) A plural noun ending in s forms the possessive with an apostrophe only.

EXAMPLES   Sailors' songs remind us of the sea.
The jars' lids had all come loose.

(3) A plural noun not ending in s adds an apostrophe and s.

EXAMPLES   Women's fashions in clothes change
yearly.

However, men's clothing fashions
seem more stable.

EXERCISE 4   Some of the following sentences are
correct. Others have errors in the use of the apostrophe to show possession. Number a sheet of paper
1–8. Write *C* for any sentence that is correct. Copy
any incorrect sentence. Write it with the correct use
of the apostrophe.

EXAMPLE   Dora Pratts party was a success.

Dora Pratt's party was a success.

1. Doras friends Eva and Jackie Ambots came.
2. Evas cousin Louis came also.
3. The womens talk covered a number of topics of
   interest.
4. Dora told about her mothers new job.
5. Eva said her cousins husband had arrived from
   France.
6. Dora served iced tea and melon slices.
7. The slices flavor was delicious.
8. The guests enjoyed themselves.

**14I An apostrophe is used to show that
letters have been omitted.**

EXAMPLES   couldn't (could not)
don't (do not)
we'll (we will)
would've (would have)

These examples are *contractions*. They are used more in speaking than in writing. Contractions are less formal than complete words spelled out.

14m **An apostrophe is used with the letter *s* to show the plural of letters, numerals, and special symbols.**

EXAMPLES Her handwriting makes *E*'s look like *C*'s.
The postwar spirit of the late 1940's may never return.

EXERCISE 5 Number a sheet of paper 1–10. Next to each number write the form that shows the possessive. Use apostrophes where they are necessary.

EXAMPLE the comb that belongs to Marcia

Marcia's comb

1. the gloves that belong to Tomiko
2. the book that belongs to Tom
3. the tickets that belong to the women
4. the cheese that belongs to the mice
5. the woods that belong to Ricardo
6. the rights that belong to the public
7. the hats that belong to the police officers
8. a knife that belongs to a butcher
9. a car that belongs to a judge
10. shovels that belong to workers

EXERCISE 6 Rewrite the following items. Put in apostrophes where they belong.

EXAMPLES   Hows it going?

How's it going?

1. Were all at home.
2. couldnt
3. Whats the time?
4. hasnt
5. Its a shame were late.
6. Well be on time.
7. Write the *Es* with a loop.
8. wont
9. Shell see you later.
10. wouldve

Italics (the Underline)

14n Underlining is used for titles of books, movies, periodicals, ships, letters of the alphabet, and important works. In printed matter these items are set in italics.

EXAMPLE   The book *The History of Art* includes notes about Michelangelo's sculpture *David*.

14o Underlining is used to make special items and foreign words stand out.

EXAMPLES   *Use caution* when opening this door.
No running near the pool.
Jeanne replied, "*Merci*," when she received the package.
I think you *must* do it.

EXERCISE 7 Number a sheet of paper 1–8. Then copy the following sentences. Use underlining wherever it is necessary.

EXAMPLE   Supership is a book that tells about life on an oil tanker.

Supership is a book that tells about life on an oil tanker.

1. One of these big ships is the S. S. Ardshiel.
2. The author argues that these ships are too big to be safe.
3. Stories about oil tankers have appeared in Time and Newsweek.
4. The Torrey Canyon was one of the first tankers to lose its gooey cargo.
5. Supership warns people about oil tankers the way Rachel Carson's Silent Spring warned about insecticides.
6. One composer read Supership and then composed a Symphony for Sludge.
7. A sculptor made a statue of a dead, oil-covered bird and called it Oilbird.
8. If people do not control oil spills and other pollution, we may be reading a new book titled Our Dying Oceans.

ENCLOSING PUNCTUATION

Special marks of punctuation are used to enclose certain parts of sentences. The most widely used marks are *quotation marks* and *parentheses*. Their common uses are presented here.

Quotation Marks

14p Quotation marks are used to enclose a speaker's exact words.

EXAMPLES   Bobby put the question, "Do we have a net?"
"No," answered Sandy, "but we can imagine it's there."

The speaker's exact words belong in quotation marks. If, however, the approximate words are used, no quotation marks are needed.

EXAMPLE

DIRECT QUOTATION   Sandy said, "Let's just hit the ball back and forth."

INDIRECT QUOTATION   Sandy suggested just hitting the ball back and forth.

14q Single quotation marks are used to enclose a quotation within a quotation.

EXAMPLES   "Did you say 'ready' or 'steady'?" asked Sandy.
"I say 'nuts'," answered Bobby as he walked away.

EXERCISE 8   Number a sheet of paper 1–8. Then copy the following sentences. Add quotation marks, single quotation marks, and commas wherever they are needed.

EXAMPLE   Grantland Rice's statement It's not whether you win or lose, but how you play the game is one of many proverbs that has entered our language from baseball.

Grantland Rice's statement, "It's not whether you win or lose, but how you play the game," is one of many proverbs that has entered our language from baseball.

1. Don't look behind you, something might be gaining on you baseball player Satchel Paige once said.
2. Slide, Kelly, slide, the fans yelled when the early baseball player Michael Kelly stole a base.
3. When a person has done badly at something, he or she may say I never got to first base.
4. Never yell You're blind at an umpire one ball player warns unless you want to get thrown out of the game.
5. Leo Durocher is supposed to have said Nice guys finish last.
6. I said something like Nice guys finish last but I didn't mean it the way people thought I did Durocher has since said.
7. Durocher said he didn't mean that nice people are always losers.

8. When Durocher saw another team and their manager, he said He's such a nice guy, and they'll finish last for him.

14r Quotation marks are used to enclose titles of chapters, articles, short stories, poems, songs, and other short pieces of writing.

> EXAMPLES Poe's story "The Gold Bug" has been popular for more than a hundred years.
>
> By next week we have to read Chapter 8, "The Dream Animal," and Chapter 9, "People of the Future."

14s A period always goes inside the end quotation marks.

> EXAMPLE Winn called down, "We'll join you in a minute."

If the quotation itself is a question or an exclamation, the question mark or the exclamation mark goes inside the end quotation marks. If not, the question mark or exclamation mark goes outside the quotation marks.

> EXAMPLE "How long is your minute?" asked Fay.
> Did Fay say, "Along"?

EXERCISE 9 Number a sheet of paper 1–6. Then copy the following sentences. Add quotation marks wherever they are needed.

> EXAMPLE   Some people will always say, I like trains better than airplanes.

> *Some people will always say, " I like trains better than airplanes."*

1. Edna St. Vincent Millay wrote a poem called Travel, which told how much she loved trains.
2. Songs about trains, such as The Atchison, Topeka, and the Santa Fe or Shuffle Off to Buffalo, have a special rhythm.
3. Did you know that a nickname for a train was The Iron Horse?
4. A book on railroad folklore has a chapter titled The Iron Horse Goes to War.
5. Railroad fans sigh, Train travel today isn't what it used to be.
6. The Decline and Fall of the Railroad would make an interesting title for a magazine article.

Parentheses

14t **Parentheses are used to enclose extra items added in a sentence.**

> EXAMPLE   Take the second step (listed at the bottom of your sheet) and record the results.

REVIEW EXERCISE A   **End Punctuation: Periods, Question Marks, and Exclamation Points**

Copy each of the following sentences on a sheet of paper. Put in periods, question marks, and exclamation points where they are needed. Circle any punctuation you add.

EXAMPLE   Winters in the western US are very long

Winters in the western US are very long

1. Cowboys used to leaf through all the books in the ranch house
2. After all, what else was there for them to do
3. They couldn't walk down to Main St and see a movie
4. What boring nights there were
5. Someone invented a game called "Know Your Labels"
6. How do you think it was played
7. Each player had to recite from memory the exact words on the labels of the cans in the kitchen
8. He had to put the commas and periods in the right places
9. Men living on ranches outside places like Abilene, Kan, and Bandera, Tex became experts at it
10. They must have been awfully glad when spring came

REVIEW EXERCISE B   Inside Punctuation: The Comma

Rewrite the following sentences on a sheet of paper, putting in commas where they are needed. Circle them.

EXAMPLE   Seven hundred years ago around the year 1200 the first Incas founded the city of Cuzco in what is now Peru.

Seven hundred years ago, around the year 1200, the first Incas founded the city of Cuzco in what is now Peru.

1. The land of the Incas has three kinds of country: deserts jungles and high mountains.
2. The Incas who founded a mighty empire were conquered by a small number of Spanish soldiers.
3. Descendants of the Incas are barrel-chested black-haired people who live high in the mountains.
4. When the Inca government was at its height great buildings and roads were built.
5. The Incas conquered many other tribes but they always asked them to join the empire before the fighting began.
6. However they would and did fight for more land.
7. The Lord Inca the most important man of all governed the people.

8. But in May 1532 the Spanish soldiers landed and the conquest of the Incas began.
9. Cuzco Peru once the Inca capital still stands.
10. "This is a fabulous city" many people say when they see Cuzco.

REVIEW EXERCISE C   Inside Punctuation: The Semicolon, the Colon, and the Hyphen.

Each of the following sentences needs either a semicolon, a colon, or a hyphen. Number a sheet of paper 1–5. Next to each number, write the words before and after a colon or semicolon and add the punctuation. If a hyphen is needed, write the syllables before and after it as they should appear.

> EXAMPLE   Here is a message to the following people the inhabitants of Midville, their leaders, and the world.
>
> *people : the*

1. As you know, we have landed in one of your football fields, spoken with your leaders, and seen one of your cities now we wish to get to know you better.
2. One of your kind has *com mu ni cat ed,* as you say, with us by radio.
3. She has said to us, "We wish to become friends with you" and now we will attempt to do this.
4. Twenty Earthlings will please arrive at our spaceship at 715 Earth time.

5. Bring these things with you warm clothing, food, cooking utensils, and items necessary for a journey.

REVIEW EXERCISE D   Inside Punctuation: The Dash, The Apostrophe, and the Underline

Each of the following sentences needs either a dash, an underline, or an apostrophe. Some sentences need more than one. Number a sheet of paper 1–5. Rewrite each sentence, adding the missing punctuation. Circle any punctuation you add.

EXAMPLE   Some people have the ability strange as it may seem to see into the future.

Some people have the ability⊙ strange as it may seem⊙ to see into the future.

1. Theyre called psychics and can sometimes see events that will happen in several years time.
2. A book called Dream Telepathy tells of experiments being done to test these peoples abilities.
3. In one experiment a chair is chosen at random before a meeting, and the psychics are asked whos going to sit in it.
4. What do these powers mean in an ordinary persons life?
5. Suppose your friends sister is psychic just suppose would you want her to tell you your future?

REVIEW EXERCISE E Enclosing Punctuation: Quotation Marks and Parentheses

Each of the following sentences uses enclosing punctuation: single or double quotation marks, or parentheses. Number a sheet of paper 1–5. Find the enclosing punctuation marks in each sentence. If they are used correctly write *correct*. If they are not used correctly, rewrite the sentence and put in the correct punctuation.

EXAMPLES "One of you in this room has committed a murder," said Vera.

correct

"Did you say, "committed a murder"?" asked Mr. Greenfish.

"Did you say 'committed a murder'?" asked Mr. Greenfish.

1. Vera suggested that Mrs. Moon tell them where she had been all evening.
2. Peter Gray said that the whole thing reminded him of a story he had read called 'The Diamond Dagger'.
3. "Everyone step forward (being careful not to trip on the rug) and stretch out your hands," said Vera.
4. When Vera said (step forward) Mrs. Moon began to protest angrily.
5. "She said," Peter Gray remarked, "that we should step forward."

UNIT FIVE

AIDS AND ENRICHMENT

Spelling
Sources of Information
Using Words

15

SPELLING

For some people spelling is easy. Other people find spelling difficult. You may be one of those who find it difficult.

Like many other skills in English, your spelling will improve if you work at it. Practice helps. Learning a few spelling rules can help, too.

Spelling rules are like helpful hints. They will not answer all your questions, but they contain useful information. In them you will find clues to the spelling of many difficult words.

RULES FOR GOOD SPELLING

15a Develop basic spelling habits.

Developing the right habits can make spelling easier.

(1)   Keep a list of troublesome words.

Some words may give you trouble time after time. Keep a list of the ones that you find hard to spell. Whenever you discover a difficult word, add it to your list.

Refer to your list regularly. When you learn to spell a difficult word, put a check beside it. See if you can check off all the words on the list.

See Master
Spelling List,
pp. 346–349

(2)   Study the hard parts of words.

Usually a difficult word has one part that gives you trouble. You may find the rest of the word easy to spell.

Commercial is an example of a difficult word. Most people can spell the beginning parts of this word. It is the ending that causes problems. What letters stand for the sound "shul"? The **cial** in *commercial* is an example of the hard part of a word.

Look at your list of troublesome words. Identify the hard part in each one. Then draw a line under it. Drawing lines under the hard parts of words will help you to concentrate on the trouble spots. Once you have mastered a word's trouble spot, that difficult word becomes easy.

(3)   See each syllable. Say each syllable. Write each syllable.

Choose a long word that gives you trouble. Say that word out loud. Listen carefully to its sounds. Can you hear the different parts of the word?

The word parts you hear are called *syllables*. Each syllable has one main vowel sound. There can also be one or more consonant sounds.

Break difficult words into syllables. Most syllables will be short word parts that are easy to spell.

EXAMPLES

GYM-NAS-TICS (gymnastics)	This word has three syllables. Only the first is likely to cause you much trouble in spelling.
	Say *gymnastics* out loud. Listen to the sound of its first syllable. Then write the word.
CYL-IN-DER (cylinder)	This word has three syllables. The last two should not cause you trouble. They are spelled just as they sound.
	The first syllable might cause you trouble. Here, **c** stands for the *s* sound. The letter **y** stands for the short *i* sound. *Sill* is a word that has the same sounds as this word part. In a word like *cylinder,* however, the first syllable is spelled *cyl*.
	Look at the word *cylinder.* Say each syllable. Write each one.

(4) Use a dictionary.

See Sources of Information, p. 303   Dictionaries break words into their syllables. If you can spell the first syllables of a word, you can find its correct spelling.

15b Learn basic spelling rules.

Spelling rules offer many useful hints. They will guide you toward a word's correct spelling. It is good, however, to remember that these rules are only guides. Most of them have exceptions. Learn the exceptions along with the rules. Together they will help you become a better speller.

(1) Regular nouns form their plurals by adding *s* or *es.*

EXAMPLES

Nouns that add **s**   hill, hills
                        track, tracks
                        battle, battles
Nouns that add **es**   fox, fox**es**
                        glass, glass**es**
                        lunch, lunch**es**

Add **es** to nouns that end in **ch, s, sh, x,** or **z.** Add **s** to all other regular nouns.

EXERCISE 1 Number a sheet of paper 1–10. Write the plural of the following nouns.

1. wire	5. bunch	9. class
2. arrow	6. box	10. spool
3. patch	7. plane	
4. racer	8. wish	

(2) **Nouns ending in _y_ after a consonant change the _y_ to _i_ and add _es_ to form the plural.**

> EXAMPLES fly, fl**ies**
> party, part**ies**

If a vowel comes before the final **y**, just add **s**.

> EXAMPLES ray, ray**s**
> monkey, monkey**s**

EXERCISE 2 Number a sheet of paper 1–8. Next to each number, write the plural of the following nouns.

1. daisy
2. tray
3. buddy
4. pastry
5. key
6. trolley
7. poppy
8. alley

(3) **Most nouns ending in _f_ add _s_ to form the plural.**

> EXAMPLES roof, roof**s**
> whiff, whiff**s**

(4) **Some nouns ending in _f_ or _fe_ change the _f_ to _v_ and add _es_ or _s_.**

> EXAMPLES calf, cal**ves**
> knife, kni**ves**

(5) **Most nouns ending in _o_ following a vowel add _s_ to form the plural.**

> EXAMPLES patio, patio**s**
> tattoo, tattoo**s**

(6) **Most nouns ending in *o* following a consonant add *es* to form the plural.**

EXAMPLES echo, echo**es**
torpedo, torpedo**es**

(7) **Musical terms ending in *o* add only an *s* to form the plural.**

EXAMPLES concerto, concerto**s**
soprano, soprano**s**

(8) **A few nouns form their plurals without *s* or *es*. Some change spelling. Some remain the same.**

EXAMPLES ox, oxen   foot, feet
man, men   mouse, mice
deer, deer   sheep, sheep

EXERCISE 3 Number a sheet of paper 1–20. Write the plural form of each of these nouns.

1. life
2. ox
3. hero
4. earmuff
5. latch
6. piccolo
7. key
8. thief
9. tomato
10. violin
11. tax
12. rodeo
13. child
14. daisy
15. cobra
16. leash
17. parachute
18. valley
19. piano
20. cliff

EXERCISE 4 Number a sheet of paper 1–10. Write the plural form of each of these nouns.

1. pass
2. batch
3. trout
4. cello
5. bluff

6. wife
7. radio
8. leaf
9. angle
10. mosquito

(9) Most compound nouns form the plural by adding *s* to the noun part, not the modifier.

EXAMPLES   basketball, basketball**s**
lady-in-waiting, lad**ies**-in-waiting

If you are not sure of a spelling, check it in a dictionary.

Prefixes

A *prefix* is a group of letters added to the front of a word or word part. The result is a new word with a new meaning.

For example, you *set* the controls on an oven. If you need to set the controls beforehand, then you *preset* them. Sometimes you may need to change the controls and set them again. Then you *reset* them. Or you may forget to set the controls at all. The controls are *unset*.

The prefixes **pre-**, **re-**, and **un-** help to make new words. These prefixes mean *before, again,* and *the opposite.*

(10) A word or root that adds a prefix does not change spelling.

Prefixes are usually added to words, such as *set*. These words can be used by themselves.

Sometimes prefixes are added to word parts. *Eject, inject,* and *reject* are examples. In these words, prefixes have been added to the letters -**ject**. A word part like -**ject** is called a *root,* or stem. It cannot be used by itself. It must join with a prefix to become a whole word.

Here are some prefixes, words or roots, and the new words they make.

PREFIX	WORD OR ROOT	NEW WORD
pro-	-pel	propel
	-duce	produce
mis-	lead	mislead
	understand	misunderstand
de-	-scend	descend
	tract	detract
re-	do	redo
	-pel	repel

EXERCISE 5 Number a sheet of paper 1–8. Next to each number write the new word formed by adding a prefix from the list to the word or root.

PREFIXES

pro-, re-, de-, mis-

EXAMPLE read

misread or reread

1. ject
2. cede
3. duce
4. spell

5. place
6. port
7. view
8. read

(11) Some prefixes change spelling when joined
to a word or root.

A word or root is spelled the same after a prefix
is added. But the spelling of the prefix sometimes
changes.

EXAMPLES

PREFIX	WORD OR ROOT	NEW WORD	
com-	-tend	contend	[The prefix
	-duct	conduct	com- becomes con-]
in-	perfect	imperfect	[The prefix
	probable	improbable	in- becomes im-]
	legal	illegal	[The prefix in- becomes il-]
	regular	irregular	[The prefix in- becomes ir-]

Suffixes

Words and roots also combine with suffixes to
make new words. *Suffixes* are added to the ends of
words or roots. Some examples are -**ful** and -**less**.
They mean *full of* and *without*. They join with a
word like *joy* to make *joyful* and *joyless*.

(12) Most words adding the suffixes *-ly, -less,* and
-ness keep the same spellings.

EXAMPLES   weak, weak**ly**
strange, strange**ly**
joy, joy**less**
blue, blue**ness**

(13) Words ending in *y* following a consonant change the *y* to *i* before adding a suffix that does not begin with *i.*

EXAMPLES   noisy, nois**ily**
sticky, stick**iness**
hurry, hurr**ied**

(14) Words or roots ending in *ie* usually change the *ie* to *y* when the suffix *-ing* is added.

EXAMPLES   die, d**ying**
lie, l**ying**

(15) Most words ending in *e* omit the *e* when adding a suffix that begins with a vowel.

EXAMPLES   scare, scar**ing**
tame, tam**ing**

(16) Most words ending in *ce* or *ge* keep the *e* when adding a suffix that begins with *a* or *o*.

EXAMPLES   trace, trace**able**
courage, courage**ous**

(17) Most words ending in *e* keep the *e* when adding a suffix that begins with a consonant.

EXAMPLES   sore, sore**ness**
place, place**ment**

(18) One-syllable words ending in a single consonant following a single vowel double the consonant when adding the suffixes *-ed, -ing,* or *-er.*

EXAMPLES dim, dim**med**, dim**ming**, dim**mer**
blot, blot**ted**, blot**ting**, blot**ter**

(19) Double the final consonant when adding *-ed, -er,* or *-ing* to words with two or more syllables ending in a single consonant following a single vowel, if the accent is on the last syllable.

EXAMPLES occur, occur**red**
begin, begin**ner**
(But *travel, traveled* because the accent is not on the last syllable.)

EXERCISE 6 Following are words and suffixes. Number a sheet of paper 1–20. Next to each number, write the new word you make by joining the word and its suffix.

EXAMPLE drop + ing

dropping

1. try + ed
2. like + able
3. move + ment
4. tie + ing
5. permit + ed
6. dizzy + ness
7. angry + ly
8. grace + ful
9. place + ment
10. notice + able
11. move + ing
12. stop + ed

13. loosen + ing   17. size + able
14. change + able   18. friendly + ness
15. prefer + ing   19. outrage + ous
16. scrap + ed   20. lie + ing

SOUNDS OF LETTERS

In the English language one sound can have a variety of spellings. The words *cough* and *cuff* end with the same sound. Both **gh** and **ff** stand for this sound. In the word *elephant,* this same sound is represented by **ph**.

15c Learn the different ways of spelling sounds.

Following is a list of common English sounds. Next to each sound are words that show different ways that sound can be spelled.

SOUND	EXAMPLES OF SPELLING PATTERNS
ch (as in *chop*)	**ch**op, wit**ch**, ques**ti**on, den**tu**res
f (as in *five*)	**f**ive, cli**ff**, tou**gh**, tele**ph**one
g (as in *gear*)	**g**ear, **gh**ost
j (as in *jump*)	**j**ump, ca**g**e, mi**d**get, sol**d**ier
k (as in *kettle*)	**k**ettle, **c**arnival, a**ch**e, lo**ck**
m (as in *math*)	**m**ath, co**mb**, swi**mm**er, pal**m**
n (as in *noon*)	**n**oon, **kn**ack, win**n**er, **gn**u, **pn**eumonia
sh (as in *shell*)	**sh**ell, mi**ss**ion, **s**ure, lo**ti**on, ma**ch**ine

t	(as in *tone*)	tone, look**ed**
z	(as in *zebra*)	zebra, **is**, des**s**ert
a	(as in *fake*)	fake, r**ai**d, w**ay**, st**ea**k, **eigh**t
e	(as in *be*)	be, s**ee**d, v**ea**l, p**eo**ple, gr**ie**f, quarant**i**ne, cloud**y**
i	(as in *pipe*)	pipe, l**ie**, b**uy**, sk**y**, **eye**
i	(as in *quick*)	quick, b**ee**n, b**u**sy, b**ui**lding
o	(as in *home*)	home, t**oa**d, w**oe**, sh**ow**, s**ew**
u	(as in *tube*)	tube, b**eau**tiful, **you**
u	(as in *dune*)	dune, s**ui**t, st**oo**l, gh**ou**l, m**o**ve, can**oe**

Homonyms

Words like *vane, vain,* and *vein* are called *homonyms*. They sound the same, but they are spelled differently and have different meanings.

Because homonyms sound the same, they may be confused. For example, *weather vanes* or *veins* carrying blood may be misspelled *vain*. Misspellings can happen when homonyms are confused.

15d Learn which spelling of a homonym belongs with the meaning you want.

See Common Confusions, pp. 255–272.

HOMONYM	MEANING
affect	to influence or to change
effect	the result of a cause
already	earlier, before
all ready	(two words) prepared, completed
capital	city, seat of government
capitol	government building

cents	pennies
scents	odors
sense	intelligence
cite	to quote or to name as an example
sight	vision, to see
site	place
cereal	grain, breakfast food
serial	something done in parts or in a series
flare	flame
flair	talent
miner	worker in a mine
minor	small, not major
pair	couple
pare	to peel
pear	a fruit
peace	opposite of war
piece	one part of something
raise	lift up
raze	cut down, level to the ground
rain	water falling from the sky
reign	rule of a king or queen
rein	strap for guiding a horse
rapped	hit, talked (slang)
rapt	fascinated
wrapped	covered
way	path
weigh	to be a certain number of pounds

EXERCISE 7 Number a sheet of paper 1–8. Next to each number write the correct word from the parentheses that belongs in the blank.

> EXAMPLE Use a sharp knife to _____ that apple. (pair, pare)
>
> *pare*

1. The man _____ on the wall with the broom handle. (wrapped, rapped)
2. The _____ was to knock off some plaster. (affect, effect)
3. To fix the wall would require only a few _____ worth of fresh plaster. (scents, cents)
4. A married _____ lived in the next apartment. (pare, pair)
5. They were eating _____ for breakfast. (cereal, serial)
6. They had _____ heard the knocking. (all ready, already)
7. It made their tempers _____. (flair, flare)
8. The damage to their wall was _____, but their feelings were hurt. (minor, miner)

REVIEW EXERCISE A Spelling Plural Nouns

Following is a list of singular nouns. Number a sheet of paper 1–15. Write the plural form of each singular noun.

> EXAMPLE dictionary
>
> *dictionaries*

1. bunch	6. ox	11. valley
2. hoof	7. life	12. clove
3. turkey	8. potato	13. cowboy
4. alto	9. fish	14. puff
5. hobo	10. cry	15. half

REVIEW EXERCISE B   Prefixes

Following are ten roots or words and a list of prefixes. Number a sheet of paper 1–10. Add a prefix to each root or word and write out the new word. Some of the prefixes can be added to more than one root, so there is more than one right answer.

EXAMPLE pro + claim

proclaim

LIST OF PREFIXES

pro-	un-	1. create	6. interpret
de-	mis-	2. -cession	7. pose
re-		3. fire	8. -duce
		4. formed	9. possess
		5. compose	10. placed

REVIEW EXERCISE C   Suffixes

Each of the following numbered words has been made by combining a root word with a suffix.

Number a sheet of paper 1–10. Next to each number write the root word and the suffix.

EXAMPLE scurried

scurry + ed

1. vying
2. outrageous
3. healthful
4. humming
5. placing

6. propeller
7. driving
8. movable
9. loving
10. kissed

REVIEW EXERCISE D Homonyms

The underlined word in each of the following sentences is a homonym. That is, it sounds like a word that is spelled differently and has a different meaning. Number a sheet of paper 1–5. Read each sentence. Then write a sentence of your own, using a word that sounds like the homonym but is spelled differently.

EXAMPLE It was with a <u>sense</u> of excitement that she got out of the car.

I have one dollar and fifteen <u>cents</u>.

1. The new senator was thrilled with her first sight of the <u>capitol</u> building.
2. On this very <u>site</u>, American presidents took the oath of office.
3. She was <u>rapt</u> with awe at the thought.

4. But the rain that began pouring from the sky interrupted her thoughts.
5. She held a piece of newspaper over her head and ran inside.

MASTER SPELLING LIST

The following list includes words frequently misspelled. Your study of this list should be by groups of words. Practice spelling ten or twenty at a time. Be sure you also know the meaning of each word. Where necessary, look up words in a dictionary.

From time to time, review words you have misspelled at an earlier time. By doing this you help to keep their spellings clear in your mind.

The hard parts of words are printed in darker letters. The darkness of the letters will help you pay close attention to the parts often misspelled.

absence	affectionate	approval
absolutely	afraid	argue
acceptance	again	argument
accidentally	aisle	arrangement
accommodate	allotment	athletic
accompany	altar/alter	attendance
accuracy	amateur	authority
achieve	analyze	available
acquaintance	annually	
acquire	anticipate	beginning
across	apology	behavior
actually	apparatus	believe
administration	apparent	benefit
admittance	appearance	benefited
adolescent	appreciate	boundary
advertisement	approach	breath (e)

buried
business

calendar
campaign
capital/capitol
cemetery
certificate
character
chief
choice
choose/chose
Christian
clothes
color
column
commercial
committee
communist
competitor
completely
conceivable
concentrate
confidential
confusion
conscience
conscious
continuous
controlled
controversial
cooperate
correspondence
courageous
criticism
criticize
cruelly
curiosity
curious
cylinder

debtor
deceive
decision
dependent
describe
despair
desperate
difference
dining
dinner
disappearance
disappoint
discipline
doctor
duplicate

eager
easily
effect
efficient
eighth
eligible
embarrass
emphasize
encouragement
entirely
entrance
environment
equipped
escape
especially
essential
exaggerate
excellent
exciting
exercise
existence
expense
experiment
extremely

fantasy
fascinate
fashionable
fatal
favorite
field
finally
financial
foreign
fortunately
forty
forward
fourth
friend
further

genius
government
gracious
grammar
guarantee
guess
guidance
gymnasium

happened
happiness
hear/here
heavily
height
heroine
hopeless
hospital
humor
humorous
hungrily
hypocrisy

ignorance
imagine

immediately

incidentally

increase

indefinite

individually

influence

ingredient

innocence

insurance

intelligence

interference

interrupt

jealous

knowledge

laboratory

laborer

laid

leisure

lessen/lesson

license

likely

listener

lively

loneliness

loose/lose/loss

luxury

magazine

magnificent

maintenance

maneuver

manufacturer

marriage

marvelous

meant

mechanic

medical

medicine

melancholy

merchandise

miniature

minimum

minute

mischief

mischievous

moral/morale

muscle

mysterious

narrative

naturally

niece

ninety

noticeable

obstacle

occasionally

occurrence

offensive

official

often

omission

omit

once

operate

opponent

opportunity

optimist

orchestra

organization

originally

paid

parallel

paralyze

particular

passed/past

peace/piece

peaceful

peculiar

performance

permanent

personality

perspiration

persuade

physical

picnicking

pleasant

politician

possession

practically

practice

preferred

presence

prejudice

preparation

pressure

privilege

probably

procedure

proceed

professor

propaganda

psychology

pursuit

quiet

quite

realize

really

receipt

recognize

recommend

referred

relieve

religious

removal

repetition

resistance

resource
responsibility
restaurant
rhythm
ridiculous
roommate

sacrifice
safety
satisfied
scarcity
scene
schedule
scholar
scissors
seize
separate
similar
sincerely
skiing
sophomore
source

specifically
sponsor
straight
strength
stretch
strictly
stubborn
substitute
subtle
succeed
successful
sufficient
summary
surprise
suspense
swimming
synonym

temperamental
tendency
therefore
thorough

though
thoughtful
tragedy
transferred
tremendous
truly

unanimous
unnecessary
useful
useless
usually

vacuum
valuable
various

weather/whether
weird
whole/hole

yield

16

SOURCES OF INFORMATION

Suppose that you want to find information about the weather in an area where you or someone you know is taking a trip. Where would you look? You can probably think of many sources.

Several hundred years ago there were far fewer sources of information about the weather. People learned by seeing for themselves. Talking to others helped, too. Most people knew only what their experiences and conversations taught them.

Today there are many more sources about the weather. Magazines offer information weekly or monthly. Newspapers offer it daily. Television and radio bring instant information right into your home.

With so many sources available, where is the best place to look for the information you want? This chapter will help you decide. It offers a guide to the sources of information.

TEXTBOOKS

Most textbooks contain special sections that help you find the information you need. The sections in a book like *Using English* are listed here.

The *front cover* usually lists the title, the author, the publisher, and the number of the book in its series. Some of the same information is often repeated on the *spine,* or back edge, of the book. The publisher is also listed here. The information on the spine makes it possible to identify books when they are stacked together on the shelves.

Many textbooks include space on the *inside cover* to identify whose property the book is and to whom it has been issued. Some textbooks include additional information on the inside cover.

The *title page* lists the title, author, and publisher of the book. The *copyright page* is usually the back of the title page. Here you will find the name of the person or company owning the rights to print the book. The latest date of publication will also be listed here. The *introduction* or *preface* includes a general explanation of the book and its purposes. Certain features may be explained. The *table of contents* offers a concise guide to the entire book. Chapter titles and contents are listed with the page numbers where you will find them.

The *text* contains the book's major contents. The *glossary* is a list of major subjects covered by the text. Glossaries often list terms, too. Entries are listed in alphabetical order with page numbers. The *index* supplies an alphabetical list of topics covered in the book. It also lists the pages that cover these topics. Some books have no glossary, while in other books the index and glossary are combined.

THE DICTIONARY

Listening and reading are the two major ways you gain information. Words are important for both of these acts. Therefore, you need to be aware of the spellings, pronunciations, meanings, and uses of words. All this information and more can be found in the dictionary.

16a Learn to use the dictionary.

Learn to use the dictionary wisely. No other book provides so much information about the English language.

(1)   Words are listed alphabetically.

The words defined in a dictionary are called the *entry words*. Some dictionaries list more than 100,000 entry words. These words are listed in alphabetical order. Words beginning with *A* or *B* are found near the beginning of the dictionary. Words beginning with *Y* or *Z* are found near the end.

When two or more words begin with the same letter, alphabetical order is determined by their second letters. *Ache* is listed after *able* in the dictionary. Both these words come before *add*. *Affect* and *age* closely follow *add*. *Awe* and *axiom* come much later, near the end of the *A* words.

A group of words may share the same first few letters. When this happens, they are alphabetized according to their first different letters.

EXAMPLES   **shadow**   **shake**
           shaggy   **shal**low
           [Each of these words begins with
           the same three letters, *sha*. The
           words are alphabetized according
           to their fourth letters.]

EXERCISE 1 Number a sheet of paper 1–10.
Write the following words in their correct alphabetical order.

    graffiti   grace
    graduate   grandstand
    grandmother   graph
    gram   graduation
    gradual   grade

(2) **Guide words at the top of each page show**
       which words are on that page.

Guide words help you find words in the dictionary. Guide words are printed at the top of every
dictionary page with entry words. The guide words
are the same as the first and last entry words on
that page. Determine whether a word for which you
are looking comes between the guide words alphabetically. If it does, you will find its definition on
that page.

Suppose you are looking for the word *lemur.*
Your dictionary is open in front of you. The guide
words on the left-hand page are *legume* and *length.*
The guide words on the right-hand page are
lengthen and *leopard.* How can you tell quickly if
you will find *lemur* on either of these pages?

Lemur begins with the same two letters as all four guide words. Its third letter is *m*. Alphabetically, *m* comes before *n*. So you will not find it on the page with *lengthen* and *leopard*. You will find it on the page with the guide words *legume* and *length*. *Lemur* comes between these two words.

EXERCISE 2 Which of the following words would you find on a dictionary page with the guide words *delicate* and *deluge*? Write the words on a sheet of paper.

delegate	dell
deluxe	delirious
delight	deltoid
delicacy	delve
delinquent	delicious

(3) Words are spelled out by syllables.

Entry words in the dictionary are broken into See Syllable, p. 409 their syllables. *Hippopotamus* becomes *hip-po-pot-a-mus*. *Spaghetti* becomes *spa-ghet-ti*.

In looking up a word, it helps to think of it as having parts, or syllables. The spelling of a word like *masquerade* may be too difficult for you. But if you know that it begins with *mas,* you can probably find it in the dictionary.

EXERCISE 3 The following pairs of words contain one word spelled correctly and one word spelled incorrectly. The first syllable of every word is correct. Number a sheet of paper 1–10. Write the correct spellings on your paper. When in doubt, check a dictionary.

1. de-ter-min
    de-ter-mine
2. hol-i-day
    hol-li-day
3. ex-pence
    ex-pense
4. sep-e-rate
    sep-a-rate
5. Feb-ru-ar-y
    Feb-u-ar-y

6. doc-ter
    doc-tor
7. un-til
    un-till
8. go-ver-ment
    go-vern-ment
9. pic-nick-ing
    pic-nic-ing
10. rec-om-end
    rec-om-mend

(4) The pronunciation of every word is given.

Dictionaries use special symbols and marks to stand for the sounds in the English language. These are called *diacritical marks*. Each entry word is spelled out with syllables and diacritical marks. If you understand these marks, you can pronounce any word in the dictionary.

Different dictionaries use different diacritical marks. A key at the bottom of every other dictionary page explains its system of marks. There is usually a section at the front of the dictionary, too, that explains its pronunciation system. Make certain you understand the system in the dictionary you are using.

> **for·ti·fy** [fôr′tə·fī] *v.* **for·ti·fied, for·ti·fy·ing**
> **1** To make strong enough to resist attack, as by building walls and forts. **2** To give added strength to; strengthen: Our support *fortified* his will. **3** To add minerals or vitamins to (a food, as milk).

(5) The part of speech is given for each entry word.

An abbreviation identifies an entry word's part of speech. For example, nouns are labeled *n*. For adjectives, the abbreviation is *adj*.

Often a word can be used for two or more parts of speech. For that entry word, the definition will list all its possible parts of speech.

(6) Unusual plural spellings are given.

Many nouns form their plurals in an unusual way. For these nouns, the dictionary entry includes the spelling of the plural. The abbreviation *pl* identifies it as the plural.

EXAMPLE   *child* (pl. *children*)

EXERCISE 4 Look in a dictionary for the plurals of the following words. Number a sheet of paper 1–6. Write the plurals next to each number on a sheet of paper.

1. ox
2. salmon
3. brother-in-law
4. salesperson
5. grandchild
6. spoonful

(7) Irregular verb forms are given.

See Verbs, pp. 40–41

Sing is an irregular verb. Its past tense is *sang,* not *singed.* Its present perfect tense is *have sung.* The entry for *sing* in the dictionary will list both these irregular forms. For every irregular verb, the dictionary will include the spellings of its past tense and its present perfect tense.

(8) Comparative and superlative forms are given for many adjectives and some adverbs.

See Adjectives, p. 21; Adverbs, p. 49

The dictionary entry for *simple* includes *simpler* and *simplest.* For many adjectives, the comparative and superlative forms are listed.

An adverb such as *bad* forms an irregular comparative and superlative. For *bad,* the dictionary entry will list *worse* and *worst.* Dictionary entries for other irregular adverbs will also list their comparative and superlative forms.

(9) Various meanings of words are given.

A farmer may work in his *field,* harvesting a crop. A doctor's *field* may be pediatrics. A magnet may create a magnetic *field*. And a particularly exciting day may be referred to as a *field* day.

Most words have more than one meaning. A dictionary lists each entry word with its meanings.

EXAMPLE

hand (noun) 1. the part of the arm below the wrist
2. a measurement of four inches
3. a style of writing
4. an employee who works with his or her hands
5. a sailor
6. the cards held by one player in a card game
7. applause

(verb) 1. to give or to pass by use of hands
2. to lead with the hand

(adj.) 1. having to do with hands

The word *hand* may have any of the above meanings. By looking at its *context,* or use in a sentence, you can determine which meaning is intended. Here is one context:

The hand climbed the mast to the crow's nest and shouted, "Land ho!"

The other words in the sentence offer clues to the word's meaning. From its use, you can tell that *hand* is a noun. Because the *hand* can climb and shout, you can tell that it is a person. You may know that a *mast,* a *crow's nest,* and the expression *land ho* have to do with ships and sailing. If you do, you can guess that *hand* is a noun with meaning #5: *a sailor.*

A different meaning of *hand* will have quite a different context. Suppose you overheard the following sentence:

> *"Let's give this young man a hand."*

Here, *hand* is obviously a noun. In this context, however, several meanings are still possible. The speaker may even be a surgeon talking about a daring transplant operation. Suppose the speaker went on to say:

> *"Come on, folks! Show him you appreciate a fine performance. Let's hear it for this young man. Give him a hand!"*

From the context in this paragraph, you can learn more about *hand.* It is something given by a group of people. It can be heard. It demonstrates appreciation for a fine performance. All these clues come together to tell you that *hand* is a noun with meaning #8: applause. The speaker could have said, "Let's give this young man some applause."

EXERCISE 5 Each of the words *litter, spring,* and *forge* has more than one meaning. One of those words belongs with each of the following definitions. Number a sheet of paper 1–8. Next to each number, write the word defined.

litter   spring   forge

1. to move ahead steadily _____
2. a fountain of water _____

3. to make a counterfeit _____
4. newborn animals from a single birth _____
5. a stretcher for carrying an injured person _____
6. to leap or bound _____
7. to dirty with debris or trash _____
8. a blacksmith's fire _____

THE LIBRARY

16b **Learn how to use the sources of information in a library.**

(1)   The librarian.

The librarian is there to help you. Ask him or her for advice. A librarian's advice can direct you quickly to the right section of the library or the right book to find the information you need.

Although you can always find help, it is good to become familiar with the library yourself. Learn its different sources of information. Discover where and how to look. Then your use of the library will be much easier.

(2)   Books of fiction.

Fiction is the opposite of fact. The stories in books of fiction are not true. They are tales invented by their authors. They often make exciting reading.

Books of fiction are usually kept on open shelves. This means that you are free to select any fiction book. You can read it in the library. Or you can check it out and take it home with you.

A particular book of fiction is simple to find. The fiction shelves are usually together in one part of the library. Books are arranged alphabetically according to the authors' last names. Books by Miska Miles will be near the middle of these shelves. Books by Byrd Baylor Schweitzer come closer to the end.

You may find several books of fiction by the same author. For instance, you may find *The Black Pearl, The Dark Canoe,* and *The King's Fifth.* These books were all written by Scott O'Dell. You will find them on the shelves in the order just listed. Books by the same author are arranged alphabetically, according to titles.

(3) Books of nonfiction.

Nonfiction is the opposite of fiction. Nonfiction books often retell true stories. They can express opinions and give facts about a wide range of subjects.

Nonfiction books are not arranged by author or title. They are arranged by subjects. Libraries group these books into ten broad subject areas. Each book is assigned a code number between 000 and 999, depending upon its exact subject. This number is printed on the book's spine. It is called the Dewey decimal number.

You use Dewey decimal numbers to locate books in much the same way you use alphabetical order. Often, however, more than one book will have the same Dewey decimal number. Then you must look at a second number on each book's spine. This number begins with the first letter of the author's last name. Books with the same Dewey decimal number are shelved together. Then they are arranged alphabetically, according to this second number on their spine.

Together, these identifying codes make up what is called a *call number.* Practice finding books by their call numbers. Become familiar with the broad divisions of the Dewey decimal system. These codes will help you find nonfiction books quickly.

THE DEWEY DECIMAL SYSTEM

BOOK NUMBERS	SUBJECTS
000–099	General information (encyclopedias and other reference sources)
100–199	Philosophy (people's beliefs about values and the meaning of life)
200–299	Religion (mythology, religious faiths)
300–399	Social Sciences (economics, history, government, and more)
400–499	Language (language histories, word backgrounds, word meanings)
500–599	Science (astronomy, biology, chemistry, and other sciences)
600–699	Technology (engineering, inventions, agriculture, and more)
700–799	The Arts (painting, music, sports, dance, and others)
800–899	Literature (poetry, plays, television scripts, and books about literature)
900–999	History (biographies, information about the past, and travel books)

Thousands of new nonfiction books are published every year. Each one of them is given a number from the Dewey decimal subject areas.

In what subject area would you find a book on Greek sculpture? Since the book would deal with sculpture, its subject area would be the Arts. Its Dewey decimal number would be between 700 and 799.

EXERCISE 6 The titles of some books you might find on the nonfiction shelves of your library are listed here. Number a sheet of paper 1–8. Next to each number, write the range of Dewey decimal numbers within which you would find the book listed.

EXAMPLE *Street Poems*

800 - 899

1. *The Black Athlete*
2. *Snakes of the World*
3. *American Political Elections*
4. *Ten One-Act Plays for Young People*
5. *The Growth of Christianity*
6. *Where Did That Word Come From?*
7. *The Changing Meanings of Right and Wrong*
8. *Days and Nights on the Oregon Trail*

(4) The card catalog.

Every library has a card catalog. It consists of cabinets containing drawers filled with index cards. On each card is information about one of the books in the library. These cards tell you what books your

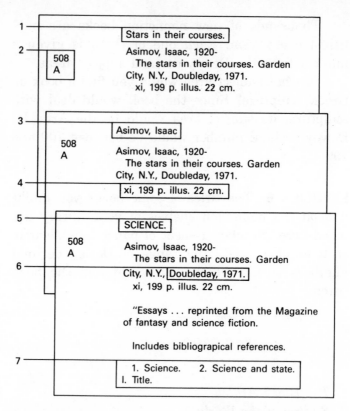

1. Title heading
2. Call number
3. Author
4. Book's physical description
5. Subject heading
6. Publisher, publication date
7. Other headings under which the book is listed.

library has to offer. They form a catalog that is always up-to-date.

Each fiction book is listed on two cards in the catalog. One is a *title card*. These cards are arranged alphabetically by titles. The other is an *author card*. These cards are also alphabetized. However, the listing is by the authors' last names.

For each nonfiction book, there are three cards in the catalog. Like each fiction book, a nonfiction book has a *title card* and an *author card*. It also has a *subject card*. These cards help you find out quickly what books your library has on a particular subject.

For example, you might be interested in magic tricks. A search through the subject catalog will tell you what books the library has on this subject. The cards you want will be filed under *M* for *magic*.

EXERCISE 7   Use the card catalog to find a nonfiction book about three of the following subjects. For each book, write the call number, the title, the author, the date of publication, and the number of pages.

1. Holidays in different countries
2. Pollution
3. Heroes of the Old West
4. The rules of a new game you want to learn
5. Slang expressions
6. Crime in the cities

(5) Reference works.

Encyclopedias are like dictionaries of knowledge. In them, you can find general information about most subjects.

Like those of a dictionary, an encyclopedia's entries are arranged alphabetically. Guide words help you to locate an entry quickly.

Encyclopedias usually contain several volumes. They are arranged alphabetically, according to the beginning letters of their entries. Guide letters on their spines help you decide which volume you need.

Suppose that you are looking for information about the game of *baseball*. You would look in the *B* volume under the entry "baseball." Here you can read about the rules of baseball, its history, background, and selected highlights or famous players. Facts about the construction of a modern baseball may also be given. And part of the entry may tell how the game was probably invented. Photographs, charts, and drawings may help make the written description clearer. For more information, the article may direct you to related articles in the encyclopedia, such as "Aaron, Henry"; "Cricket"; and "Doubleday, Abner." Some encyclopedia articles list other books that may be useful to read.

Atlases are reference books for geographical information. Maps usually form a large part of their content. Useful information accompanies the maps. You may learn facts about an area, such as its population, climate, and natural resources.

New *almanacs* are printed every year. In fact, they are like yearbooks of facts. They contain up-to-date information about many very different subjects, including:

> sports champions
> winners of famous awards
> names of government officials
> patterns in the weather
> yearly rates of death and birth
> important events of the past year

(6) Periodicals.

Periodicals are one kind of nonbook material. They are printed regularly over short periods. This is where the name *periodical* comes from.

Some examples are newsletters, newspapers, and magazines. These may be published daily, weekly, monthly, or quarterly each year.

Periodical magazines can be a valuable reference source. Because they are published regularly, periodicals are timely. They often contain information too recent to be in any of the books on the shelves. First, however, you must learn how to find their information.

The *Readers' Guide to Periodical Literature* will help you. It is like a card catalog for these publications. New volumes of this guide are published twenty-two times a year. They index articles and stories from more than one hundred of the most popular periodical magazines.

Become familiar with the *Readers' Guide*. Here is a sample of the information you will find there.

CAMPING
Camper on the beach; motorhomes at the seashore. F. Woolner. il Field & S 82:46+ My '77
Float trip camping N. Strung. il Field & S 82:52-4+ My '77
　See also
Camp cookery
　　　　Educational aspects
OBIS and ACA—the impossible equation does match. D. Buller. il Camp Mag 49:10-11 Ap '77
　　　　Outfits, supplies, etc.
Camping: field-use reports of new gear. E. A. Bauer. See issues of Outdoor life
Revolution (maybe); lightweight equipment and clothing. S. Netherby. il Field S 82:40+ My '77
　See also
Camp cookery
　　　　Canada
Bowhunter's camp; northwest Canada. F. Bear. il por Field & S 82:64-6+ My '77
　　　　Montana
Camping with big game; upper Gallatin River area. B. McRae. il Field & S 82:58-60+ My '77
　　　　Wyoming
Rocky Mountain high time of your life. V. Landi. il Outdoor Life 159:70-5+ My '77
CAMPS
　　　　Administration
Strong staff: the key ingredient. D. Shellenberger. il Camp Mag 49:6-8+ Ap '77
　See also
Camp directors
　　　　Counselors
　See Camp counselors

(7) Audiovisual materials.

Ask your librarian if your library contains audiovisual materials. Many libraries have a selection of cassettes or records. At some libraries, filmstrips and even motion picture films are available.

These audiovisual materials can be quite entertaining. In addition, they offer you one more source of information.

A BASIC LIST OF CONTENTS OF THE LIBRARY

Almanacs: Yearbooks of events and facts about everything from weather predictions for the next year to the name of the winner of last year's Kentucky Derby.

Atlases: Books of geography containing maps and often written information about the places shown in the maps.

Audiovisual materials: Audio recordings on disks, tapes, or cassettes; filmstrips; motion picture films; prints; microfilm; video recordings.

Bibliographies: Lists of books, usually arranged alphabetically by titles, authors, or subjects, including information about the publishers. In an annotated bibliography, there are also brief comments about the contents of each book.

Books

    Fiction: Stories made up by writers, including short stories and novels.

    Nonfiction: The opposite of fiction, covering a wide range of topics, including biographies and instructional materials.

    Collected works: Plays, television scripts, poems, songs, musical pieces, photographs, and art reproductions.

Dictionaries: Alphabetical listing of words giving their meanings, pronunciations, uses, and other practical information.

Encyclopedias: Dictionaries of knowledge containing an alphabetical arrangement of factual articles.

Indexes: Subject matter, such as topics and names, listed alphabetically, with page numbers.

Pamphlets: Loosely-bound, paper-covered booklets containing nonfictional information.

Periodicals: Newsletters, newspapers, and magazines that are published over regular intervals.

OTHER SOURCES OF INFORMATION

16c Make use of other sources of information.

Today there are many sources of information. In fact, there are so many that you might forget or not know simple ways that people once learned. You can still gain a great deal of knowledge from your experiences. You can also learn just by talking to other people. Other people could include the mechanic at the corner service station. From him or her you might learn important things about your car.

The people all around you offer much knowledge: a lifeguard, a police officer, a chef, a carpenter. Each of these people knows something you do not know. In their fields, each is an expert. You can learn a great deal just by talking with them, and they can respond to your questions—something that library material can never do.

If you keep your eyes open, you may find other sources of printed information. Notice the billboards. Read the words on cans and boxes. Any printed material offers you information. Become a label reader. Compare prices and contents. Study the claims an advertiser makes. Look in the *Readers' Guide* for articles about products that interest you.

The federal government publishes hundreds of booklets of information every year. Many of them are free or inexpensive. You can obtain a list by writing to the Superintendent of Documents, Government Printing Office, in Washington, D.C.

State governments also print informational material. Large businesses publish pamphlets of general information about their special fields.

It is important that you learn to use the library's sources of information well. It is also important for you to keep your eyes and ears—and mind—open to experience. There are sources of information all around you.

REVIEW EXERCISE A   Textbooks

Each of the answers from the list belongs with the following definitions. Number a sheet of paper 1–5. Next to each number write the letter of the answer that belongs with the definition.

ANSWERS

A. the cover
B. the copyright page
C. the glossary
D. the introduction or preface
E. the index
F. the table of contents

EXAMPLE Gives a general explanation of the book

D

1. Lists the title and author
2. Supplies an alphabetical list of topics covered in the book
3. Lists chapter titles, contents, and page numbers
4. Tells the name of the person or company who owns the rights to print the book
5. Lists major subjects covered by the text; often gives lists of terms, with definitions and examples

REVIEW EXERCISE B   Alphabetical Order and Guide Words

All the words in a dictionary are listed in alphabetical order. Guide words at the top of each page tell you if the word you are looking for comes between them alphabetically and can be found on that page. Number a sheet of paper 1–10. Next to each number, write the following words in alphabetical order. Then write the correct set of guide words next to each word.

EXAMPLE

ALPHABETICAL LISTING	GUIDE WORDS
badger	*bacteria – badly*
baker	*bait – balance*

1. complexion
2. conspire
3. conservative
4. crop
5. conjugate

6. cup
7. cradle
8. choke
9. cycle
10. curate

GUIDE WORD LIST

conical—connect
consequence—considerate
crack—crake
complemented—comply
consonant—constellation

cupid—cure
choice—choler
cyanide—cyclic
crook—cross
cuneiform—cuprene

REVIEW EXERCISE C Using the Dictionary

One word of each following pair is spelled correctly. All of the words have more than one meaning or definition. Number a sheet of paper 1–10. Next to each number write the correct spelling of the word that belongs in the blank.

EXAMPLE ac-cownt
ac-count
a bank _____

WORD LIST

con-duc-tor
con-duc-ter

bowl
boul

shoul-dor
shoul-der

set-tle-ment
set-le-ment

tai-lor
tae-lor

1. a railroad employee _____
2. the hollow of a spoon or pipe _____

3. the edge of a roadway _____
4. a person who directs an orchestra _____
5. to roll a ball down an alley _____
6. to jostle or push aside _____
7. a resolution of differences _____
8. one who makes clothes _____
9. to make or adapt to a special need _____
10. a colony, newly established _____

REVIEW EXERCISE D   The Library

The following questions can be answered from the list of information sources. Number a sheet of paper 1–10. Next to each number write the answer to each question.

EXAMPLE   What is the number on the spine, or back edge, of a nonfiction book in the library called?

call number

INFORMATION SOURCES

an atlas, the Dewey decimal system, audiovisual materials, periodicals, the *Readers' Guide to Periodical Literature,* the librarian, an almanac, in the card catalog, in alphabetical order, a pamphlet, the call number

1. In what reference book would you find a map of Outer Mongolia?
2. Where would you find the title, author, or subject of every book in the library?

3. What is the numbered system used to classify books at the library?
4. In what reference book would you find the amount of rainfall that fell on Michigan last year?
5. What reference book would list magazine articles printed about most subjects?
6. How are fiction books arranged in the library?
7. Who can tell you where things are in the library?
8. What are records, tapes, films, and similar materials called at the library?
9. What is a paper-covered booklet containing nonfiction information called?
10. What are newspapers, magazines, and newsletters published at regular intervals called?

REVIEW EXERCISE E Finding Out

Pick a subject you have always wanted to know something about. If you can't think of one off-hand, choose one from the following list. Then list at least two sources of information that can tell you some of what you would like to know. Do not forget to include people you have asked who are experts.

SUBJECT LIST

clowns	auto repair
roller derby	famous women
Ireland	African dancing
football stars	fashions
ancestors	

17

USING WORDS

Everyone uses words so often that few people stop to think how important they can be. Yet if you consider a few examples, the importance of words becomes clear. The word *stop* is one example. Placed on a sign at a crossroad, this word can mean the difference between safety and an accident. Think, too, how important are the words that stand for persons and things around you. They make it possible for you to talk about the world.

Problems occur with words, however. One reason is that people may call different things by the same name. The word *globe,* for example, can mean a light bulb, a model of the earth, or a container for goldfish.

Another reason for problems with words is that several different words may stand for the same person or thing. An example is the set of words for a picture. Here are a few: *drawing, image, sketch, illustration,* and *scene.*

This chapter presents a few basic facts about the way people use words. It gives you some guidelines for making words work better for you.

THE MEANING OF WORDS

17a A word may have more than one meaning.

An example is the word discussed earlier, *globe*. Another example is the word *cut*. Notice the use of *cut* in the following sentences:

1. She had a *cut* on her finger.
2. Follow this *cut* through the hills.
3. We will have to make a *cut* in the play script.

In Sentence #1 the word *cut* refers to "a break in the skin made by a sharp object." In Sentence #2 the same word means "a kind of valley." *Cut* in the third sentence refers to "a part removed from the play."

Be aware of the fact that many words have different meanings. As you build your knowledge of words, you can watch for different meanings for the same words. In this way you will strengthen your control of English.

EXERCISE 1   Write the following ten words in a column on a sheet of paper. Next to each word write another word or group of words that shows its meaning.

EXAMPLE truck

truck – a vehicle for transporting things

1. glass
2. box
3. bark
4. tie
5. handle
6. mine
7. stick
8. rock
9. goal
10. track

EXERCISE 2 Write the ten words from Exercise 1 in a column on a sheet of paper. Next to each word write a meaning different from the one you used in Exercise 1.

17b More than one word may be used to stand for a single meaning.

You may think that everyone knows what a *sofa* is. The word *sofa* refers to a padded bench with arms and a back. It is often found in the living room. However, not everyone calls a sofa a "sofa." Some people call it a "couch." Still others call it a "settee." A few people actually call a sofa a "squab."

Different words that mean the same thing are called *synonyms*. You probably have known about synonyms for many years. Nonetheless, thinking about synonyms again may help you deal more effectively with word problems.

Here are more examples of synonyms:

crime, wrongdoing, felony
joy, ecstasy, happiness
lamp, light, torch

EXERCISE 3 The following two columns contain synonyms. Number a sheet of paper 1–10. After each number write the word from Column A. Next to each word write a synonym from Column B.

EXAMPLE raise

raise   lift

A	B
1. movie	ripped
2. file	dwelling
3. horse	show
4. torn	rasp
5. fear	mug
6. house	tremble
7. shake	ground
8. cup	steed
9. latch	anxiety
10. earth	lock

17c The meaning for a word is often shown by its context.

A word without other words around it can easily be mistaken in its meaning. In the *context* of surrounding words, however, the meaning becomes clear. Alone the word *run* can have one of a number of meanings. In context, it means something particular.

EXAMPLE The colors in that shirt will *run* in the wash.

In the above context, *run* means "spread" or "wash out." In other contexts, *run* has different meanings.

EXAMPLES Last year there was a *run* on the market.
Did the clock *run* fast?

Every time you use words in English, there is a risk you will be misunderstood. One way to help prevent misunderstanding is to put words into clear contexts.

When you hear others use words that might be confused, or when you read them, check the context. From the context you can usually understand the meanings.

EXERCISE 4 Write each of the following words in contexts of your own making to give them meaning. After each context write the definition of the word.

EXAMPLE pan

> *The critics will **pan** this movie.*
> *to give a low critical rating to*

1. cap
2. light
3. book
4. bench
5. thin
6. color
7. throw
8. ship

EXERCISE 5 Choose one of the meanings for each underlined word. On a sheet of paper, write the word and its meaning next to each number.

EXAMPLE Leon Watson was <u>infatuated</u> with Henrietta Arfsten.

bankrupt   foolishly in love
overweight

infatuated — foolishly in love

1. He <u>ran</u> a high temperature.
   stepped quickly   increased   had
2. When he was away from her, he felt <u>forlorn</u> and miserable.
   sad   weary   foolish
3. Leon <u>speculated</u> about his chances of getting Henrietta to marry him.
   gambled   thought   wore glasses
4. She <u>spurned</u> his attentions and would have nothing more to do with him.
   turned aside   stuck with a sharp object   urged

17d Many words change in many ways.

The English language has gone through many changes in time. In fact, English is still changing. It will probably continue to change.

(1) Words change in their meanings.

Humor means something funny. The word comes from ancient Latin. In that language it meant *liquid*. How, you may ask, can a word that meant *liquid* have changed to mean *funny*? The story is only one illustration of the way words change their meanings.

Several hundred years ago *humor* was used in England to refer to a liquid in the body, like blood or lymph. It was thought that a person was sad or happy depending upon the amount of a certain kind of liquid in the body. Later, whoever could see the funny side of life was said to be "in a good humor." This meant that the good fluid in the body was in plentiful supply.

In time, the word *humor* more and more came to be used for anything funny, laughable, or "humorous."

The following examples show how other words have had their meanings changed:

WORD	PRESENT MEANING	OLDER MEANING
lunatic	insane person	touched by moonlight
purse	a bag to hold money	animal hide
camera	an instrument for taking pictures	a room
crouch	a stooped position	a bent hook

(2) Words change in their forms and pronunciations.

If you suddenly were taken back four centuries in a time machine and put among English-speaking people, you would have great trouble understanding what they were saying. The words they spoke have become our modern English, but pronunciations of many words were quite different then.

If you were to read something written then, too, you would see how strange the words look. Below is part of a page of a book printed in 1582.

Y good cuntriemen and gentle readers, you cannot possiblie haue anie more certain argument of the great desire, which I haue to please you, and the earnest care, which I haue to win your liking, then this verie speche directed vnto you, and that of set purpos. For if I had trusted vnto my self alone, and had thought mine own iudgement sufficient enough, to haue bene the rule of my right writing, which when I had pleased, I should nede no further care, to content anie other, I might haue spared this pains in requiring your frindship, and haue left curtesie to som

Change in sounds and forms of words have been going on since history was first written. Other changes are going on now. As you study English, you have a chance to understand the importance of those changes.

17e Different groups of people who speak the same language may use a number of different words, word forms, or pronunciations to mean the same things.

The special form of a language is called a *dialect*. English has many different dialects. In these dialects different words may have the same meaning, for example, *pan, skillet* and *spider* may all mean the same utensil. Dialects may also use different word forms to mean the same thing, such as *dived* or *dove* to describe a swimming activity in the past tense. Dialects may also use different pronunciations of the same word.

If a dialect is clear and understandable to other speakers of the language, it passes the most important test. That test is one of communication. If the dialect communicates facts and feeling, it serves its purpose.

17f No dialect is better or worse than another; it is only different.

Remember that if a dialect is clearly understood by others, it is not bad. It succeeds in communicating. That is the main reason for having a language, no matter what dialects exist.

Keep in mind, however, that you want to learn which dialect of English does the best job of communicating. One dialect may work better in certain situations.

Whatever you learn about the different forms of English will help you make better use of language. You can speak and write more effectively in many different dialects.

Some of the best known dialects of English are spoken in Scotland, Ireland, and North America. Within the United States many different groups of people speak different dialects.

Even within one region, different dialects may exist side by side. If people move to a new region, they take their dialect with them. Many people of Spanish-speaking background live in the United States. Some have kept a Spanish flavor to their English. They speak a *cultural dialect* of English.

Another cultural dialect is Black English, spoken by millions. It, too, has the special characteristics of a dialect of English. Each dialect has its place and its uses. If it didn't, it would die from lack of use.

Despite the presence of many dialects, *standard English* remains the dialect most widely used. People such as editors, broadcasters, and government leaders recognize that standard English communicates to the greatest number of people. For this very reason it is called standard English.

REVIEW EXERCISE A   Words and Meanings

Following is a list of words that have more than one meaning. One of their meanings is given. Number a sheet of paper 1–10. Next to each number, write a sentence using each word according to the definition given.

EXAMPLE   light (not heavy)

The package was bulky but light.

1. plant (a factory)
2. meet (a gathering)
3. reel (a spool)
4. marble (to streak)
5. novel (new and unusual)
6. face (to confront)
7. bear (to shoulder or endure a burden)
8. firm (a company)
9. down (feathers)
10. beat (the rhythm in music)

REVIEW EXERCISE B Synonyms

Each of the numbered words has several synonyms. Number a sheet of paper 1–10. Next to each number, write at least one synonym for each word. Try to do this without looking in the dictionary. Then, if you cannot think of a synonym, look up the word in the dictionary.

EXAMPLE cool

chilly

1. robber
2. work
3. blossom
4. mob
5. dress

6. complain
7. power
8. end
9. blunder
10. request

REVIEW EXERCISE C Words in Context

Decide what the meanings of the underlined words are by their context—the way they are used in the sentence. Number a sheet of paper 1–10. Next to each number, write the meaning of the word as it is used in the sentence. You may choose the meaning from the list here:

LIST OF MEANINGS

unprotected
apt to
excessively cruel
a scientist who studies the mind or behavior
distributed

employing harsh or insulting language
imitation or simulated
jailed
made to feel less human
defiant
unresisting; obedient

EXAMPLE   An interesting experiment was
           performed by a psychologist at
           Stanford University, Dr. Phillip G.
           Zimbardo.

*a scientist who studies
the mind or behavior*

1. A mock prison was set up.
2. Volunteers were either incarcerated or they
   were assigned to be guards.
3. Prisoners were depersonalized; all of their be-
   longings were taken away from them.
4. Guards were issued uniforms.
5. As time went on, they became abusive toward
   the prisoners.
6. The prisoners were at first rebellious.
7. But they became more and more passive.
8. Some guards became cruel and sadistic.
9. The experiment showed how liable people are
   to act as they think they are supposed to, no
   matter how they really feel.
10. People are very vulnerable to outside pres-
    sures.

GLOSSARY

This glossary lists special terms appearing in the text. Most terms here are followed by definitions. A few terms are cross-referenced to other terms that do have definitions. Examples are included in many cases to illustrate terms.

From time to time terms are followed by references to sections of the text. In the text the terms are treated in more detail.

adjective   A word that describes a noun. (See also **article**.) See **1g.**

The *red* car had a *long* antenna.

Its wheels were *yellow*.

An adjective helps *compare things*. Most adjectives change form to show comparison.

One *short* way is through Clayton.

A *shorter* way is on Old Mill Road.

The *shortest* way is over Buck's Pass.

adverb   A word that *describes* sentence *actions*. An adverb tells *where, when,* or *how* something happens. It usually does this by describing the verb in the sentence. An adverb can also describe some other part of speech. See **2e.**

These adverbs tell *where* the action happens.

Lift your arms *up*.

Swing them *around*.

These adverbs tell *when* the action happens.

Rosita will win *tomorrow*.

She knows it *now*.

These adverbs tell *how* the action happens.

We can *clearly* see the balloon.

They arrived *safely*.

agreement   The forms of words that show the same number. See **10a.**

A pronoun agrees with its antecedent in gender and number.

David opened *his* lunch bag.

A verb agrees with its subject in number.
He *does* this every day at noon.

antecedent   The word or group of words referred to by a following pronoun.

The old grey house on the corner is empty. It has been that way for years.

antonym   A word that means the opposite of another word.

up/down

old/young

apostrophe A mark that looks like a comma above the line to show possession, missing letters, or the plural of numbers. See **14k (1)–(3), 14l, 14m.**

Babe's coat   shouldn't   x's

appositive A word or group of words placed next to another to identify someone or something or to explain a meaning or idea.

Shari telephoned Lu, *her best friend.*
One night we say heat lightning, *a flickering light in the sky.*

article The words *a, an,* and *the.* An article is a kind of adjective.

auxiliary verb (See **helping verb.**)

case The form of a pronoun that shows its relation to other parts of the sentence. See **1f.**

SUBJECTIVE CASE usually serves as the subject of a sentence.

We heard the horn.

OBJECTIVE CASE usually serves as the object of the sentence or the object of a preposition.

Its sound startled *us.*

POSSESSIVE CASE shows ownership.

Our driver just smiled.

clause A group of words with both a subject and a predicate. A clause can be a sentence or part of a sentence. See **4a, 4b, and 4c.**

INDEPENDENT CLAUSE A clause that can stand alone as a complete thought.

The truck backed up slowly but *its wheels spun fast in the snow.*
The truck backed up slowly. Its wheels spun in the snow.

DEPENDENT CLAUSE A clause that depends upon an independent clause to complete its thought.

As the truck backed up slowly, its wheels spun in the snow.

colloquial Acceptable words or forms in informal conversation, but usually not acceptable in formal speech or writing.

Get on with it.
Take it easy.

comparison The forms of an adjective or adverb that show more or less about the words they describe. (See also **modifiers**.) See **1h** and **2f**.

POSITIVE small, slow

COMPARATIVE smaller, slower

SUPERLATIVE smallest, slowest

completer A word or words that complete a statement about the subject of a sentence. A completer comes after the verb. It is part of the predicate. (See also **predicate**.) See **5k–5l**.

Completers are words or phrases that can fit in sentence blanks like these:

Sansha chopped _____.
She appeared _____.

NOUNS AND NOUN WORD GROUP COMPLETERS
Sansha chopped *the log*.

ADJECTIVE COMPLETER
She appeared *strong*.

ADVERB COMPLETER
We are *here*.

complex sentence A sentence with an independent clause and a dependent clause. (See also **clause**.) See **5e**.

Ramon made meat sauce while the macaroni was boiling.

compound A word or group of words made up of two or more parts that could stand alone.

COMPOUND WORD *basketball, maid-of-honor*

COMPOUND SUBJECT *Old wagons* and *new cars* rolled in the parade.

COMPOUND OBJECT He scooped *rice* and *barley*.

COMPOUND PREDICATE Kangaroos *sit in the shade* or *hop across an open area*.

compound sentence A sentence made up of two or more independent clauses. See **5d**.

Betsy hopes to go to college, but she is not sure where she would like to be.

compound-complex sentence A sentence made up of two or more independent clauses and at least one dependent clause. See **5f.**

George drives the motorcycle and Arlene rides behind him whenever they take a trip.

compound verb Two or more verbs in a clause or sentence. See **5b (4).**

Velma *unrolled* and *smoothed* the blueprints.

conjunction A word that connects words, phrases, or clauses. Two kinds of conjunctions are *coordinating conjunctions* and *subordinating conjunctions.* See **2i.**

COORDINATING CONJUNCTIONS connect words, phrases, or clauses. The most common coordinating conjunctions are *and, but,* and *or.*

Mutt *and* Jeff
We should move inside *or* the rain will soak us.

SUBORDINATING CONJUNCTIONS connect ideas not equal to each other. Some examples are *after, although, as, because, before, like, since, though, unless, until, when, where, while.*

She always drinks a glass of milk *before* she eats a meal.
After she has had lunch, she takes a nap.

connector Word used to connect other words or groups of words. Some examples are conjunctions, such as *and, but, after;* and connecting adverbs, such as *then, therefore,* and *afterward.*

consonants All alphabet letters that are not vowels (*B, C, D,* for example). Consonant sounds are made in speaking by closing or bringing together parts of the throat, mouth, teeth, tongue, or lips.

context The words surrounding a word that help define it. See **17c.**

contraction A word form using an apostrophe to show missing letters.

> *can't, don't, could've*

dangling modifier A modifying word or word group without a subject to modify. See **6c.**

> *Soaked and frozen,* the wind made conditions all the more difficult. [This sentence does not say who is soaked and frozen. It is not the wind.]

> CORRECTED *Soaked and frozen,* Jolly found the wind made conditions all the more difficult.

dash A line like a long hyphen used to show a continuation of related ideas in a sentence. See **14j.**

dependent clause (See **clause.**)

determiner (See also **article.**) Determiners are words like *a, an, the, one, some, their.* A determiner is a kind of adjective that always is followed by a noun.

> *a* rock, *an* arm

Determiners help tell whether a noun is singular or plural.

one cat, *several* cats

diacritical marks   Marks used with letters to show how they are pronounced.

Examples are $\bar{\text{a}}$ [as in *say*], $\breve{\text{e}}$ [as in *set*], $\ddot{\text{a}}$ [as in *father*].

diagraming   A way of showing how parts of a sentence relate to one another. Two main types of diagraming are sometimes used. One type is a traditional diagram. The other is a tree diagram.
Any diagram of a sentence is only one way of showing the relationships among its parts.

TRADITIONAL DIAGRAMING   Six sentences are diagramed below. Each diagram shows how added parts of a sentence fit together.

(1) The musician played the guitar.

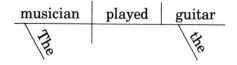

[The simple subject belongs first on the horizontal line. Under it on a slanted line belongs its modifier. The verb follows the simple subject, separated by a vertical line through the horizontal line. The direct object follows the verb, separated by a vertical line resting on the horizontal line.]

(2) The young musician played the guitar.

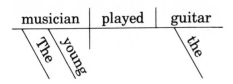

[Additional modifiers of the subject belong on additional slanted lines.]

(3) The young musician in the band played the guitar.

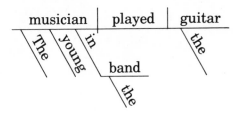

[A prepositional phrase modifying the subject belongs on slanted and horizontal lines as shown in (3) above.]

(4) The musician had played the guitar.

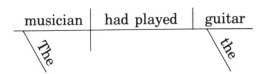

[Auxiliary verbs belong with the main verb on the horizontal line.]

(5) The musician played the guitar skillfully.

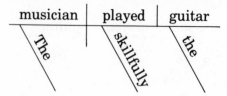

[An adverb belongs on a slanted line under the verb it modifies.]

(6) The young musician in the band played the electric guitar skillfully.

[The completed diagram is shown in (6) above.]

(7)

[All parts of the sentence are shown in (7) above.]

TREE DIAGRAMING

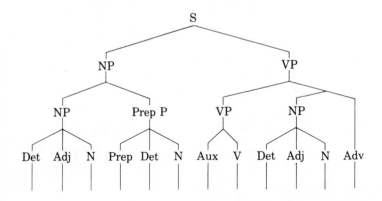

The young musician in the band has played the electric guitar skillfully.

A tree diagram gets its name from its shape. Turn it upside down and it looks a little like a tree. The abbreviations used in the tree diagram have the following meanings. These meanings are not all the same as those in traditional grammar. Follow your teacher's direction in using these meanings.

S: Sentence

NP: Noun phrase [A noun phrase is often the complete subject or the object of a sentence. It may have another, smaller phrase in it.]

VP: Verb phrase [A verb phrase can be the complete predicate of a sentence. It can have a verb phrase and a noun phrase in it.]

Prep P: Prepositional phrase

Det: Determiner
Adj: Adjective
N: Noun
Prep: Preposition
Aux: Auxiliary [a helping verb]
V: Verb
Adv: Adverb

dialect   The special features of a spoken language used by a group of people. Examples of features are in choices of words and pronunciation. See **17e.**

> *cornpone* for *cornbread*
> "pahk" for "park"

double negative   The incorrect use of two words that mean "no" in the same sentence. The most common negatives are *no* and *not*. Other negatives are *none (no + one), nothing (no + thing),* never *(not + ever),* and *neither (not + either).* See **10p.**

Here are examples of double negatives:

1. We didn't do nothing.
2. They're not never going to finish.

CORRECTIONS
1. We didn't do anything.
2. They're never going to finish.

expletive   A word without meaning used as the subject of a sentence.

> *It* is clear.
> *There* is nothing to say.

Also, an expletive is an interjection that expresses strong feeling.

Why *in the world* are you late?

exposition Writing that expresses, explains, or "exposes" one's ideas, for example, a newspaper editorial, an essay, or a research paper.

fragment An incomplete sentence, one without either the necessary subject or predicate. See **6a**.

Stuck in the mud [Who or what is stuck in the mud?]

CORRECTED The camel is stuck in the mud.

gender Male or female or neuter (neither).

MALE *He* wept.

FEMALE *She* laughed.

NEUTER *It* broke.

helping verb Words that are used with main verbs. The most common helping verbs are listed here. See **2a (5)**.

be: am, are, is, was, were, being, been
do: do, does, did, done
have: have, has, had

Here are some other common helping verbs:

can, could, may, shall
will, would, might

Helping verbs help the verbs express their actions.

Mike *was* eating a hamburger.
He *had* finished a shake.

Helping verbs also help show time.

> His appetite *will* return.
> He *has* gobbled two lunches.

idiom   A word or phrase used in a special way.

> He *banked on* the possibility of future success. [He depended upon it.]

independent clause   A group of words having a subject and predicate able to stand by itself without need of other words to finish its meaning. [See also **clause**.] See **4b.**

indirect object   The secondary receiver of sentence action.

> Carla gave *him* a wallet. [To whom did Carla give a wallet? Answer: *him*.]

infinitive   The standard or base form of a verb, often with *to*.

> to wait, to watch

The infinitive is sometimes used as a noun.

> *To wait* long hours is not easy.

inflection   The change in the form of a word to show a change in meaning or grammatical use.

> dog [singular], dogs [plural], dogs' [plural possessive]

> sing [present], sang [past], sung [past participle]

interjection A part of speech showing strong feeling. An interjection is not grammatically related to the sentence. See **2j**.

> *Oh, heck,* the faucet leaks!

irregular verb A verb that does not add **ed** to form the past tense. (See also **verb**.) See **2d**.

italics Slanted letters printed to draw special attention. See **14n–14o**.

linking verb A verb that links the subject to the subject completer. See **2a (4)**.

> *appear, become, fell, look,* and forms of the verb *be.*

main clause An independent clause.

metaphor A figure of speech in which one item is compared to another.

> The market was a *beehive* of activity.

misplaced modifier A modifying word or phrase too far from its subject to be clear in meaning. See **6c**.

> *Scrubbing hard,* the counter was finally cleaned by the men. [This seems to say the counter did the hard scrubbing.]

> CORRECTED   *Scrubbing hard,* the men
>   finally cleaned the counter.

modal auxiliary   A verb used as a verb helper that does not change form.

can, could, might, ought

modifiers   Words used to describe someone, something, or some action. [See also **adjective** and **adverb**.]

mood   The purpose of the speaker as shown in the form and use of the verb. The three moods are (1) *indicative,* to state something; (2) *imperative,* to order or request something; and (3) *subjunctive,* to show a condition that is not true or is desirable.

> (1) INDICATIVE MOOD   Young people enjoy life more than anyone.
> (2) IMPERATIVE MOOD   Take the opportunity while you can.
> (3) SUBJUNCTIVE MOOD   If we were younger, we might not feel this way.

nominative   The subjective case. (See also **case**.)

nonrestrictive clause or **phrase**   A group of words that tells something more about someone or something in the same sentence. A nonrestrictive clause or phrase is not necessary to make the sentence complete, but it adds to its meaning.

> The astronauts, *safely into orbit,* began to plan for their next maneuver. [phrase]
> The astronauts, *who were safely into orbit,* began to plan for their next maneuver. [clause]

noun   A word or group of words used to name a person, place, thing, or idea. See **1a**.

> Names of persons: Laurie Engels, Kinsha
> Omedo
> [proper nouns]
> Names of places: Golden Gate, Chicago
> [proper nouns]
> Names of things: paper, oil, garden
> [common nouns]
> Names of ideas: spirit, tradition
> [common nouns]

number   One or more than one person or thing. In English, singular or plural number is shown in most nouns by the addition of **s** or **es**.

> train/trains, watch/watches

A few nouns change their spelling in special ways.

> man/men, goose/geese

Number is shown in most pronouns by a change in form.

> this/these
> that/those
> he, she/they
> her, him/them
> hers, his/theirs

object   The result of action or the receiver of the action in a sentence. See **5k.**

> DIRECT OBJECT   The bloodhounds found *him*.

> INDIRECT OBJECT   The police gave *him* help.

The object of a preposition is a noun or pronoun which is related to another word by the preposition. See **2h.**

The police gave some help to *him*.

objective case   Pronouns show the objective case when they serve as the objects of a sentence or of a preposition. (See also **case**.)

The committee agreed to give the prizes to *her* and to *them*.

paragraph   A paragraph is a group of sentences beginning with an indention. The sentences should all be about one idea. There should be enough sentences to make the idea clear to the reader. See **7a**.

The topic of a paragraph is often written in a topic sentence. The topic sentence usually comes at the beginning of a paragraph. See **7b.**

The cowboy's bandanna seemed to have a hundred uses. In hot weather this bright square of cloth kept the sun off the cowboy's neck. In cold weather it kept his ears warm. It could tie his hat on his head. If he was hurt, it could be a sling or a bandage. He could dry dishes with it. He could wave it as a signal. He could strain muddy water through it. And at the last, it would cover his face when he died.

participle   The **ing** or the **ed** form of a verb that can be used as an adjective. A few irregular verbs form their participles in irregular ways. (See also **phrase**.)

happening [present participle]
happened [past participle]
broken [past participle of irregular verb
break]

parts of speech   English sentences can have eight
main kinds of words in them. These eight kinds of
words are called parts of speech. These words do the
work of the sentence. They help show meaning.

The eight parts of speech are *noun, pronoun, verb,
adjective, adverb, preposition, conjunction,* and *interjection.* (See separate listings.)

persuasive speaking or **writing**   Speaking or writing that attempts to convince someone to hold a
certain opinion or carry out a certain action.

phrase   A group of words belonging together, but
not making a complete statement. See **3a**.

PREPOSITIONAL PHRASE   under the box

VERB PHRASE   having started

NOUN PHRASE   a terrible storm

plural   More than one. The plural is shown by
words that mean more than one *(many, ten)*. It is
also shown in the forms of nouns *(man/men)*, pronouns *(her/them)*, and verbs (she *runs*/they *run)*.

possessive   A form of a noun or pronoun showing
that someone owns something or that things belong
close together.

the *girl's* slipper [possessive noun]
his plan [possessive pronoun]

predicate   The part of a sentence that tells about the subject. See **5b (2)**.

Marie *appeared quite unhappy.*
Al *drove to the edge of the road.*

PREDICATE ADJECTIVE   (See **completer.**)

PREDICATE NOUN   (See **completer.**)

prefix   A prefix is one or more syllables added to the front of a word or root to affect its meaning. See **15b (10)–(11)**.

indirect, **at**tain, **un**readable

preposition   A part of speech that points out how two words are related. Most prepositions show time or place or direction. See **2g**.

She stayed *after* the bell.
Mickey sat *behind* the desk.

prepositional phrases   (See **phrase.**)

pronoun   A word that can stand for a noun or pronoun. Usually, a pronoun stands for a group of words in which the noun is the main word. See **1d**.

An engineer in the cab of the locomotive waved at the people.
He waved at the people. [*He* stands for *an engineer in the cab of the locomotive.*]

There are three cases of pronouns. The first is the *subjective case.* It usually shows the doer of the action in a sentence.

> *They* waved back.
> *He* smiled.

The second case of the pronoun is the *objective case.*

> He gave *them* another wave.

The third case of a pronoun is the *possessive case.*

> He saw *their* smiles.

The common kinds of pronouns are *personal, demonstrative, indefinite, interrogative, reflexive,* and *relative.* See **1f.**

punctuation   The marks used with words to show how they relate and how they are to be read. See Chapters 13–14.

root   The basic part of a word. Parts are added to it to change its meaning. (See also **prefix** and **suffix**.)

> in*habit,* re*possess, station*ary

run-on sentence   Two or more sentences run together without correct punctuation or connecting words. See **6b.**

> The praying mantis is an insect of strange appearance it seems to rest in a kneeling position.

> CORRECTED   The praying mantis is an insect of strange appearance. It seems to rest in a kneeling position.

sentence   A group of related words needing no other words to complete its thought. A sentence has a subject and a predicate. See **5a**.

> SENTENCE   The drinking fountain squirted water into the air.

> FRAGMENT   Squirted water into the air (See also **fragment**.)

sentence combining   A method of joining two or more sentences into one. (See **clause**.)

singular   Only one of anything. (See **plural** for a comparison.)

slang   A word or phrase not yet accepted for general use by most educated people.

> I can *dig it*. [I understand what is meant.]

subject   A noun (or its equal) that the rest of its sentence says or asks something about. The subject of a sentence is the *who* or *what* that belongs with the predicate. See **5b (1)**.

> *Dust* swirled around the town.
> *Cars* disappeared in the cloud.

subject completer   (See **completer**.)

subordinate clause   A dependent clause. (See also **clause**.)

subordinating conjunction   (See **conjunction**.)

suffix   One or more syllables that add meaning to a word or root. A suffix is added to the end of a word or a root. See **15b (12)–(19).**

> swift*ly,* hope*ful,* spend*able*

syllable   A letter or group of letters containing a vowel that is pronounced as one unit. A syllable may be a single vowel.

> in-tent, i-den-ti-fy

Most syllables contain a vowel sound plus a consonant sound or sounds.

> up-set [2 syllables]
> ar-ri-val [3 syllables]
> cor-re-spond-ence [4 syllables]

synonym   A word that means the same as another.

> trolley/street car, thin/slim, looks/appearance

syntax   The arrangement of words and parts of a sentence.

> The post office sent her a notice.
> The post office sent a notice to her.
> She was sent a notice by the post office.
> [All three sentences mean the same. However, the syntax, or order of words, is different in each.]

tense   Time as shown by the form of a verb. See **2b.**

> PRESENT   she *runs,* they *run*
>
> PAST   she *ran,* they *ran*
>
> FUTURE   she *will run,* they *are going to run*

topic sentence　(See **paragraph**.)

transformation　The changes in form that can be made in sentences and word groups.

unity　In composition, making sentences refer to the same topic or subject.

verb　A part of speech that shows action *(run)*, states something *(is)*, or shows condition *(seems)*. Most verbs change their form to show time *(run — ran)*. (See **tense**.) Other changes show number (One woman *was* there. Most *were* not.) See **2a.**

A verb tells the action in a sentence. Or it tells that something exists. Exists means "is" or "to be."

> *action:* flies, breaks, mends
> *existence:* is, are, was, seem

verbal　A form of a verb used as another part of speech. (See **infinitive** and **participle**.)

vocabulary　The words and their meanings used in a language.

voice　The form of a verb that shows who or what is doing something.

> ACTIVE VOICE　Fern *raced* Jenra.
>
> PASSIVE VOICE　Jenra *was raced* by Fern.

vowel　The letters *A, E, I, O, U,* and sometimes the letters *Y* and *W.*

INDEX

TAB KEY INDEX

CORRECTION SYMBOL	DEFINITION	CHAPTER
ad	adjectives and adverbs	10
adj	adjective	1
adv	adverb	2
agr	agreement of subjects and verbs	10
ap	apostrophe	14
cap	capital letter	12
cl	clause	4
comp	incomplete or false comparison	
conj	conjunction	2
cxt	context	2, 17
dm	dangling or misplaced modifier	6
dn	double negative	10
frag	fragment	6
g	good use	
glos	glossary	
info	sources of information	16
inj	interjection	2
ital	italics	14
k	awkward sentence	
let	letter writing	9
n	noun	1
nc	not clear	
p	error in punctuation	13, 14
paral	parallelism	
phr	phrase	3

TAB KEY INDEX
(Continued)

CORRECTION SYMBOL	DEFINITION	CHAPTER
plan	planning and writing a composition	8
prep	preposition	2
pro	pronoun	1
ref	reference of pronouns	10
ro	run-on sentence	6
sp	spelling	15
ss	sentence structure	5
verb	verb	2
ww	wrong word	11
¶	paragraph	7
./	period	13
?	question mark	13
!	exclamation mark	13
,/	comma	13
;/	semicolon	14
:/	colon	14
-/	hyphen	14
"/	quotation marks	14
( )	parentheses	14
[ ]	brackets	
—	dash	14

A
B
C
D
E
F
G
H
I
J